BEHOLD THE BUDDHA

Religious Meanings of Japanese Buddhist Icons

James C. Dobbins

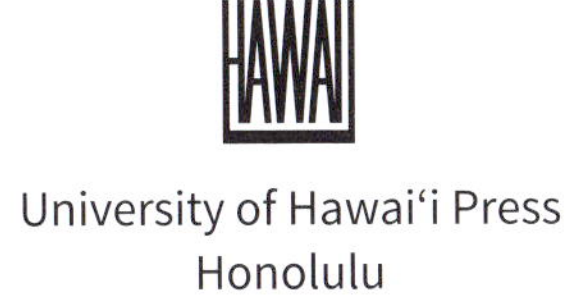

University of Hawai'i Press
Honolulu

Printed in the United States of America

25 24 23 22 21 20 6 5 4 3 2 1

Library of Congress Cataloging-in-Publication Data

Names: Dobbins, James C., author.
Title: Behold the Buddha : religious meanings of Japanese Buddhist icons / James C. Dobbins.
Description: Honolulu : University of Hawai‘i Press, [2020] | Includes bibliographical references and index.
Identifiers: LCCN 2019020047 | ISBN 9780824879990 (pbk. ; alk. paper)
Subjects: LCSH: Buddhist art and symbolism—Japan. | Buddhism and art—Japan. | Buddhist gods in art.
Classification: LCC BQ5115.J3 D63 2020 | DDC 294.3/4370952—dc23
LC record available at https://lccn.loc.gov/2019020047

University of Hawai‘i Press books are printed on acid-free paper and meet the guidelines for permanence and durability of the Council on Library Resources.

Cover art: Seated Amida Nyorai, 12th cent. By permission of Kyoto National Museum.

Design by Nord Compo

In memory of my parents
Mary Alice Smith Dobbins
and C. Ray Dobbins

CONTENTS

ILLUSTRATIONS

ACKNOWLEDGMENTS

Inspiration for this book originally came from my students at Oberlin College. During my first semester on the faculty a few wanted to know more about the Buddhist images in Oberlin's Allen Memorial Art Museum. Since then, I have taken classes there once a semester to introduce them to the function and meaning of Buddhist icons. It has given them a palpable sense of the religion apart from its philosophical ideas and popular practices.

My own attraction to museums, as well as repeated trips to Japan, subsequently led me to undertake a few small research projects on Buddhist images, and in the early 2000s I laid plans to write this book. Work on it proceeded sporadically for many years, interrupted by long periods of service to the college and the profession and by other large research projects. Major progress occurred during two periods of generous research support—in 2006–2007, by the National Humanities Center, and in 2015, by Oberlin College. Along the way many individuals and institutions assisted and accommodated me: Otani University, the Kyoto and Nara National Museums, various museums in the United States and abroad, and dozens of temples in Japan. This book has also benefited from the open access policy for the reproduction of images in the public domain adopted by the Metropolitan Museum of Art in New York, the Los Angeles County Museum of Art, and a few other organizations.

Final production of the book was supported by subventions from the Metropolitan Center for Far Eastern Art Studies, the Bukkyō Dendō Kyōkai, and Oberlin College. Preparation of the illustrations was done by Steve Buchanan. The University of Hawai'i Press performed magic transforming my raw manuscript into an attractive volume, especially with the guidance and expertise of Stephanie Chun and Stuart Kiang. Over the years many colleagues, friends, and family members have encouraged me in this work. In particular

I want to thank my wife, Suzanne Gay, and my parents, to whom the book is dedicated. I also wish to express appreciation to Jacqueline Stone, Robert Sharf, William Bodiford, Richard Jaffe, Nobuyoshi Yamabe, Takami Inoue, Samuel Morse, Melissa Rinne, Patricia Graham, Mimi Hall Yiengpruksawan, and numerous others who have supported me in ways great and small. The successes of the project owe much to them. The shortcomings belong to me.

BEHOLD THE BUDDHA

INTRODUCTION
Art Museums

Art museums are one of my favorite places. Serene, immaculate, they evoke in me a contemplative frame of mind and a sense of shelter from the world. I love to walk their pathways that usher me from one visual encounter to another. In them I slowly, unconsciously, find myself opening up to things in a way that I do not typically do on the street. Each object I meet offers its own brief surprise—sometimes pleasing, sometimes perplexing. Museums, with their sophisticated lighting and protective enclosures, allow me to examine closely the things that engage me the most, and discovering their details increases a feeling of intimacy toward them (fig. 1). Over the years

Fig. 1. Gallery of Hōryūji Treasures, Tokyo National Museum. Small Buddhist images from the Hōryūji Temple, dating from the sixth to the eighth century, are displayed in protective cases with individualized lighting.

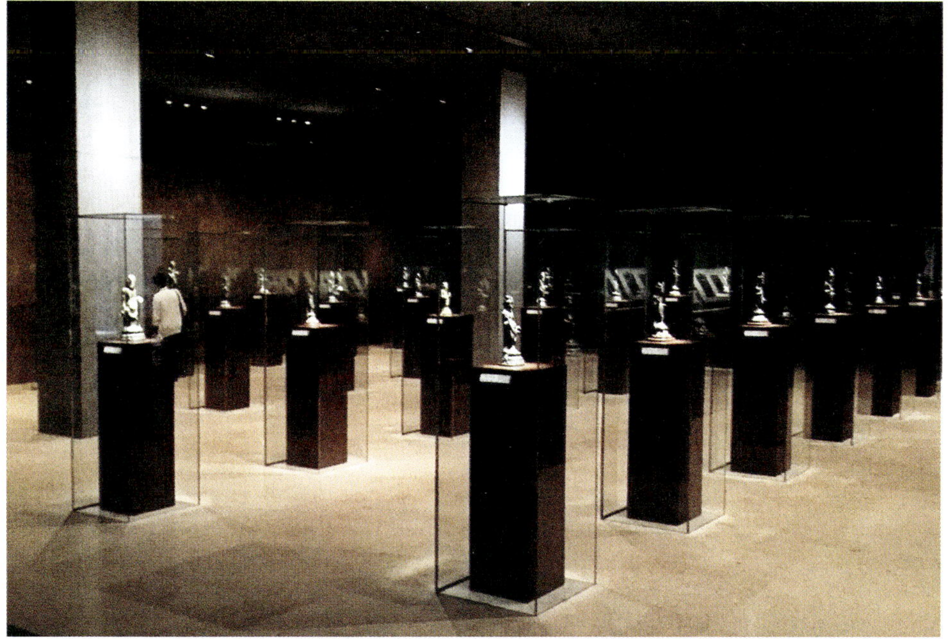

I have had the good fortune of living near several wonderful museums: the Allen Memorial Art Museum in Oberlin, the Cleveland Museum of Art, and, during several residencies in Japan, the Kyoto National Museum and the Nara National Museum. Through many visits they have become cherished sites in my life, each containing a few objects that have turned into old friends, so to speak.

My early enchantment with museums coincided roughly with the years that I first lived in Japan. Museums there are, by and large, like ones in the United States except, naturally, they have far more Asian objects on display. Among them are many statues and paintings of the Buddha and other Buddhist figures. Such objects are common in Western museums too (and now on the internet and in pop culture as well), but I first took serious note of them while living in Japan. At the same time, I also began visiting Buddhist temples—part of my youthful aspiration to immerse myself in Japanese culture. When entering them, I reflexively looked at the Buddhas in the temples as I would ones in museums: with curiosity, attention to detail, and interest in their identity, age, and aesthetic appeal. Many famous temples in Kyoto and Nara have adapted to this museum mentality: they open their doors to the public during regular business hours, they charge an admission fee, and several have transformed their private storehouses of Buddhist treasures into makeshift museums. My original impression of these temples was that their Buddhist images were no doubt exceptional but were exhibited less skillfully than in museums. The lighting was poor, the access limited, and the surroundings overly embellished and distracting (fig. 2).

Since then I have come to realize that museums, notwithstanding my enduring love for them, may not offer the best setting for experiencing Buddhist images as religious entities. There is a prevailing museum sensibility that processes these objects in such a way that their meanings and significance in a religious context are often masked—or, at least, not allowed to arise. Museums do identify them as Buddhist objects and may even expand the labels to describe their religious function, but usually matters of historical provenance,

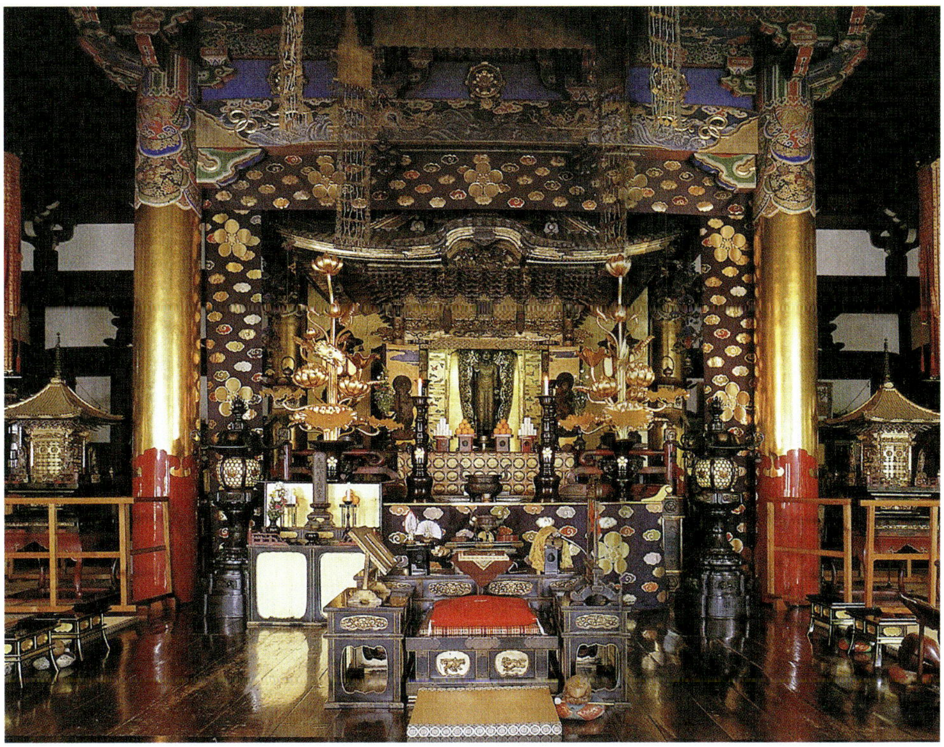

Fig. 2. **Grand altar of Seiryōji Temple, Kyoto.** The central icon, a five-foot standing image of the Buddha, is enclosed in an elaborate shrine cabinet with a screen that is normally rolled down, obscuring the view. The altar is adorned with an incense burner, food offerings, candlesticks, artificial flowers, lampstands, and decorative tapestries. In the foreground is a platform where the officiating priest sits during religious services. Figures 21 and 66 are closeup views of the icon.

workmanship, and aesthetics dominate. Curiously, the shortcomings I found in the display of icons at Buddhist temples were precisely those that obstructed me from enjoying them as museum pieces. Unconsciously, I was transposing the concerns of a modern sensibility onto the premodern sites that had generated and defined the objects in the first place. Over the years I have come to realize that Japanese temples, despite their deficiencies in displaying images for the convenience and enjoyment of the viewer, preserve an earlier way of seeing Buddhist icons that is difficult to replicate in a museum setting.

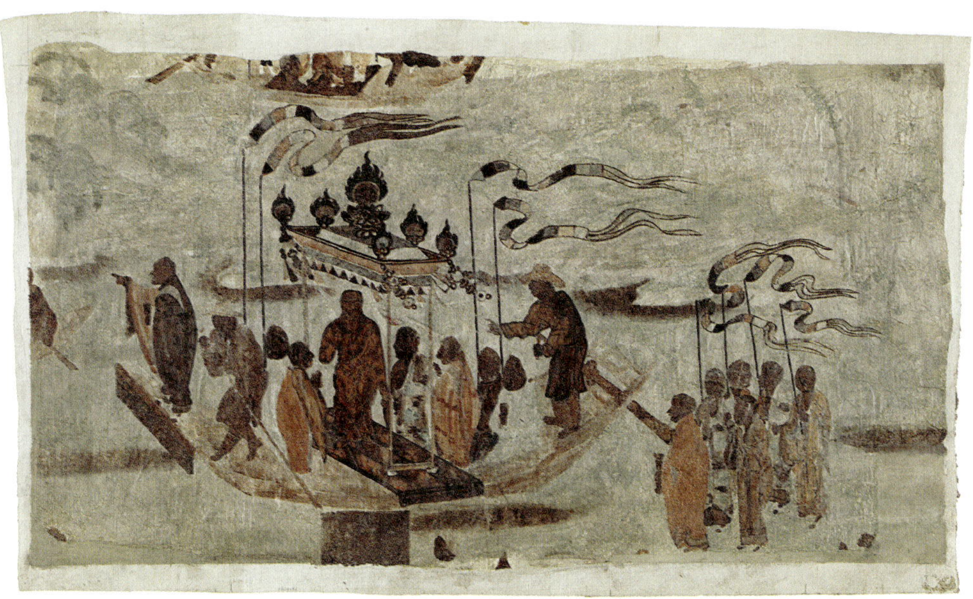

Fig. 3. **Mural fragment from Dunhuang, 7th cent.** A painting entitled *Eight Men Ferrying a Statue of the Buddha* acquired by Langdon Warner at Dunhuang in 1924. It depicts the recovery of a renowned statue of Śākyamuni Buddha from a river near Yangzhou in the early fourth century.

In recent decades museums have become the target of a postcolonial critique.[1] As institutions, they arose in an age—specifically, the nineteenth and twentieth centuries—when the West dominated large parts of Asia. In many instances, museums became the guardians of "trophies" from colonial incursions, and on occasion they actively participated in the acquisition of Buddhist treasures. For instance, the celebrated—and also quite culturally sensitive—Asian art specialist Langdon Warner (1881–1955), who served variously at the Boston Museum of Fine Arts, the Cleveland Museum of Art, the Philadelphia Museum of Art, and the Fogg Art Museum at Harvard University, led an expedition to the Buddhist cave complex at Dunhuang in remote western China in 1924, and brought back a three-foot Buddhist sculpture and a dozen small plaster patches of murals from chapel wall paintings, which are now preserved at Harvard's Sackler Museum (fig. 3).[2] Sad tales—some known, but most not—may stand behind many of the Buddhist images exhibited today. Although Japan itself was not subjected to colonial occupation, many Buddhist treasures from temples did flow into museums both outside the country, from sale and export, and inside it, as emblems of a rising cultural nationalism. In the early twentieth century, the museums superintended their Buddhist objects conscientiously, sometimes protecting them, albeit unwittingly, from social and political upheavals. In their most generous moments, museumgoers in the West treated such objects as aesthetic treasures from far-off lands. But in more condescending moments, they looked upon them as exotic artifacts from a strange religion. The former attitude endures in current museum culture, while the latter still appears sporadically. Because this colonial heritage is so pervasive, I myself feel an occasional tinge of guilt by association even though (or perhaps because) I continue to enjoy the objects it has brought to American museums.

Today museums and museumgoers are driven by somewhat different assumptions from those in vogue at the beginning of the twentieth century. In this age of internationalization, and especially in the wake of Japan's postwar economic miracle and China's social and economic transformation, a healthy respect for Asia is widespread. There is a kinder and gentler response to Buddhist images than the Christocentric one that prevailed in the US a century or so ago. This does not represent a newly created attitude, but one that has evolved gradually from the colonial past. Despite this more tolerant and deferential perception of Buddhist images, their religious significance and function are still not conveyed well in the museum context. Astute museum exhibitors and curators are fully aware of this. They understand that religious objects are transformed in meaning when placed in a museum setting, and that museums create their own ambiance and meaning-giving mechanisms which may be at odds with the religious character of these objects.[3] To compensate for this, some museums have experimented by replicating Buddhist-style installations of icons in exhibition spaces (fig. 4), sometimes even with altar settings and ritual implements. And in a few instances these museums have invited Japanese priests to perform Buddhist ceremonies before a recreated altar.[4] These are intended to alert visitors, if only briefly, to how the object would be treated in a Buddhist

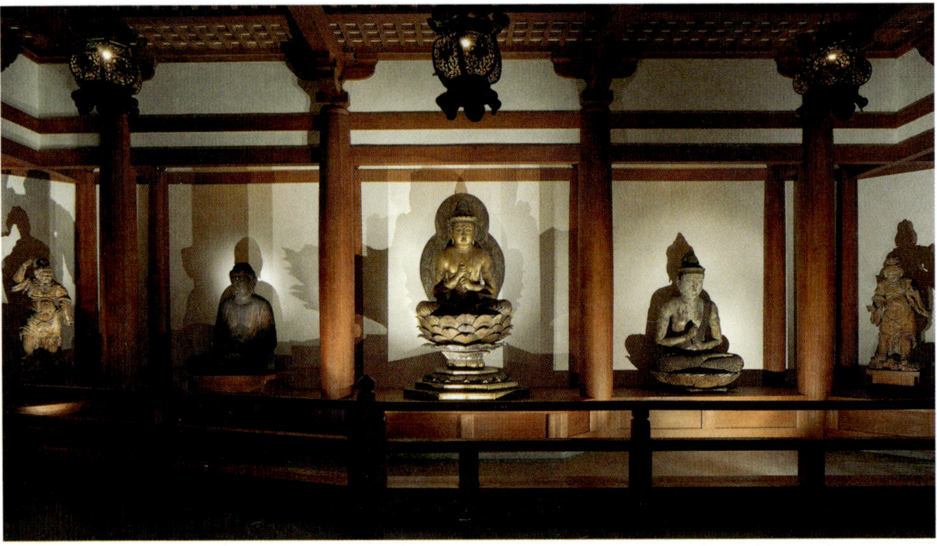

Fig. 4. **Buddhist Temple room, Museum of Fine Arts, Boston.** The wooden pillars and wall brackets of this special gallery help evoke the atmosphere of a Japanese temple. The gallery was inspired in part by the main hall of Hōryūji Temple (fig. 31). Subdued lighting contributes to its reverential and contemplative atmosphere. Photo © 2020 Museum of Fine Arts, Boston.

setting. Notwithstanding such special installations and events, it is still difficult to convey to museumgoers the range of religious meanings that suffuse a Buddhist image in an actual temple.

This book is an attempt to outline the vast array of meanings that icons have carried in traditional Buddhism, specifically meanings that predate the advent of museums. They include the various identities of Buddhist figures, the stories behind them, their appearance and symbolism, the magical "living" qualities recognized in them, their treatment in ritual settings, and their influence on the larger religious landscape of Japan. The site where these meanings are best expressed is the Buddhist temple itself, not only historic ones but also those built in recent times to the extent that they preserve the layout, practices, and outlook of traditional Buddhism. Images enshrined in such settings are surrounded by objects, sounds, smells, and activities quite different from those of a museum. In seeking to convey something of that ambiance, this work attempts to transport the reader to another time and space and to reconstruct—or, more precisely, to reimagine—the earlier Japanese experience of Buddhist icons. If I had to apply a timeframe to this premodern consciousness, it would extend roughly from 700 to 1800, just before museums began to appear in world culture. Needless to say, an immense variety of beliefs, rituals, and images evolved over those centuries, and, admittedly, I have elided them into a broad, open-ended construct representing the premodern religious worldview. In this, I must ask the indulgence of art specialists, for this study aims at revealing the religious perceptions of images rather than the characteristics and stages of Buddhist art over the sweep of Japanese history.

One word of caution both to myself and to the reader: what I present in this book should not be taken as the "real" meaning of Buddhist icons. As with all objects, they have a changing meaning depending on context, audience, and other cultural variables. Certainly icons, as material objects, bear tangible physical features, but how these features are understood is contingent on numerous factors independent of the objects themselves. What this means is that the pleasures or perplexities experienced by the museumgoer looking at an image of the Buddha today are no less "authentic" than the reverence and awe experienced by a twelfth-century Japanese encountering the same image in a Buddhist temple. They are profoundly different experiences, and one person might look at the other as miscomprehending the image. But each view is true to what the object is in that context, delineated by the particular cultural capacities and conceptual options that each setting has to offer.[5]

The following chapters are an attempt to uncover and explicate the many layers of religious meaning found in Japanese Buddhist icons. I begin by outlining the West's historical encounter with such images and elucidating Buddhism's own understanding of them. I then turn to the connection between icons and religious narrative: stories that define and shape the religion and reverberate through every aspect of it. Next, I explore the attributes and symbolism of these images as related to these stories. From there, I consider a wide variety of Buddhist figures and the way they diversify core Buddhist themes—dedicating three chapters to Buddhas, Bodhisattvas, and Buddhist divinities, respectively. Next, I examine temple settings and rituals as a primary mode of engagement with icons, wherein they are recognized as living religious entities. And finally, I look beyond the Buddha image to identify a similar power lodged in other religious objects—relics, scriptures, inscriptions, revered people, and so forth—that constitute the complex sacred landscape of premodern Japan. In all these explorations, the goal is to highlight the religious perception of these objects and the religious response to them. That, I propose, is what it means to "behold the Buddha" (fig. 5).

I would like to add that my original hope in assembling illustrations for this volume was to include as many images as possible from temples themselves, especially of the most renowned Buddhist icons in Japan. In the end I have had to rely on images of diverse pedigrees, many from museums in both Japan and the West. There are several reasons for this. One is that photography is severely restricted in most Buddhist temples, especially of enshrined icons. Another is the difficulty and considerable expense of gaining permission to publish reproductions of Japan's most famous Buddhist images. As a result, the selection of illustrations may not be the most representative from an art historical perspective. But my goal here is not to showcase the art per se but to illustrate points about Buddhism as a religion. With that in mind, these illustrations, I believe, serve their purpose.

I should emphasize also that this book does not seek to propose any new scholarly theory, instead deriving its information and analyses from an extensive literature on Buddhism and art. Its originality lies perhaps in how it combines these ideas. I draw, respectively, on the traditional strengths of scholars of religion (sensitivity to religious narratives, doctrines, beliefs, practices, and rituals) and art historians (close attention to formal qualities of images and their historical development). In fact, the impulse to write this book comes in part from a wave of scholarship appearing over the last few

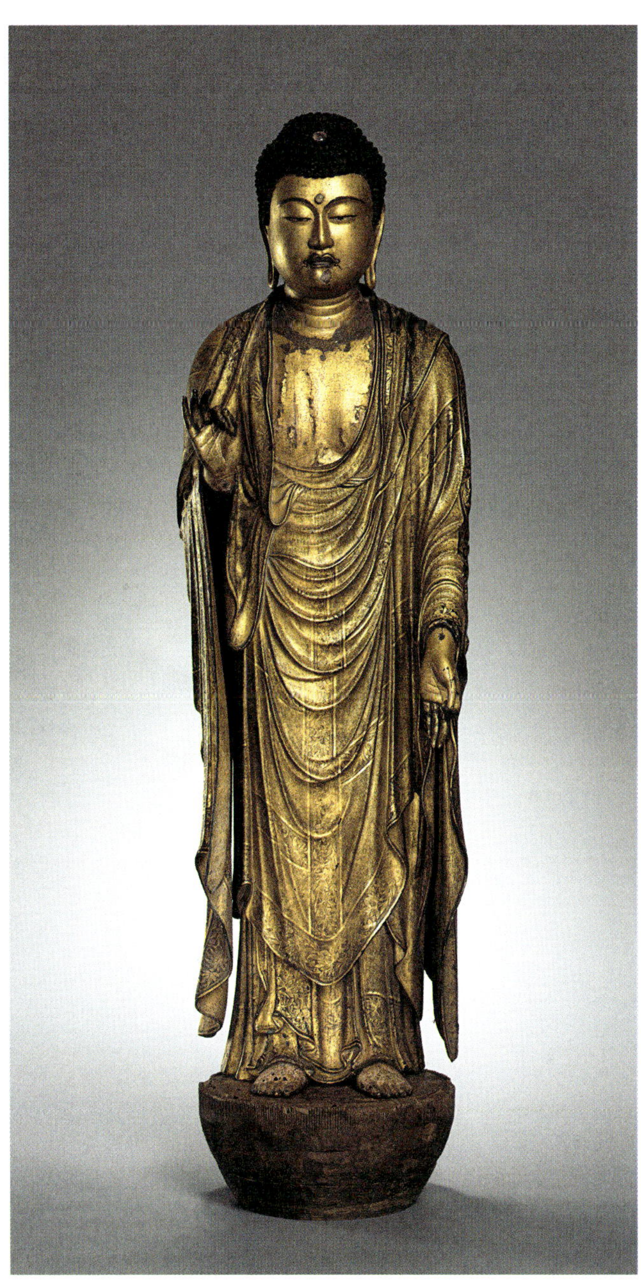

Fig. 5. Buddha of Infinite Life and Light (Amida), 13th cent. An archetypal image of the Buddha in a standing pose bearing most of the standard physical features in both attire and bodily marks. It is representative of the type of icon frequently encountered in a Japanese temple, and of the appearance Buddhists would bring to mind when recollecting the Buddha.

decades representing interdisciplinary collaborations between Asian art historians and scholars of Buddhism. It is gratifying to witness this permeability between our disciplines. Still, I must apologize to art historians if I do not adhere to the conventions and concerns of their field, for I am asking different questions and seeking different answers of the iconic objects that we both study.

Finally, for practical reasons I have restricted the scope of this work to Japan without attempting to review the vast store of Buddhist iconography in other parts of Asia, though it is just as rich and diverse and consequential. I hope the book will be of value, first, to readers interested in Japanese Buddhism who may be attracted to its texts and philosophical insights while knowing less about its sacred imagery. Second, I hope the work can serve as a handbook for people traveling to Japan and visiting Buddhist temples, helping them identify and understand the multitude of images confronting them and the complex settings in which they appear. Finally, I hope that museumgoers themselves find their experience expanded and enriched by the information contained in this work. After all, the museum encounter is an ever-evolving experience.

PART I

MAKING SENSE OF BUDDHIST IMAGES

CHAPTER 1

ATTRACTION AND AVERSION TO BUDDHIST ICONS

Most anyone traveling to Japan's ancient capital of Nara will visit the magnificent Tōdaiji, the Great Eastern Temple. It stands as a monument to the high civilization imported from China through which Japan's ruling elite sought to define itself in the eighth century. Now, as then, the temple is one of Japan's foremost treasures. It reflects how much the national identity of the country has been intertwined with Buddhism throughout history. Visitors to the Tōdaiji will approach the temple via a long and wide stone-paved avenue extending from south to north. They first encounter a grand gate, the Great South Gate (Nandaimon), which looks more like a building in its own right with a passageway through the middle. Upon mounting the steps of the gate, they immediately confront massive images of two ominous-looking guardian figures in alcoves on each side. Their ferocious faces and muscular posturing provoke a sense of foreboding in those coming to visit the temple (fig. 59).

Next, people continue along the stone-paved approach about three hundred yards more to the central temple complex, which is surrounded by a high, roofed wall with an intermediate gate. After entering a portal at the far left, they proceed into a vast courtyard and find themselves standing at the south end of a long walkway leading to the main temple building. There the stately Hall of the Great Buddha (Daibutsuden) towers majestically before them (fig. 6). At first glance it does not look radically different from other Japanese Buddhist temples: large wooden pillars, cantilevered eaves, gracefully curving roof lines, and orderly rows of roof tiles. But quickly it becomes apparent that the structure is immense, purportedly the

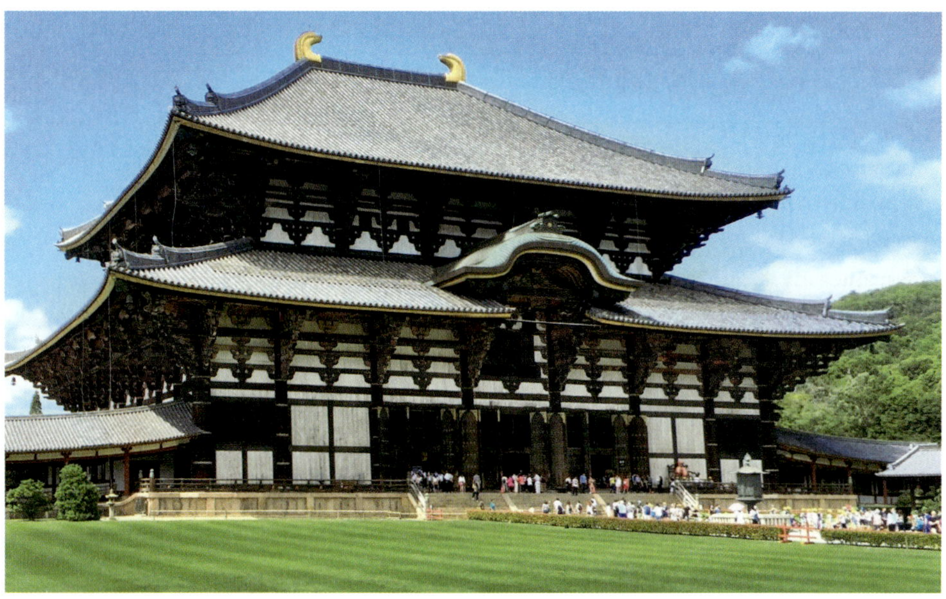

Fig. 6. Great Buddha Hall. Tōdaiji Temple, Nara. This is the hall in which the Great Buddha of Nara is enshrined. It is said to be the largest wooden building in the world. Originally constructed in the mid-700s, it was twice destroyed by wartime fires, in 1180 and 1567. The second reconstruction, delayed for more than a century, resulted in the current building, which is somewhat narrower than its predecessors.

largest wooden building in the world. This realization is confirmed with each pace taken toward the front porch, until one is standing dwarfed by the massive wooden doors at the entrance.

When people finally step inside the building, they are first struck by the darkness of the cavern they have entered. But as their eyes adjust to the light, they realize with a mixture of astonishment and awe that a gigantic bronze image of the Buddha is situated right in front of them, five stories tall (fig. 7). Face placid and eyes half closed, the Buddha seems emotionless and remote, even though his presence is immediate and overwhelming. Once people regain their composure, they slowly and respectfully walk around the enormous stone platform on which the Daibutsu, or Great Buddha, rests. Little by little, they take in the details of this religious and cultural icon of Japan. The Buddha is posed in a cross-legged sitting position. His robes are draped in an orderly fashion across his shoulders, and cascade down over his lap. In demeanor he seems inward looking and contemplative except for the gestures of his powerful hands. He holds the right one up, palm out, offering assurances and goodwill, and he rests the left one, palm up, on his knee with the fingers uncurled graciously. His head bears a number of peculiar details: snail-shell-like ringlets dotting his scalp depicting close-cropped hair; huge drooping earlobes; and a mysterious round dot between his eyebrows. Behind the Buddha is a giant gilded mandorla backdrop, bearing representations

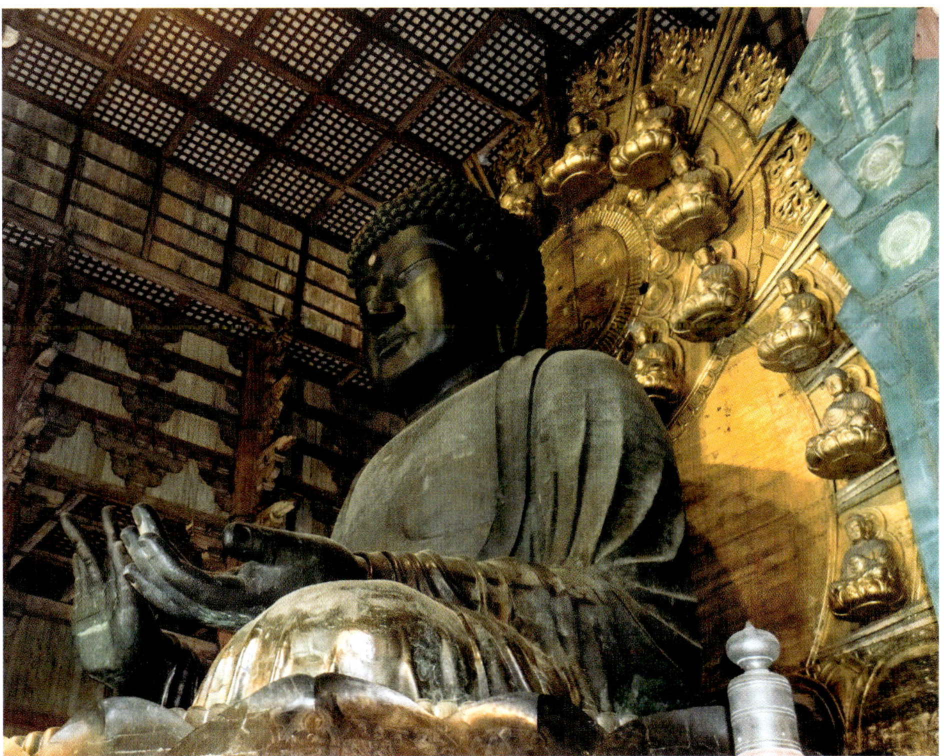

Fig. 7. Great Buddha. Tōdaiji Temple, Nara. The Great Buddha of Nara, a bronze image rising forty-eight feet above its pedestal, bears the appearance, adornments, pose, and gestures found in traditional Buddhist iconography. The practice of building monumental images of the Buddha was widespread in the Buddhist world—India, Central Asia, China, and elsewhere. The Great Buddha of Nara was recast in the late 1600s after the temple's destruction by fire a century earlier.

of light rays that emanate from the Buddha and supporting other miniature images of the Buddha that create a frame around his massive body. The entire statue sits on a broad, low lotus-flower-shaped pedestal, and on each lotus petal around the scalloped perimeter is etched the image of another Buddha surrounded by a celestial host hovering over many layers of heavens and multiple worlds (fig. 37). Flanking the Great Buddha on each side are two other immense images, Bodhisattvas (figures on the path to Buddhahood), both with manifold adornments of their own, some of which are similar to the Buddha's. If it were not for the enormity of the Great Buddha, these Bodhisattvas would appear as daunting icons in their own right. Anyone circumambulating the Great Buddha and observing this grand display will leave the hall dazzled and mesmerized, but also perhaps perplexed. This historic icon of Japan carries within it multiple layers of meaning. I will return to it repeatedly to illustrate various features of Buddhist images. Readers, I hope, will develop a familiarity with it as if they were revisiting the Tōdaiji Temple each time.

THE WESTERN GAZE

Some Christian and Jewish observers, with recollections of scriptural references to graven images, may have a feeling of discomfort when confronted with Buddhist icons. They might wonder what manner of religion would create such a colossus as the Great Buddha of Nara. I myself, in my first encounters with Buddhist images decades ago, also found something unsettling about them. Their faces looked placid, emotionless, and remote, and I questioned how religious ideals might be expressed in them. These responses may arise, consciously or not, from an age-old polemic that portrays venerated objects as idols. Early Jesuit missionaries visiting Japan in the sixteenth and seventeenth centuries identified the Daibutsu, or Great Buddha, of Kyoto (which no longer exists) in this way (fig. 8):

This metal idol, which they call Daibutsu, might well be included among the seven wonders of the world, and I fancy that it is comparable to the most wonderful of them all. It is made entirely of bronze and is so singularly tall that however extravagantly it might be praised (and they certainly extolled it) it was quite impossible to visualize what I eventually saw. . . .

They were building the temple [around it] when I passed and I understand from letters since received that they have yet to finish the work. I learned that more than 100,000 carpenters and all kinds of workmen were engaged in the operations—only the devil could have devised this waste in order to make the Emperor use up his wealth and riches.[1]

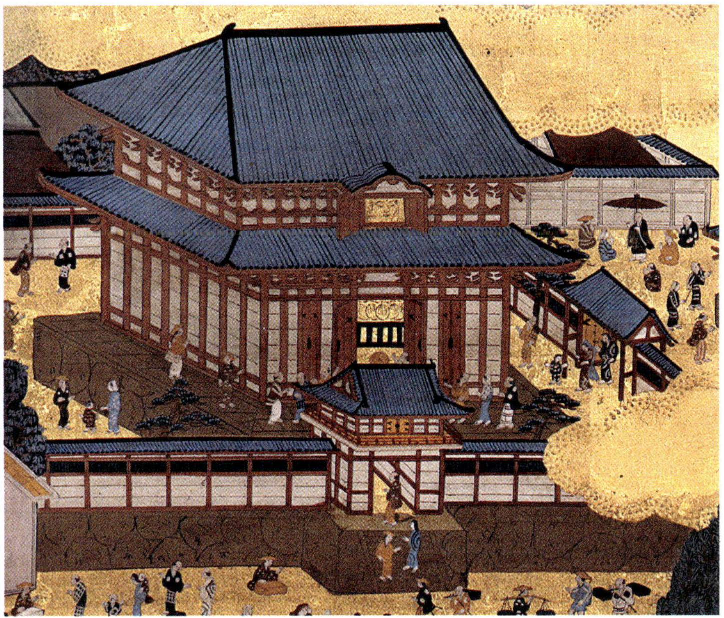

Fig. 8. Great Buddha Hall of Hōkōji Temple, Kyoto. Detail of *Rakuchū Rakugai Zu Byōbu*, 18th cent. This is how the main hall of Hōkōji Temple might have appeared when Jesuit missionaries encountered it in the late sixteenth and early seventeenth centuries. Its Great Buddha, which no longer exists, can be seen though the window above the door, and the scalloped lotus-petal base on which it rests is visible through the door. This depiction appears on a pair of decorative folding screens showing historic sites in the capital of Kyoto.

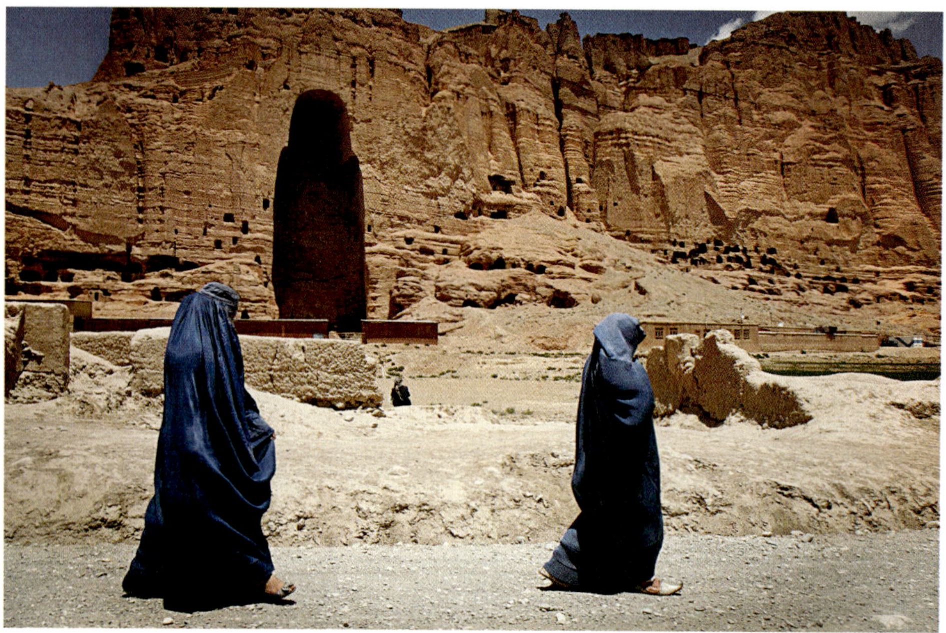

Fig. 9. **Destroyed Buddha of Bamiyan, Afghanistan.** The empty cavity in the cliff face is what remains of one of the great stone-carved Buddhas of Bamiyan. Originally constructed in the sixth century, it towered 174 feet above the ground. The Chinese Buddhist priest Xuanzang (602–664) mentioned the Bamiyan Buddhas in his travel diary when he saw them in 630 en route to India on his fourteen-year pilgrimage.

Clearly the Jesuits found the actual image magnificent, but they were inescapably tethered to the concept of idolatry, replete with negative presuppositions, when they beheld it.

Idolatry is itself an ancient theme in religious thought. The Jews of the Hebrew Bible used it to criticize the beliefs and practices of rivals and adversaries,[2] and Christians, even while developing a cult of saints with a rich and inviting ensemble of Christian icons, invoked idolatry as a standard condemnation of pagans.[3] The concept also became prominent in Islam, influencing the way that Muslim conquerors who swept into South Asia from the eighth through the eleventh century reacted to local Buddhist and Hindu temples. Notwithstanding a demonstrated history of using figurative images in Islam, the rhetoric of idolatry continues to be a potent discourse today, as evidenced by the Taliban's destruction of the giant stone Buddhas of Bamiyan in March 2001 despite international appeals, as it sought to repress the local Hazara population of Afghanistan (fig. 9).[4] Because the accusation of idolatry is predicated on the assumption that the veneration of images—the belief that a physical object is synonymous with God—arises from some distorted and pernicious impulse, it is treated as a grave religious error.[5] Accusations of idolatry often prompted denunciation and blatant attack in the premodern world, while in modern times responses have more typically ranged from quiet condescension to open contempt. Because idolatry as a concept carries within it a confessional and polemical subtext, it would seem to have limited usefulness as an analytical category in the study of religion. And yet the term did creep into "objective" scholarship during the early twentieth century as scholars attempted to classify and explain the iconography of Asian religions.[6] Nowadays the more benign language of "images" and "icons" tends to prevail in its place.

In the late nineteenth and twentieth centuries, more tolerant and generous approaches to Buddhist images began to emerge, offering an alternative to the rhetoric of idolatry. These approaches arose in tandem with the West's increasing fascination with Buddhism, which was part of a modern reconstitution of religion taking place worldwide. Through a process of demythologization and winnowing of so-called superstitions, the perception of Buddhism that came to dominate was that of a rational and humanistic religion without a God, aimed primarily at self-discipline and personal transformation.[7] This reassessment produced several different but related interpretations of Buddhist icons. The first is that Buddhist images arose to accommodate a lower level of religious awareness, one that sought an object of veneration as the centerpiece of religious activity. Icons were created, that is, to satisfy the yearnings of people who did not understand Buddhism's central message of spiritual self-cultivation, and they functioned as heuristic devices to lead people gradually to this realization.[8] Such an interpretation, while well meaning, tends to treat icons as unsophisticated appendages of the religion, and its condescending view of them is faintly reminiscent of the earlier stance toward idolatry.

A second interpretation arising from the humanist view of Buddhism is to treat icons as symbols of the great truths and principles of the religion. Thus, images of the Buddha are not intended to portray him as a god, for there is no God in this modern demythologized understanding of Buddhism. Rather, the images are commemorative and symbolic expressions reminding people of who the Buddha was, and they point beyond themselves to the process of self-perfection that everyone must undergo. As a search for universal ideals, this humanist view of Buddhism has certainly created an openness to the religion that did not exist before. It has also furthered an appreciation of icons by linking them to the edifying values found in Buddhism—principally, a life of self-examination and the virtues of wisdom and compassion. But one unfortunate result of this approach is that the icons themselves are moved quickly from center stage, and the abstract beliefs and ideals of Buddhism are highlighted as the true expression of the religion. That is, Buddhist images are treated as signposts guiding people to great truths that, when realized, allow them to set aside the icons themselves.[9] I cannot help but wonder if this response—to shift attention from icons to abstract principles—has also been influenced by the anti-iconic discourse of earlier times.

A third approach to Buddhist images may be described as aestheticism. This response can be found in museum culture today, though it is not the only response at work there. It is to treat icons as emblems of Asia's high culture and to focus on their form, appearance, expressive detail, and presentation. It is to love them for their visual richness and their aesthetic qualities. This approach too has brought a sympathetic treatment of Buddhism into the modern period and, more than the others, has allowed the icons to remain center stage in an appreciation of the religion. In fact, it has given rise to great celebrations of Buddhist art at major museums all over the world. But there is a danger in relying on aestheticism as the primary mode of approaching Buddhist images. It is that the meaning of

Buddhist icons *as icons*—that is, as religious objects that carry a religious message and evoke a religious response—tends to get lost.[10] For that reason, it is important to look beyond aestheticism when seeking to understand Buddhist images.

BEHOLD THE BUDDHA

All these approaches have value, and it would be wrong to think that any of them is invalid or without basis in the religion. Certainly, throughout the history of Buddhism icons have been recognized in one context or another in all these roles—as heuristic devices and as symbolic expressions of great truths and as aesthetic objects. Together these approaches have provided a strong antidote to any lingering impressions of Buddhist icons as idols. Despite their value, such approaches still fall short in capturing the complex and multifaceted religious dimensions of Buddhist icons, especially as they were understood in premodern Japan.

If I had to propose a guiding theme for exploring the religious dimensions of Buddhist icons, it would be to "behold the Buddha." I realize this may sound superficial, but it hints at the kind of sensibilities that surrounded icons before the advent of museums. In its most literal sense, "seeing the Buddha" might refer to meeting the historical Buddha in person—that is, standing in his presence, bathed in his wisdom and compassion, and receiving the enlightening message of the Dharma, the teachings and truths that he has propounded. Certainly, the Buddhist scriptures proclaim what a rare and wondrous event it is to be born during the lifetime of the Buddha and to encounter his teachings directly.[11] For those not so fortunate, there were other ways of beholding the Buddha. For instance, contemplative practices were developed in which one could arrive at a mental picture of the Buddha revealing both his physical and spiritual attributes. In fact, the Buddhist expression "to see the Buddha"—in Japanese, *kenbutsu* or *kanbutsu*—typically refers to these meditative exercises and visions.[12] Yet another way of beholding the Buddha was in the form of an icon. Despite the tendency to regard such objects as commemorations of his life or as aids to meditative visions, ritual interaction with icons represented an independent and equally compelling mode of encountering the Buddha (fig. 10). In that sense, icons were as much an embodiment of the Buddha as his visionary appearance in meditation and his original physical incarnation were. The Buddha that one beheld in any of these modes was considered identical and interchangeable with his other manifestations. To that extent, icons did not offer a competing embodiment of the Buddha but rather one that was concordant with those experienced by other means.

Various thinkers in Buddhist history have attempted to theorize the nature and status of an icon. It was recognized of course as an extraordinary entity, described in popular accounts with such terms as "auspicious" (*medetashi*), "profound" (*imiji*), "splendorous" (*shōgon*), "solemn" (*ikameshii*), and "honored" (*tōtoshi*). Moreover, ritual interaction with icons could trigger a religious awakening—in the words of the great Buddhist master Kūkai (774–835, fig. 86), "With a single glance [at the images], one becomes a Buddha."[13] At the same time, icons were known to have a problematic or paradoxical nature. To the extent that the Buddha transcends all characteristics, abiding in an utterly undefinable state, and that all discernible objects in the world are actually "empty," meaning devoid of essence, it should be impossible to capture the Buddha in a palpable form. In that respect an icon is a contradiction in terms. But to the extent that it can evoke a realization in the observer of the Buddha's inexpressible nature, it can function as a physical representation of the unrepresentable, so to speak. Put in terms of Buddhist doctrine, the Buddha is thought to have the capacity to manifest himself in a multitude of different ways, as expressed in the thirteenth-century collection *Sand and Pebbles*, by the priest Mujū Ichien (1226–1312):

> The true body (*shinjin*) of the Buddha is formless and ineffable (*musō munen*). Great compassion is his original vow, and he appears in various

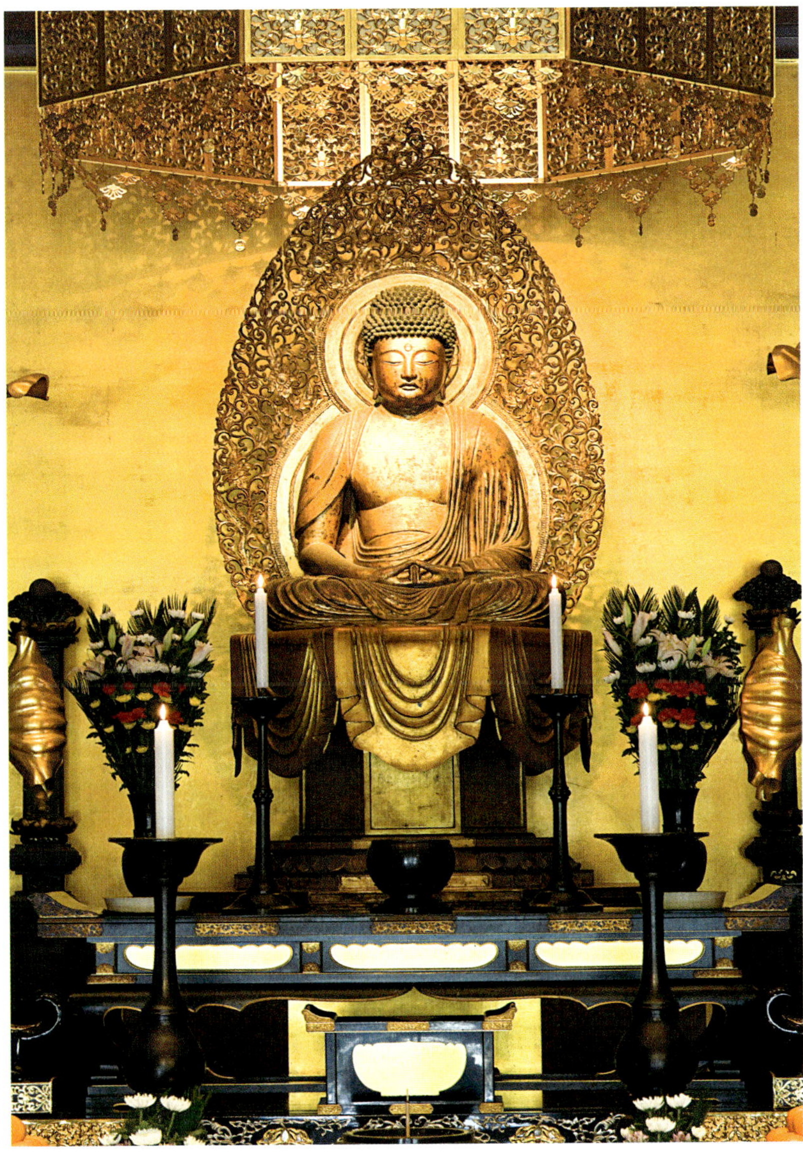

Fig. 10. **Seated Buddha Amida, 14th–16th cent. Zōjōji Temple, Tokyo.** This image of the meditating Buddha Amida is enshrined as the central icon in the main hall of Zōjōji Temple. The rituals performed in his presence follow the traditions of the Jōdo school of Buddhism in Japan.

> guises by virtue of the good seeds of merit which we have sown in previous lives. Whatever form he takes is a physical manifestation of the Buddha (*ōjin*). In conforming to the level of belief and understanding of the devotee, the Buddha simply assumes the form of wood and stone for those who think in terms of wood and stone. Even at the level of wood and stone, he who thinks on the Buddha will be benefited by the Buddha. When reverence and faith are genuinely deep and one feels sincerely close to the Buddha, then he is not at all far from the benefits of his living manifestations.[14]

Such explanations are typical of the interpretations offered by religious intellectuals who sought to speak for and justify the already widespread veneration of icons in Buddhism.

My purpose in these pages, however, is not to analyze icons through the filter of Buddhist doctrine but instead to present them simply and plainly as living religious entities. Historically, among practicing Buddhists, icons were considered alive. Specifically, they were seen as the living embodiment and instantiation of the Buddha in this world of palpable objects (and, by extension, of the Buddha's Dharma, and of Nirvana, his perfect state of enlightenment and liberation). This view, needless to say, has the potential to resurrect suspicions of idolatry. But it is consistent with the belief that the Buddha appears in the world in mysterious ways. Icons are just one of his manifestations. People encountering Buddhist images today might recognize their special character just as premodern believers did—that is, they might "behold" the Buddha—or they might simply regard icons as they would any inert object. Yet their inability to see the Buddha's identity in the object would not detract from his "real" presence there—not, at least, in the eyes of those who experience the icon as alive.

The materialist mindset of modern culture tends to treat things reductionistically. I hope to resist that impulse in this consideration of Buddhist images. Though it may feel unnatural, it might be possible by an act of the imagination—a suspension of disbelief and a leap of faith—for people today, briefly, to behold the Buddha in the icons they encounter.

CHAPTER 2

THE BUDDHIST IMAGE AS SACRED STORY

Images of the Buddha have a narrative quality about them, as if telling a story or describing a momentous occurrence. That story discloses the events that make the Buddha what he is and establishes his connection to the world. It thus constitutes a sacred narrative that undergirds the religion as a whole. Observers who are attuned to it while engaging the icon are able to "behold" the Buddha and "hear" his story. Those who are not may find the image just another interesting object—or perhaps a perplexing one.

The role of story, or sacred narrative, in religion has been a topic in religious studies for decades. In its simplest form, it revolves around the idea that a powerful component in the structure of a religion is its narrative base, that is, the sacred story that expresses and embodies its core values, goals, and ideals. Neither philosophical principles nor moral truths can be a substitute for it, for they cannot exert the same emotive influence that the story does. In fact, philosophy and ethics are in a sense dependent on the sacred story for their power and legitimation. Such an analysis of religion presupposes that the narrative mind-set—that is, the propensity to think in story-like structures—is widespread in human experience. Children learn structured thought through hearing stories and telling them again and again. Humans organize their lives in story-like patterns: "First this happens. Then I will do that. This will lead to that result. And it will all end up this way." These narrative structures permeate countless dimensions of human activity: memories, hopes, moral stances, daily work schedules, jokes, diaries, obituaries, tragedies, and so forth. It should not be surprising, then, to find stories built into religion and into Buddhist icons specifically.

In assuming the narrative quality of icons, one ramification is that people, whether consciously or not, are constantly searching for an underlying story when they look at icons. What this means is that a purely aesthetic viewing of an icon is impossible. Narrative questions inevitably arise: What is this image? Who is the figure? What are they doing? Why are they doing this? Just to ask the name of a depicted figure is to set in motion an inquiry into the story that gives it meaning. One can think of no more tragic fate for an icon than to lose its story. Imagine a monument, like the statue in Percy Bysshe Shelley's poem "Ozymandias," that is abandoned in the desert where no one knows its name or what it is about.

An important corollary to this is that, while religions tend to have a core sacred story, there are usually variants and spin-offs from it. In short, religions comprise not just one narrative but many, and they are in an intricate interplay with each other. One story line may dominate, but it may be expressed in many forms—embellished, abbreviated, or disguised. Moreover, other stories interweave with the core story, forming parallels, contrasts, resonances, elaborations, echoes, and refrains. The narrative corpus of the religion is the sum total of these stories, producing a complex blend of religious symbols and meaning. Buddhism's vast iconographic store is shaped as much by variant and ancillary stories as by its primary one.

This approach to icons—identifying them as the repository of a sacred story—is fraught with many problems, especially in light of contemporary literary and cultural criticism. It is no longer deemed acceptable to claim that a specific message or meaning is inherent in a particular object, whether it be a literary text, a work of art, or a religious icon. Multiple meanings surround these objects, originating as much from the people encountering them as from the objects themselves. Not even creators and authors can imbue an artistic or literary object with an unimpeachable meaning, for their intent can be lost or transformed or superseded once other people interact with it. The meaning, then, emerges from this interaction, and a Buddhist icon bears a sacred story only to the extent that those observing it bestow that reading on it.

This is not to say, though, that the meaning of a Buddhist image is unanchored or lies only in the eye of the beholder. Objects and people do not float in a vacuum, and meaning is not created randomly and without context. Rather, icons exist within interpretive communities, in which the significance of the thing at any particular moment is shaped by the shared understandings of the community that responds to and sustains it. Tissues of knowledge and interpretive traditions build up around icons and are passed on to subsequent generations along with the objects themselves. These meanings are not fixed and immutable. Variations can arise, and there may in fact be competing interpretations, as well as long-term evolutionary changes. But by and large there is a prevailing constellation of meanings that surrounds an icon at any one time. And this set of meanings—rehearsed, preserved, and perpetuated by the supporting community—is often keyed to a narrative, thereby giving the icon its sacred story. The meanings of the Buddhist images explored in this book are those found in a wide variety of interpretive communities in premodern Japan.[1]

THE LIFE OF THE BUDDHA

If Buddhism has a core narrative, it is none other than the story of the Buddha Śākyamuni (J. Shaka), who is thought to have lived in India around the sixth or fifth century BCE. This narrative, replete with mythic elements and questionable episodes, has been examined in the modern period by scholars who have sought to construct a historically verifiable biography of Śākyamuni, only to be stymied by the problematic nature of the sources they must use. Scholars have subsequently expanded their interest to the Buddha of mythic lore, for it is this mythic figure that has shaped Buddhism the most over time.[2]

The legendary story of the Buddha's life ripples throughout the religion in various guises, functioning as a narrative foundation for beliefs, practices, doctrine, and iconography. Virtually all Buddhist icons presuppose it either overtly or implicitly, and derive a certain richness and depth from it. The story thereby gives cohesion to the wide variety of images found in Buddhism. In fact, there may be an archetypal structure embedded in the story of Śākyamuni that is faintly replicated in the stories of other Buddhist figures. The structure is founded on three identifiable dimensions or phases in the Buddha's life, namely, his religious quest, enlightenment, and compassionate life thereafter. To the extent that images of other figures reflect these dimensions, they too partake in Śākyamuni's story in one way or another.

In Japan the story of Śākyamuni's life has circulated in diverse versions and formats, but one of the earliest and most pervasive was a classical Buddhist text known as the *Sutra on Past Causes and Present Effects.*[3] It became popular in Japan from the seventh or eighth century and inspired lavishly illustrated scroll editions of the text. A long tradition of Buddhist narrative art had flourished in India and China, where illustrated narratives were an established means of celebrating momentous figures of the religion and recounting their crowning achievements. So it was only natural that Śākyamuni's life would become the subject of such works in Japan too. The following synopsis of the Buddha's life is based primarily on this sutra.

Śākyamuni was born amid miraculous signs as the son of a ruler in a small kingdom at the foothills of the Himalayas. Before his birth his mother, Queen Māyā, dreamed that the Buddha-to-be descended from the heavens riding a white elephant and entered her side. He had been residing in a heaven known as Tuṣita (J. Tosotsu) waiting for the right moment to appear in the world after many previous rebirths as a Bodhisattva preparing for Buddhahood. Ten months later, as Māyā traveled from the palace, Śākyamuni was born from her right side as she stood holding on to the branch of a tree in Lumbinī garden. He immediately took seven steps, raised his right hand in the air, and declared, "I, among all deities [in heaven] and humans [on earth], am the greatest and most revered. Countless rebirths will now come to an end. During this lifetime I will benefit all humans and deities."[4] Streams of pure water poured down from the heavens to bathe his body and there was rejoicing throughout the firmament. This event is ritually reenacted at many Japanese temples each year on the eighth day of the fourth month, which is recognized as the birthday of the Buddha. Commonly, an image of the infant Śākyamuni, standing in a large basin, is installed on an altar and people come to the temple and pour fragrant water over him, replicating the heavenly streams that showered him (fig. 11). Queen Māyā died seven days after his birth and Śākyamuni was reared by her sister Mahāprajāpatī.

His father, King Śuddhodana, consulted seers about the unusual infant, who identified thirty-two auspicious physical features on his body, some of which are reproduced in Buddhist iconography. Based

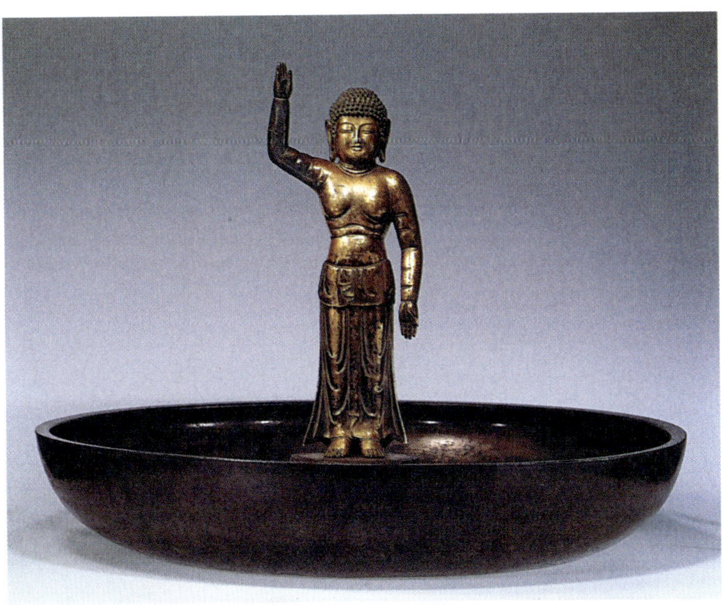

Fig. 11. Śākyamuni Buddha at birth, 8th cent. Tōdaiji Temple, Nara. The infant Śākyamuni declares that he is the most revered in heaven above and earth below. This type of image, with the figure standing in a basin, is installed on a special altar each year to have fragrant water poured over the icon to commemorate his birth.

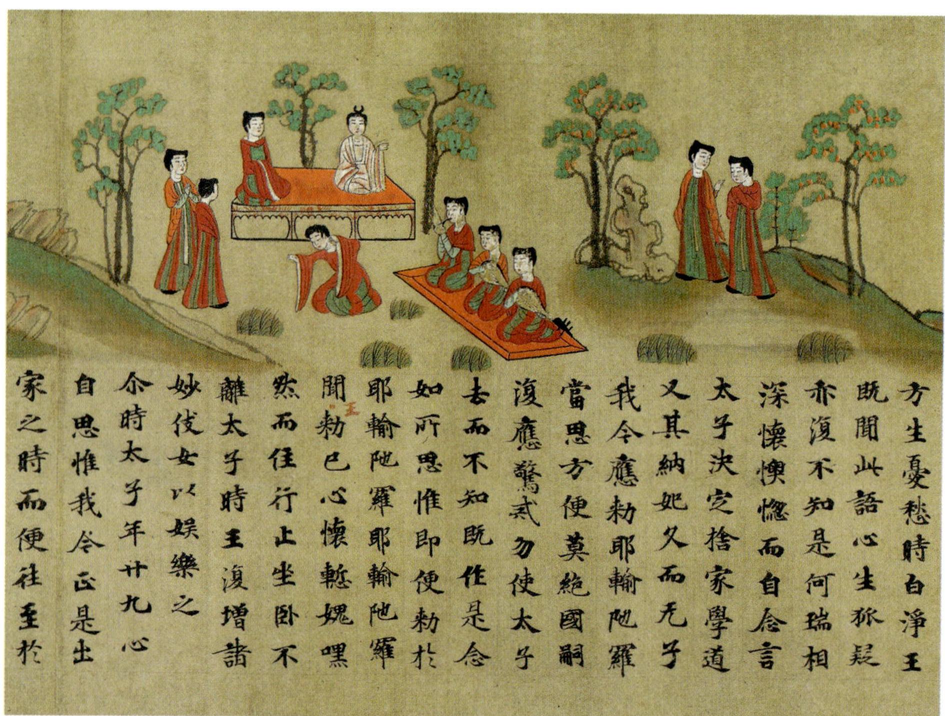

Fig. 12. Śākyamuni entertained by palace maidens. Section from *Eingakyō*, 8th cent. The prince and his wife Yaśodharā are entertained by a dancer and three musicians. This narrative scroll places illustrations in the upper register and the text of the *Sutra on Past Causes and Present Effects* in the lower.

in part on these signs, the seers predicted that either he would become a "chariot-wheel-turning" (or world-conquering) king or he would attain enlightenment, "turn the wheel of the Dharma," and save all living beings. Hearing this, his father sought to shelter him from spiritual influences and steer him toward kingship. As a result, the prince lived an insulated life, residing in three luxurious palaces provided by the king: one for the cold season, one for the hot, and one for the mild. A retinue of maidens skilled in singing and dancing served him, and seldom did he tarry from the comforts and pleasures of the palace (fig. 12). In due course, he became a student and surpassed his own teachers in all fields of knowledge. He also became proficient in the martial arts, outstripping others and accomplishing superhuman feats. When he came of age Śākyamuni was anointed crown prince, but his thoughts turned gradually to the sufferings of living beings after a brief

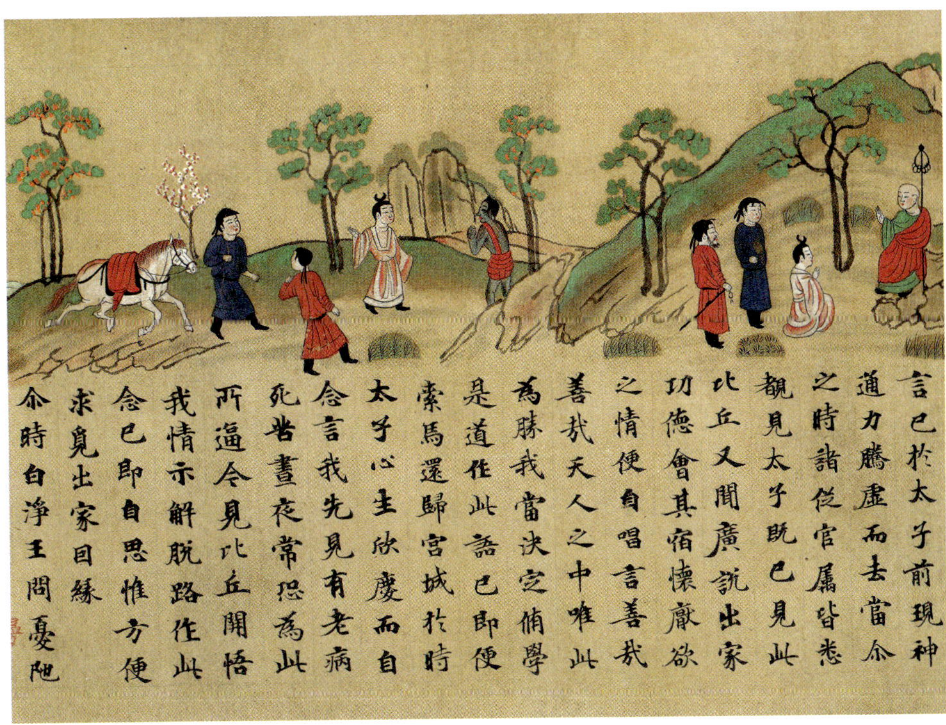

Fig. 13. Śākyamuni encountering the monk. Section from *Eingakyō*, 8th cent. On his fourth sojourn from the palace, Śākyamuni comes upon a monk (*far right*) who expounds on the virtues of a homeless life, inspiring him to embark on a path of renunciation.

experience of meditative trance, which by chance he fell into while sitting under a tree watching laborers working in the fields. Not even his subsequent marriage to the most beautiful and refined lady of the land, Yaśodharā, could diminish these feelings of sorrow and pity.

One day, as the story goes, the young prince decided to make a series of rare sojourns on horseback to gardens outside the palace, and in doing so he encountered figures conjured up by the deities to inspire him religiously. First, he happened upon a feeble old man and was moved to ponder the ravages of old age and decrepitude. Then he encountered a sick man and reflected on the frailty and vulnerability of the body. Finally, he confronted a dead man and contemplated the inescapable fate awaiting everyone. In each case, these encounters triggered deep reflections in Śākyamuni, and he came to realize the insubstantial and fleeting nature of youth, health, and life itself. On a fourth sojourn from the palace, he met an itinerant monk (fig. 13) who, in his freedom from possessions and worldly ties, seemed to offer an alternative in the face of impermanence and uncertainty. From that time, Śākyamuni set his sights on following the example set by the monk. But when he requested his father's permission to do so, the king was reluctant to give it (fig. 14). Instead, he attempted to confine the prince to the palace, showering him with even more extravagant luxuries and pleasures.

At the age of twenty-nine (or nineteen according to some accounts), in an act known as the great departure or renunciation, Śākyamuni abandoned his princely estate and set out on a religious

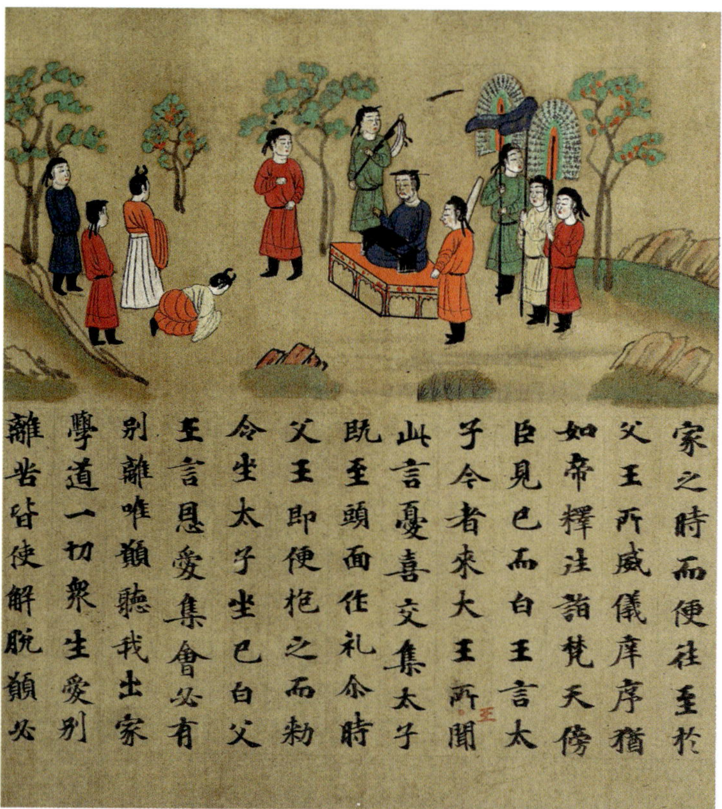

Fig. 14. Śākyamuni seeking consent to become a religious mendicant. Section from *Eingakyō*, 8th cent. Śākyamuni, bowing to his father, seeks permission to leave the palace to pursue a homeless life. The king weeps and implores him to stay.

quest that would culminate in his enlightenment and Buddhahood. In doing so he left behind a son, having fulfilled his obligation to provide an heir to the family. Because the king was resolute in opposing his departure, the deities in the heavens conspired to help Śākyamuni by causing a great sleep to fall over the members of the palace. With quiet determination, he then took his leave and, accompanied by his groomsman, rode his steed to the edge of the kingdom. There he dismounted, cast off all his adornments and opulent attire, cut off his hair, and donned humble robes. Resolving not to see his family again until he had reached his spiritual goal, he embarked on a homeless life and an austere religious quest.

This departure marked the beginning of a six-year period of religious searching. During this time Śākyamuni first sought the guidance of two ascetic teachers. But when he realized that his goal surpassed even theirs, he set out on his own to confront the riddle of worldly suffering. The course he took led him through the mortification of his body. He reduced his food intake to a single sesame seed or grain of rice a day, transforming his torso into an emaciated form resembling a withered tree. He would sit in meditation for prolonged periods, depriving himself of sleep and practicing strenuous forms of breath control. As a sign of humility, he dressed in rags and sought to tame the incessant yearnings and desires of mind and body. Śākyamuni became so proficient in these austere practices that he attracted five followers of like spiritual bent. But despite his accomplishments, the asceticism in which he excelled did not endow him with a sense of peace or understanding or liberation, as he had expected. In fact, it seemed to fuel yet another strong emotion in him, aversion. Therefore, six years into his search Śākyamuni decided to end his extreme asceticism. Rather than revert to the extravagance of his earlier life, he adopted a middle path between overindulgence and self-deprivation. At ease with his decision, Śākyamuni washed himself in the river and took nourishment from the alms offered by a cow-herding maiden. Buddhist iconography celebrates this turning point with images of a gaunt "Śākyamuni emerging from the mountains" (fig. 15).

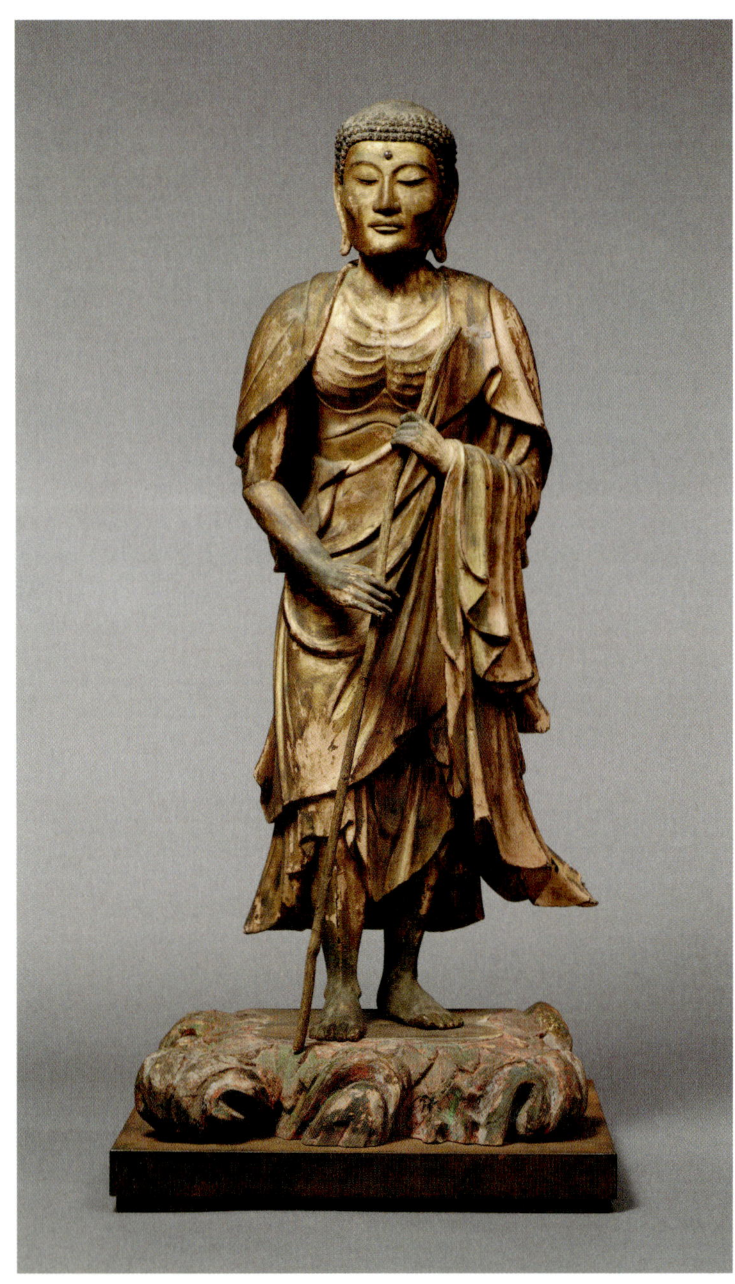

Fig. 15. Śākyamuni emerging from the mountains, 14th cent. After embarking on his religious quest, Śākyamuni subjects himself to austerities for six years, leaving his body gaunt and emaciated. This image commemorates the moment when Śākyamuni abandons his harsh asceticism and "emerges from the mountains."

Forthwith the Buddha-to-be sat down cross-legged in meditation under the so-called bodhi or enlightenment tree, vowing not to rise until he had attained complete realization. But one of the deities of heaven, Māra, the god of desire, sought to distract him from his goal. Māra first used temptation—sending his alluring daughters to kindle carnal desire—and then intimidation—dispatching fearsome armies of demons to attack him—but Śākyamuni was undeterred and pressed forward in his quest (fig. 16). During long, intense meditative explorations he first comprehended the dynamics of rebirth and suffering, how all living beings transmigrate through endless cycles of reincarnation—as humans, deities, starving ghosts, animals, or denizens of various hells. He next discerned the intricate web of causes and conditions that locks everyone in this incessant turmoil—grounded in ignorance, engendering attachments, and suffering myriad deaths, all people according to their

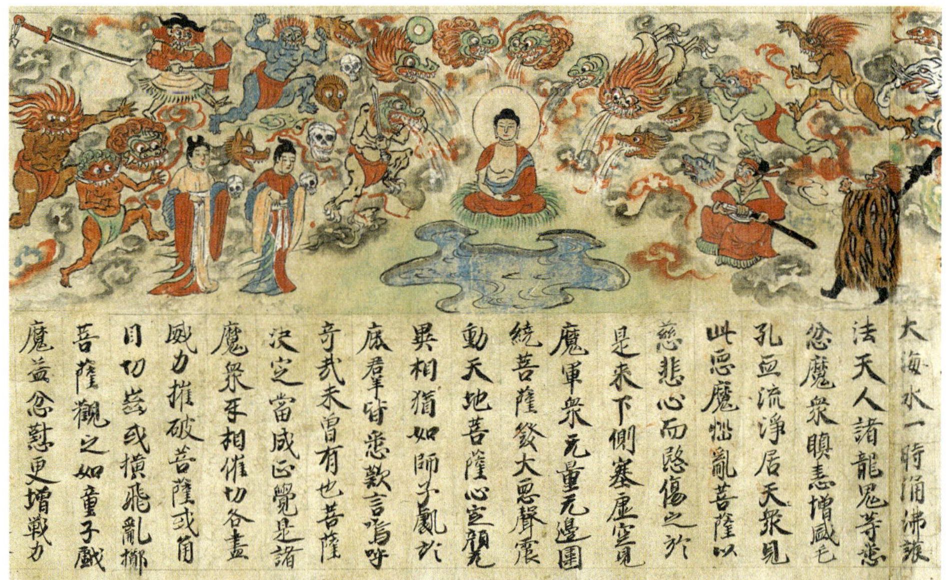

Fig. 16. Śākyamuni Buddha's enlightenment. Section from *Eingakyō*, 13th cent. Śākyamuni sits resolutely in meditation while Māra, the god of desire, tries to tempt him with his daughters (*left*) and frighten him with assorted demons and furies.

own rightful retribution. At the same time Śākyamuni realized that, just as these events build on themselves, they can also be undone. And this undoing he understood as the key to liberation, to breaking the cycle of ignorance, attachment, and endless rebirths. This sublime realization, coupled with the inner emancipation that it endows, is known throughout the Buddhist world as enlightenment or Nirvana. From the moment Śākyamuni plumbed this liberating truth at the age of thirty-five he became the Buddha. In iconography this enlightenment event, the culmination of his religious quest, is captured in the pose of the Buddha in a state of perfect meditation.

At this point Śākyamuni questioned whether ordinary humans, so deluded and enmeshed in their own petty concerns, could possibly grasp the profundity of this truth. But with the urging of the deities of heaven (except for Māra), who saw Śākyamuni as the greatest hope for the liberation of all beings, he rose from his meditation seat and embarked on a lifelong career of proclaiming this truth, the Dharma. What made Śākyamuni the Buddha was not simply his own spiritual liberation but also his unceasing efforts to bring others to liberation. His first encounter was with two merchants who greeted him as a sage, offering alms as a sign of reverence. From there the Buddha proceeded to Deer Park near Benares, where his former followers were sojourning.

These five ascetics had broken with Śākyamuni after his decision to abandon asceticism. Upon encountering them he expounded for the first time the teachings of Buddhism, thereby "setting the wheel of the Dharma turning." Specifically, the Buddha proclaimed the middle path to enlightenment, a course that lies between the extremes of self-gratification and self-mortification. He also revealed the manifold forms of suffering in the world and the chain of causes that produce them. And then he explained the Four Noble Truths:

> Suffering is what you should know. Habitual behavior is what you should cease. Nirvana is what you should attain. The path is what you should practice. To wit, I realize there is suffering and therefore

cease habitual behavior. Thereupon I attain Nirvana practicing the path. As a result, I achieve supreme and perfect enlightenment.[5]

His articulation of these truths in three parts at Deer Park has come to be known as the three turnings of the wheel of the Dharma. The five followers were immediately awakened and took up the Buddhist path. They became the first arhats, or enlightened monks, and the first adherents of the Buddha's new religious order, the Sangha. Thus, at Deer Park the so-called Three Treasures (*sanbō*) of Buddhism—the Buddha, the Dharma, and the Sangha—were actualized.

The import of the Buddha's teachings is that human beings are caught in a web of cravings and attachments and constantly long for permanence and happiness. Such desires drive people to actions, or karma, that result in more deep-seated longings and, depending on their deeds, in an endless series of rebirths. Despite people's pursuit of stability and comfort, life is characterized by continual change and disappointments. The goal, therefore, should be to realize the fleeting nature of things and to break out of the self-perpetuating cycle of attachments. To do so one must realize that even the inner self, which people fall back on and cling to in desperation, is also a conceptually fabricated object of one's hopes and desires. Once illusions about the self and the world are overcome, a person experiences emancipation and supreme understanding—in short, enlightenment. The path leading to this goal consists, first, of ethical actions, which help reverse and neutralize self-serving and self-deceptive impulses. Second, it entails meditation—that is, quieting the mind of its incessant yearnings so that it can perceive the world with clarity. Third, it involves the cultivation of wisdom—specifically, comprehending the Dharma so as to see things as they truly are, without distortion or self-interest.

Throughout the remaining years of his life, the Buddha spread his teachings widely to people in diverse circumstances and walks of life—old and young, male and female, rich and poor, lowly and powerful, urban and rural, pious and worldly, socially engaged and reclusive. His commitment to spread them demonstrated that compassion for others was as deeply embedded in his religious consciousness as dispassion for things. The implication is that detachment from the world and compassion for living beings both arise out of the selflessness of enlightenment. People were attracted to the Buddha as much because of his sagely aura as because of the persuasiveness of his teachings. To stand face-to-face in his presence—that is, to behold the Buddha—was to encounter the Dharma incarnate. People perceived him not simply as a great teacher but also as the palpable embodiment of these ideals, a living manifestation of their truth. This is one reason images of the Buddha were always considered symbols of much more than just a man.

Among those immediately drawn to the Buddha were religious renunciants and seekers much like Śākyamuni himself. Beyond his five converts at Deer Park were the three Kāśyapa brothers and their followers, forest ascetics who venerated fire as sacred. Śākyamuni won them over with his spiritual serenity and miraculous powers, including his ability to defeat a demonic dragon and capture it in his begging bowl. There were also the renowned monks Śāriputra and Maudgalyāyana, who forsook their own master and joined Śākyamuni after hearing of his teaching that "all things arise from causes and conditions and no people are the master of themselves." Among the Buddha's disciples, Śāriputra emerged as the greatest in wisdom and Maudgalyāyana as the greatest in supernatural powers. In addition, the monk known as Kāśyapa the Great, famous for both his religious knowledge and the breadth of his practice, sought out Śākyamuni as a teacher and was awakened by his teachings. Kāśyapa is sometimes mentioned as the eldest of his disciples and the one who presided over the so-called First Council when the Buddha's teachings were collected and recited after his death. These are only a few of the many renunciants who became Śākyamuni's disciples, some of whom are portrayed in Buddhist iconography. The lifestyle they took up consisted of distancing themselves from domestic life, taking vows of celibacy, forswearing harm to any living being, begging for food and other material support, keeping minimal possessions, and living a life of morality, discipline, mental cultivation, and self-control. Adherents who dedicated themselves to this path comprised the earliest Buddhist Sangha, the order of monks and nuns. Those who attained enlightenment were known as arhats.

Besides this group there was another constituency in the Buddha's following: ordinary people who, instead of separating themselves from society, remained tied to their family and community, but were nonetheless drawn to the spiritual aura of the Buddha and dedicated themselves to the selflessness, wisdom, and liberation he preached. The two passing merchants who offered alms and homage to Śākyamuni immediately after his enlightenment are good examples. In response to these two the Buddha predicted they would receive good fortune, have a felicitous rebirth, hear the sublime teachings, comprehend the truth, and attain highest realization. The culmination of this encounter was the merchants' taking the Three Refuges—in the Buddha, the Dharma, and the Sangha—a religious vow common to both clerical and lay Buddhists. Also, the Buddha preached to crowds when he sojourned near Rājagṛha, the capital of the kingdom of Magadha in ancient India. There not only the townspeople but also the king, Bimbisāra, together with his ministers and high-caste brahmins, showed their reverence for the Buddha, sought his teachings, and received the Three Refuges without opting for the homeless life of a renunciant (fig. 17). Following this meeting, Bimbisāra was moved to donate a pleasure garden in a bamboo grove to the Buddha and his Sangha, where they frequently went into retreat during the rainy season. Such support of the Sangha with alms and gifts became typical of lay Buddhists, but many also adopted an ethical lifestyle, performed devotions to the Buddha, cultivated clarity of mind, and aspired to enlightenment. Throughout history the construction of icons and temples was often sponsored by Buddhist lay followers who found great spiritual meaning in these images and religious sites.

The story of Śākyamuni's death at the age of eighty is not recorded in the *Sutra on Past Causes and Present Effects* but is found

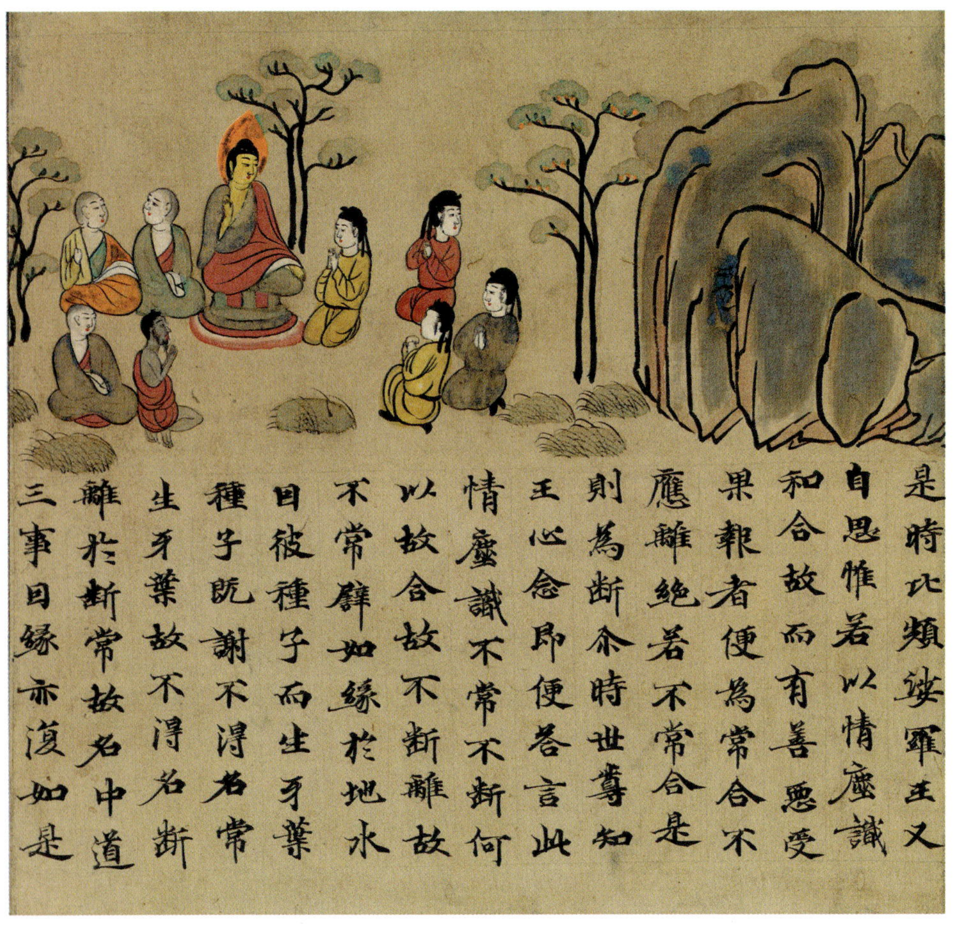

Fig. 17. Śākyamuni Buddha preaching. Section from *Eingakyō*, 8th cent. The Buddha preaches to renunciants and lay people alike. Monks appear in robes with shaved heads (*left*), together with a bearded ascetic in red, while lay people are in ordinary clothes with caps and long hair (*right*).

in a group of so-called Nirvana texts, most prominently the *Sutra on the [Buddha's] Great Nirvana Without Remainder*.[6] According to it, Śākyamuni traveled with his entourage to a quiet spot near the town of Kuśinagara in northern India when he saw his death approaching. There his devoted attendant, the young disciple Ānanda, laid out a bed, and Śākyamuni reclined on his right side facing west with his head to the north under a canopy of twin *śāla* trees, which flowered and scattered blossoms out of season. At that point he gave his followers a last opportunity to ask him questions. Ānanda, seized with grief, expressed affection for his master. Śākyamuni comforted him, assuring him that he too would attain enlightenment. A wandering ascetic named Subhadra approached the Buddha, received his final teaching, and became his last disciple. Then the clans and families of the nearby Malla tribe approached to witness his passing, as did deities from the heavens. In the end, the Buddha urged his disciples to be diligent in their religious endeavors, reminding them that all composite things are transient—a message conveyed this way in one popular account from twelfth-century Japan: "You must know that soon I will enter Nirvana. Whatever flourishes must decay; whatever is born is destined to die."[7] Entering into a state of meditation, he moved through successive levels of trance and at last passed into "Nirvana without remainder" (Skt. *parinirvāṇa*), as the Buddha's death is euphemistically known. The earth shook, and most of those in attendance wept, lamenting the demise of this conqueror of worldly suffering. But those who were enlightened remained composed, reconciled to his passing. The Buddha's death is widely commemorated in Japanese temples each year on the fifteenth day of the second or third month. Many display a large scroll painting of the deathbed scene showing his close disciples and other followers, rulers and residents from the surrounding area, animals and creatures of all species, and deities and spirits of both heaven and earth—including the Buddha's mother, Queen Māyā, descending from the heavens—all gathered around the recumbent Buddha under the *śāla* trees (fig. 18). At some temples a short text is recited, known as the *Sutra of Teachings Bequeathed by the Buddha*, reputed to be the Buddha's last instructions.[8]

After the Buddha's death his body was cremated and his remains, or "relics" (Skt. *śarīra*, J. *shari*), were divided up and interred in great burial mounds known as stupas, located in various regions. These places, along with those of his birth, enlightenment, first teaching,

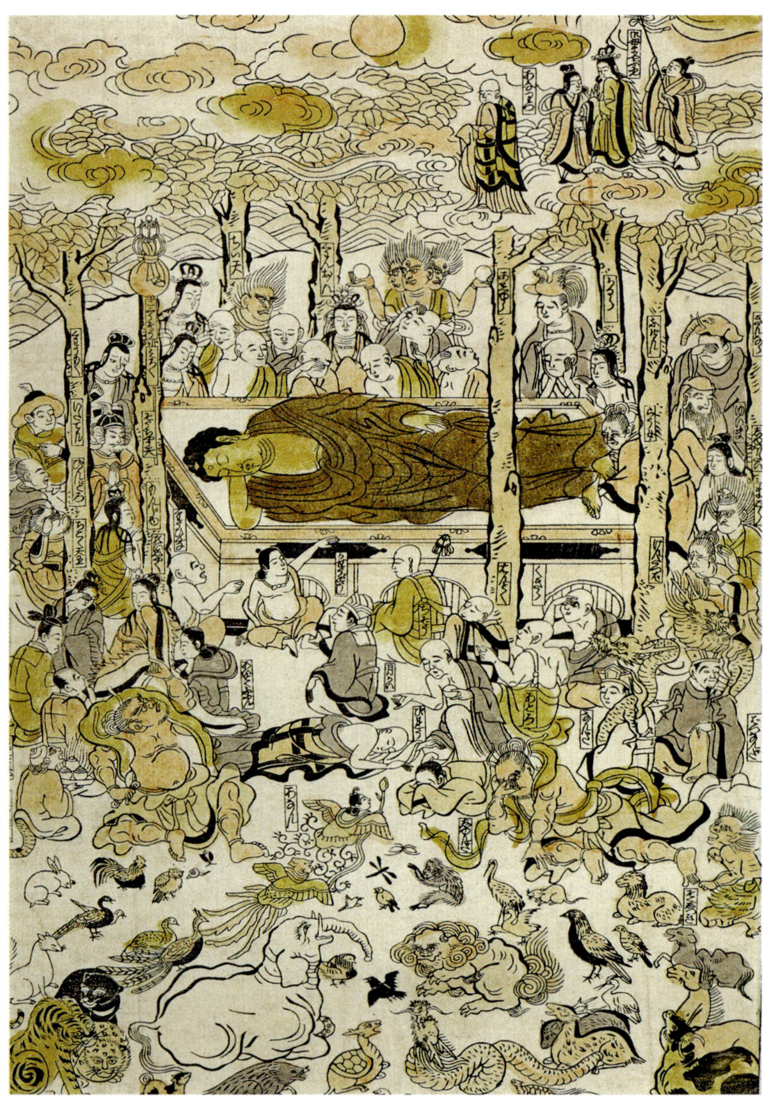

Fig. 18. **Death of the Buddha, 18th cent.** The Buddha lies on his right side with his head to the north under the flowering branches of the *śāla* trees while all manner of creatures gather round to witness his passing. This woodblock print shows the classic layout and composition of the larger deathbed depictions of the Buddha that are installed in some temples for ceremonies during the annual commemoration of his death.

and death, subsequently became sacred spots where Buddhist pilgrims flocked and many sought final interment. They considered these locations to be sites of the Buddha's abiding presence, where people could encounter him and receive spiritual merit from proximity to him. Devotional centers of this type, together with monasteries where monks and nuns pursued study, training, discipline, and mental cultivation, were the institutional bases for Buddhism as it unfolded after Śākyamuni's death. The story of his life as recounted in sutras and ancillary texts provided a narrative foundation for the subsequent expansion and elaboration of Buddhism and, indeed, for the development of Buddhist iconography itself.

THE EMERGENCE OF ICONS

The appearance of actual images of the Buddha in India occurred several centuries after his death. A few rare examples have been dated to the first century BCE, but only in the next couple of centuries did figural images become common. In fact, in early religious depictions the Buddha is often omitted altogether. Instead, objects closely associated with his story appear: a meditation seat under a bodhi tree, or a Dharma wheel, or a stupa, or his unique footprints. Most scholars have interpreted these scenes as aniconic representations of the Buddha and have given various reasons for them—most prominently, that the Buddha in Nirvana transcends physical representation. In such depictions the Buddha might be said to have a "presence in his absence" (fig. 19).[9] Other scholars have suggested that these scenes simply portray sacred sites where Buddhists worshiped and have questioned the claim that early Buddhists eschewed actual depictions of the Buddha.[10] Whatever the case, figural images appeared from the first century BCE alongside aniconic ones and ultimately dominated Buddhist iconography, becoming a standard marker of the religion.

According to one theory proposed in the early twentieth century, Greco-Roman influences gave rise to the first portrayals of the

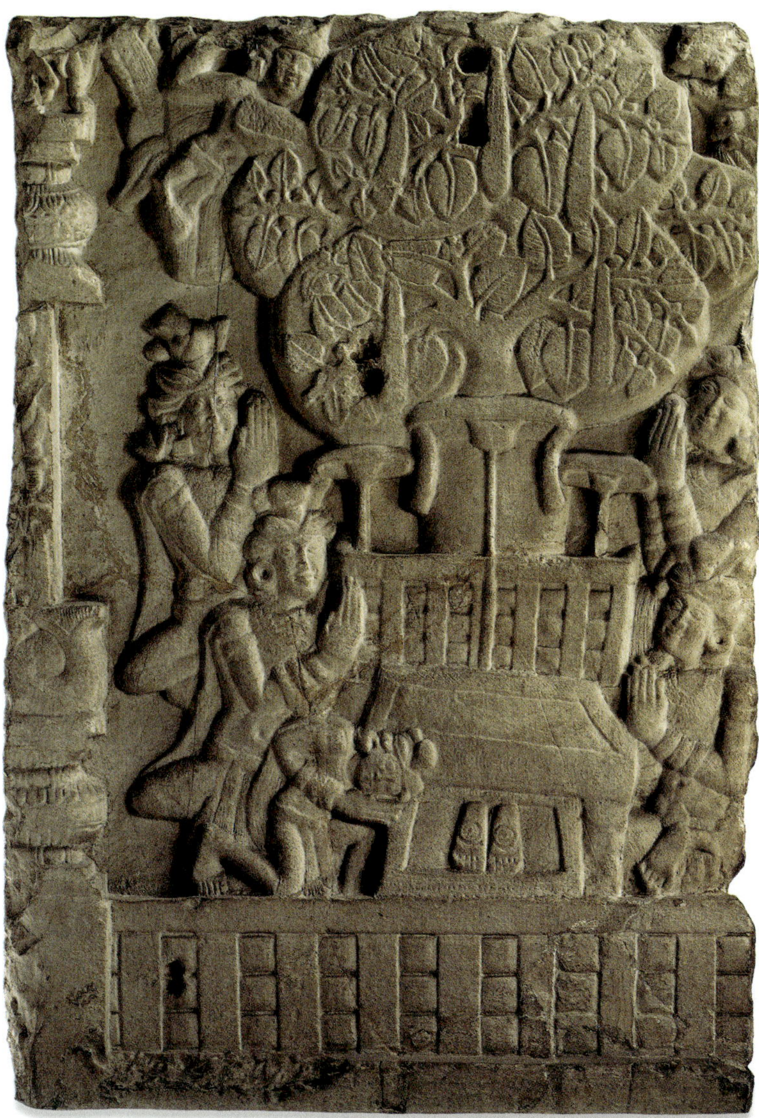

Fig. 19. Empty seat under the bodhi tree, 1st cent. BCE. Amarāvatī Stupa, India. This scene of the seat under the bodhi tree, with worshipers on each side and celestial musicians above, symbolizes the Buddha's enlightenment. The footprints below reveal Dharma wheels on the soles, one of his thirty-two physical marks. This type of image is widely interpreted as an aniconic representation of the Buddha.

Buddha in a region known as Gandhara in the Peshawar valley northwest of modern India. Buddhist icons appeared there during the first to the third centuries CE bearing many stylistic characteristics of Roman sculpture and portraiture (fig. 20). But there are also strong counterarguments that sufficient conditions existed in India proper to inspire iconic representations of the Buddha without external influences from Gandhara.[11] Once images of the Buddha did appear, they became ubiquitous in the religion and synonymous with it. In Buddhist settings of all types—monasteries, stupas, and pilgrimage sites—icons of the Buddha or other Buddhist figures were typically enshrined in places of honor and reverence. Moreover, the transmission of Buddhism to China and Japan was clearly associated with the spread of Buddhist images in conjunction with other sacred objects that were vital to the religion. Chinese recount the apocryphal dream of Emperor Ming of the Han dynasty (first century CE) in which he saw a golden man—suggestive of a gilded Buddhist image—flying through the air and landing at the palace, presaging the arrival of icons, texts, and monks.[12] Japanese, for their part, date Buddhism's arrival to 552 when an image of Śākyamuni Buddha was presented to the ruler of Japan along with religious texts and ritual implements from the ruler of the Korean kingdom of Baekje.[13]

There is also a legend on how icons originated in Buddhism that goes back to an early strata of scripture and circulated widely in variant forms in China and Japan. The account is of King Udayana of the Indian kingdom of Kauśāmbī, who was a convert to the Buddha's teachings. He was disheartened when the Buddha took leave for an extended period to proclaim the Dharma to deities in one of the heavens, including to his mother Queen Māyā. Therefore artisans were dispatched to the heaven to construct an exact likeness of the Buddha from fragrant sandalwood (a precious material in India subsequently treasured for Buddhist images). Once it was completed, the king had it installed in a place of honor and took great comfort in its company while the Buddha was absent. When he returned, the Buddha exchanged greetings with his iconic double and prophesied that the image would generate great

Fig. 20. Śākyamuni Buddha, 2nd–early 3rd cent. This statue of the Buddha from the Gandhara region of present-day Pakistan displays traditional characteristics of Buddhist iconography, such as a dot between the eyebrows, elongated earlobes, a protuberance of the head (represented here as a topknot of hair), a halo, and a gesture of assurance. The facial features and treatment of the hair and robes bear striking similarities to Greco-Roman sculpture.

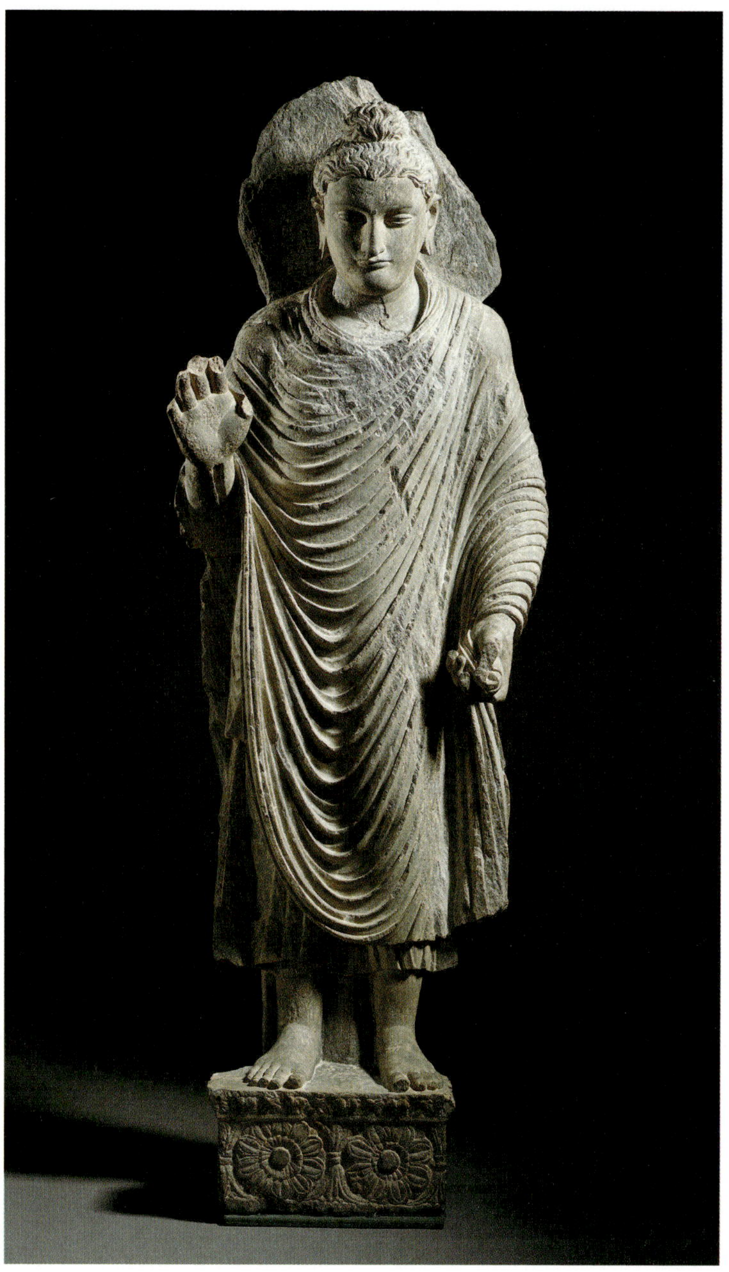

spiritual merit and help spread his religion in the future.[14] The image thus functioned as a surrogate of the Buddha not only for the king but also for ensuing generations. This story subsequently became linked to Buddhist images in China and Japan. The travel diary of Xuanzang (602–664), the great Chinese pilgrim to India and translator of many Buddhist scriptures, records that he encountered Udayana's image of the Buddha while in India and had a replica made, which he carried back to China. The Japanese Buddhist priest Chōnen (938–1016), who in turn traveled to China, had a replica of Xuanzang's Buddha made and transported it to Japan in 986. That icon survives today in the Shakadō, or Śākyamuni Hall, of the Seiryōji Temple in Kyoto (fig. 21). Throughout its history the image has been treated as the living presence of Śākyamuni in the temple, and tales of miracles and miraculous encounters connected with the icon circulated widely in premodern Japan.[15] The mythic aura of the Seiryōji Śākyamuni is in fact paradigmatic of premodern Japanese Buddhism, and I will return to it to illustrate a number of points about Buddhist icons.

Across the sweep of Buddhism's dissemination in Asia believers have experienced Buddhist icons as powerful and charismatic entities equivalent to the Buddha himself. During his lifetime, people felt changed by encountering the Buddha and considered it a special privilege to stand in his presence. After his death, the sites connected with his life together with his relics and stupas were all thought to retain the Buddha's presence and to offer another way of encountering him. Buddhist icons in turn were recognized as yet another form of the Buddha's presence and another way to behold him, since icons supposedly preserved the Buddha's true likeness. It is easy to forget—in a world now saturated with photos, reproductions, and all manner of visual images—how rare it was to encounter realistic representations of humans in premodern times. In that environment icons of the Buddha were treated as miraculous revelations and were thought to embody the power and aura of the Buddha himself.

Even though icons occupied an exalted place in the religion, it would be wrong to think that Buddhists were oblivious to the

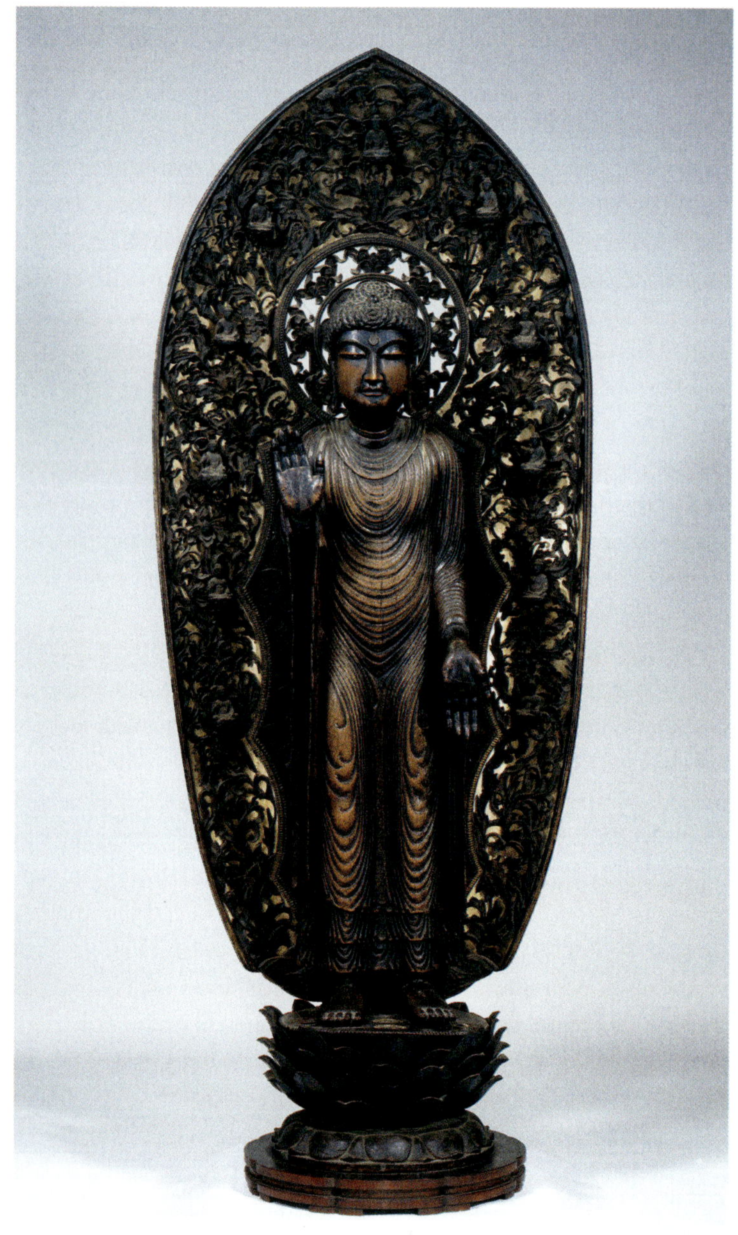

Fig. 21. Śākyamuni Buddha, 10th cent. Seiryōji Temple, Kyoto. This five-foot wooden image was brought from China to Japan in 986 and enshrined in the Seiryōji Temple. In style it is known as an Udayana Buddha since it supposedly bears the exact likeness of Śākyamuni that was preserved in King Udayana's original sandalwood statue of the Buddha. In appearance it reflects stylistic traits found in Chinese and Indian iconography and differs substantially from other Buddhist images in Japan. The countenance, pose, and symmetrical treatment of the folds in the Buddha's robes became hallmarks of subsequent replicas of the Seiryōji Buddha elsewhere in Japan (fig. 32).

contingent and constructed nature of images. On the contrary, they were aware that these were fabricated objects and that their special significance and very identity arose from the fragile interaction between people and images. Buddhist teachings are filled with expositions on the constructed nature and mutual dependence of all things—ideas articulated in the Buddhist doctrine of emptiness. But the realization of the emptiness of things, of both persons and objects, did not result in a nihilistic suspicion of reality but rather in a vision of their interrelatedness. Hence, to Buddhists it seemed natural that the Buddha could not be separated from his Dharma, nor from his relics or sacred sites or icons. At some level people knew that icons are not to be regarded as absolute, but at the same time they felt comfortable approaching them with absolute acceptance. This precarious stance—a cognitive balancing act, so to speak—did not detract from the spiritual quality of icons but in fact heightened it. To engage the icon and to recognize its sacred identity was an evanescent event that could evaporate in an instant. But it was within this brief, elusive, interactive moment that Buddhists believed they could behold the Buddha in the icon.

Behind every icon lies the story of the Buddha. The three phases of his life—the Buddha's religious search, enlightenment, and subsequent spread of the Dharma—can actually provide a convenient rubric for analyzing icons. Heuristically and for simplicity's sake, it is possible to distill these three into the following dimensions of Buddhahood: (1) quest, (2) enlightenment, and (3) compassion. Every image of a Buddha reflects at least one of these modes of being a Buddha. Typically, an image might convey one of the three predominantly, but in some cases multiple modes might be expressed in the same icon. When extended to other aspects of Buddhism, this threefold classification also provides a rubric for analyzing many facets and dimensions of the religion: stages in a person's spiritual development, the function and meaning of rituals, themes in religious texts, activities of Buddhist institutions, and so forth. In short, it may be possible to map these three elements—quest, enlightenment, and compassion—onto a host of Buddhist phenomena. The life of the Buddha thus inspires an archetypal structure that helps explain the religion as a whole as well as its many parts. For the purposes of this study, this means that, whenever one approaches a Buddhist icon, it will usually evoke these aspects of the Buddha's story in one fashion or another.

As Buddhism spread and diversified, Śākyamuni came to be identified as the historical Buddha of this world, a status that left open the recognition of other mythic Buddhas. It is noteworthy that the life stories ascribed to them bear a striking resemblance to Śākyamuni's. All were assumed to have a noble background and auspicious physical marks, to renounce their high station and embark on a spiritual quest, to overcome worldly attachments and attain Nirvana, and to endeavor thereafter to bring all living beings to enlightenment. From a scholarly perspective, it seems clear that Śākyamuni's life story was projected onto these newly recognized Buddhas. But from a believer's perspective, the assumption is the opposite. Śākyamuni was merely following the prototypical trajectory—quest, enlightenment, and compassion—that all Buddhas take whenever they appear in the world. This assumption is conveyed in the word Tathagata (J. *Nyorai*), a common substitute for the term Buddha. Tathagata, according to one interpretation, means "the one who has thus come," indicating someone whose life-course has been "thus"—that is, like that of all other Buddhas. Hence, the story of the Buddha's life was considered a primordial form pervading the universe whenever and wherever Buddhas appear.

Without the story of the Buddha's life, the power and significance of Buddhist icons become elusive. Cut off from it, the image exudes mystery but seems to withhold its meaning from the human gaze. Once suffused with his life story, the icon's meaning breaks forth and the viewer is placed in a dynamic relationship with the Buddha. Not all Buddhists know every detail of Śākyamuni's life, but even the bare rudiments—quest, enlightenment, and compassion—are enough for the icon to come alive. In the end this life of the Buddha functions as the subliminal backdrop to the panoply of iconic images that pervade the religion.

CHAPTER 3

THE EXPRESSIVE DETAIL

Buddhist Symbolism and Iconography

When looking at an actual image of the Buddha, people are confronted with an object that is both intriguing and perplexing. Its human qualities—tranquil face, erect posture, orderly clothing, expressive hands, dignified pose—offer various points of intersection with the human experience. People feel a kinship to the figure because they can identify with its physical appearance and the human feelings it conveys. Simultaneously, there is something foreign about the image, suggesting that the Buddha belongs to a separate world. The icon's elusive gaze and its curious physical features—the dot between the eyebrows, the unusual shape of the cranium, the drooping earlobes—all give the impression that the figure is in some way different. It is this tension, the experience of familiarity and unfamiliarity at the same time, that gives the Buddhist image its power and effect (fig. 22).

Trying to make sense of this mesmerizing but enigmatic object requires examination of its details as well as reflection on its overall appearance. The point of departure for doing so is the story of the Buddha's life. Icons in a sense embody the life of the Buddha. Elements of his story are inscribed on its body in highly abbreviated and stylized form. Hence, understanding an icon is to a certain extent a process of deciphering it in the light of the Buddha's biography. This is not, however, to reduce the icon to a simple representation of the Buddha's life, for there are other influences and dimensions—social, cultural, artistic, and narrative—that have also contributed to its form and function. Particular cultures and individual artists have sometimes added features to icons apart from what the Buddha's story says. Nonetheless, his legendary biography provides a starting point for unpacking the icon's meaning.

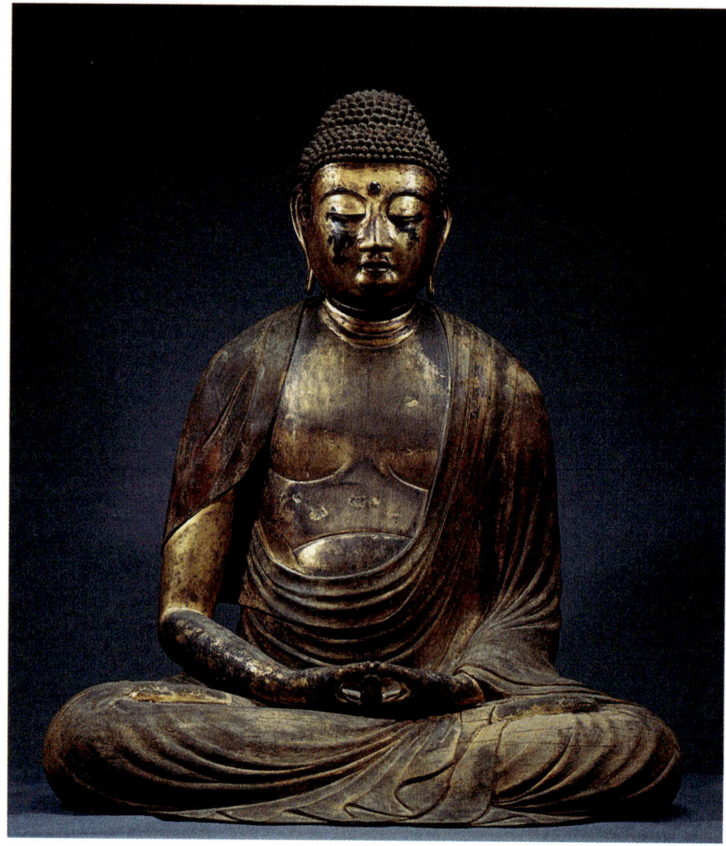

Fig. 22. Meditating Buddha, 12th cent. This seated image of the Buddha Amida bears the standard characteristics of a Buddha's appearance: simple robes, uncovered head, close-cropped hair, and lack of jewelry or adornments. This look is commonly associated with monks and clerics.

One of the first questions to ask when examining an icon is whether it is a Buddha or a Bodhisattva. The term Bodhisattva literally means a being of enlightenment, and it indicates a Buddha-in-the-making, someone who has vowed to become a Buddha and is on the path to Buddhahood. Originally, the word was used to refer to Śākyamuni during the thirty-five years of his life that preceded his enlightenment, as well as his countless lifetimes before that. The assumption behind the Bodhisattva concept is that to become a Buddha is an immense and protracted process requiring cultivation over a huge expanse of time. An entire genre of Buddhist literature, the so-called Jataka tales, emerged to recount the past lives of Śākyamuni and the virtues he fostered in each life as part of his quest for Buddhahood. Subsequently, as multiple Buddhas and Bodhisattvas came to be recognized, the meaning of the term Bodhisattva was expanded to include not just Śākyamuni but anyone who has embarked on such a quest. Strictly speaking, a Bodhisattva corresponds to the quest phase of Buddhahood whereas a Buddha represents the compassion phase, with enlightenment functioning as the pivot between the two (though, as will be seen, there is not always a hard and fast division between the three). In Buddhist iconography Bodhisattva images generally appear with jewelry and adornments, exquisite garments, headdress or crown, and styled hair—details harking back to the royalty of ancient India—and hence in the guise of a lay person (fig. 23). Buddha images, with a few exceptions, are presented with close-cropped hair, clerical robes, and no ornamentation—that is, in the guise of a monk or cleric (fig. 22). Based on these visual indicators, it is usually possible to quickly identify an icon as a Buddha or a Bodhisattva, and the observer's response to the image may reflect the respective status of the figure. But beyond these initial cues, the particular identity and significance of an image are further expressed in a variety of physical features including posture, size, bodily marks, hand signs, objects held, and accompanying display.[1]

POSTURE, SIZE, AND PHYSICAL MARKS

The pose and posture of an icon offer clues to its message and meaning. The vast majority of Buddhist images are presented in a standing or a sitting position, postures that help define the significance and activity of the figure. For instance, a meditating Buddha invariably assumes a sitting position (fig. 10). A Buddha conveying compassion (figs. 5 and 7) or a teaching Buddha, on the other hand, can appear in either a sitting or a standing position. The pose helps determine how the Buddha is to be understood. In addition to the standing and sitting posture, images of the Buddha are occasionally shown lying down. These are

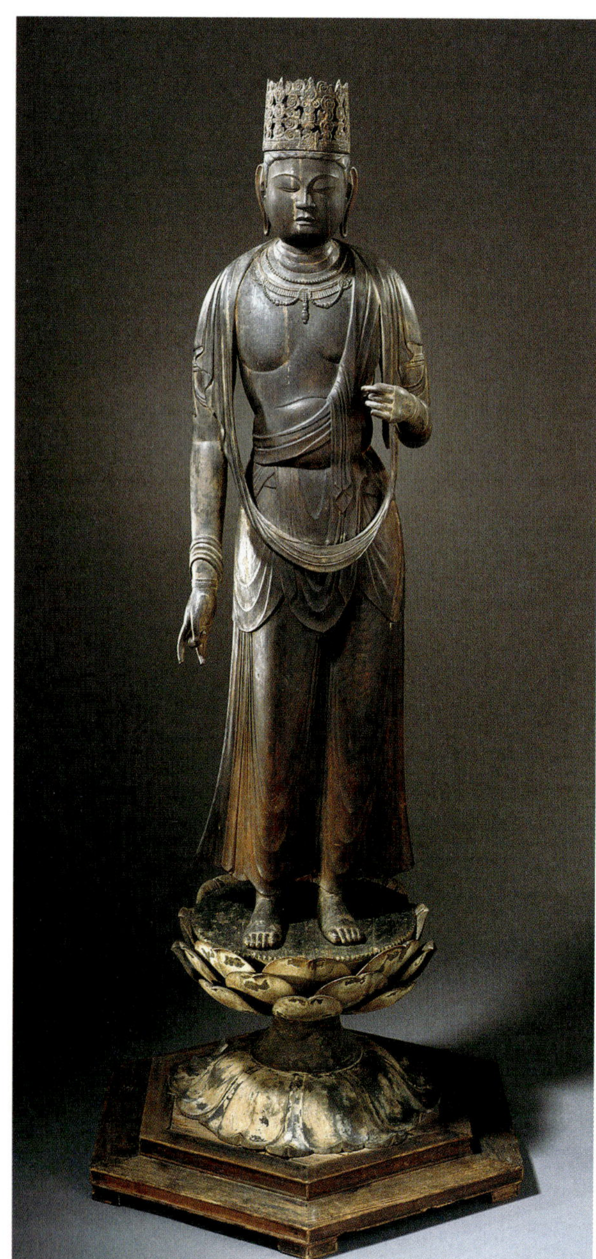

Fig. 23. Bodhisattva, 12th cent. This image of the Bodhisattva Kannon is dressed in exquisite garments, adorned with necklaces, bracelets, and armbands, and crowned with a headdress—all signs of royalty in ancient India. Such features, typically associated with lay people, are distinguishing marks of most Bodhisattva images.

sometimes identified in Western literature as a reclining Buddha, but strictly speaking they represent the Buddha on his deathbed (fig. 18). This is one of the special iconographic poses tied to a specific episode in the Buddha's life and is used to commemorate it. Actually, most images of the Buddha have, among other functions, a commemorative dimension. They point to some event or phase in the Buddha's life and vicariously transport the observer back to it.

The size of an icon, at least in some cases, may also reflect common beliefs about the Buddha. According to tradition, Śākyamuni was towering in height. This view is based on the ancient Indian notion that the idealized person is approximately sixteen feet tall, over twice the height of anyone else and thus inspiring awe in others. Occasionally attempts were made in Japan to replicate this characteristic of the Buddha, resulting in sculptures almost sixteen feet tall (*jōroku*) in the standing position and eight feet (*hasshaku*) in the sitting position. Needless to say, there is wide variation in the dimensions of icons, ranging from colossal Buddhas (*daibutsu*), to so-called "life-size" sixteen-foot ones (*jōrokubutsu*), to "half-size" eight-foot ones (*hanjōrokubutsu*), to images equivalent to the height of the devotee commissioning them (*tōshinbutsu*), and finally to miniature ones that can fit inside a life-size one (*tainaibutsu*). Though not many temples have had the resources to create sixteen-foot icons, those few that exist have a powerful effect, dwarfing believers in their presence.

Another striking aspect of Buddhist icons is the array of peculiar details that adorn them, all considered to be auspicious marks (*sōgō*). These are traceable to the belief that the Buddha was born with a set of physical characteristics that distinguished him from ordinary human beings. Only individuals destined to become a Buddha or a "chariot-wheel-turning king" were thought to be endowed with them. In the story of Śākyamuni's life, the seers predicted the infant's destiny based on these bodily attributes. Virtually every image of the Buddha has at least a few of these characteristics, which Buddhist texts typically call the thirty-two marks (*sanjūnisō*).[2] Among them is a protruding, inverted-bowl-shaped crown of the head, known in

Sanskrit as the *uṣṇīṣa* (J. *chōkeisō* or *nikkeisō*). To the untrained eye it looks like a skullcap or miniature turban, but in fact it constitutes one of the Buddha's anatomical features. Sometimes it is identified as the spot where the Buddha's spiritual powers are concentrated, highlighted by a jewel at its base in the front. Another characteristic is the round dot between the Buddha's eyebrows, called an *ūrṇā* in Sanskrit (J. *byakugō* or *byakumōsō*). Originally described as a small white tuft of hair, it came to be viewed in Buddhist lore as a magical mark, as the jeweled wisdom eye of the Buddha from which he would emit a beam of light whenever he was about to reveal a new and enlightening teaching. Yet another characteristic is the soft, tight ringlets on the Buddha's head, derived from the belief that each hair on his body swirls to the right in a clockwise direction (*mōjōkōsō* or *shinmōusensō*), resulting in snail-shell-like curls. Two other characteristics are the golden hue of the Buddha's skin (*konjikisō*) and an aura of light emanating from his body (*jōkōsō*). These are often represented iconographically by the gold leaf applied to Buddhist images and by a halo around the Buddha's head and a nimbus surrounding his body. Still another characteristic is the small, "thousand-spoke" wheel imprinted on the palms of his hands and the soles of his feet (*senpukurinsō*), symbolizing the wheel of the Dharma (figs. 19 and 25). Finally, one other characteristic is a webbing of the skin between the Buddha's fingers and toes (*shusokumanmōsō*). There is some speculation that this characteristic was projected back onto the Buddha after sculpted images of him emerged in India, on the ground that the webbing helped keep the fingers and toes of statues from breaking off. Among the thirty-two marks, some were only rarely adopted for iconographic depiction—for instance, arms so long that the Buddha's hands could touch his knees when standing up straight (*ryūshumashitsusō*) or a concealed sexual organ (*onzōsō*), kept retracted within the Buddha's body (fig. 24).

These thirty-two marks are sometimes paired with another list of physical features known as the eighty minor characteristics (*hachijisshugō*),[3] which also apply to the Buddha but not to the

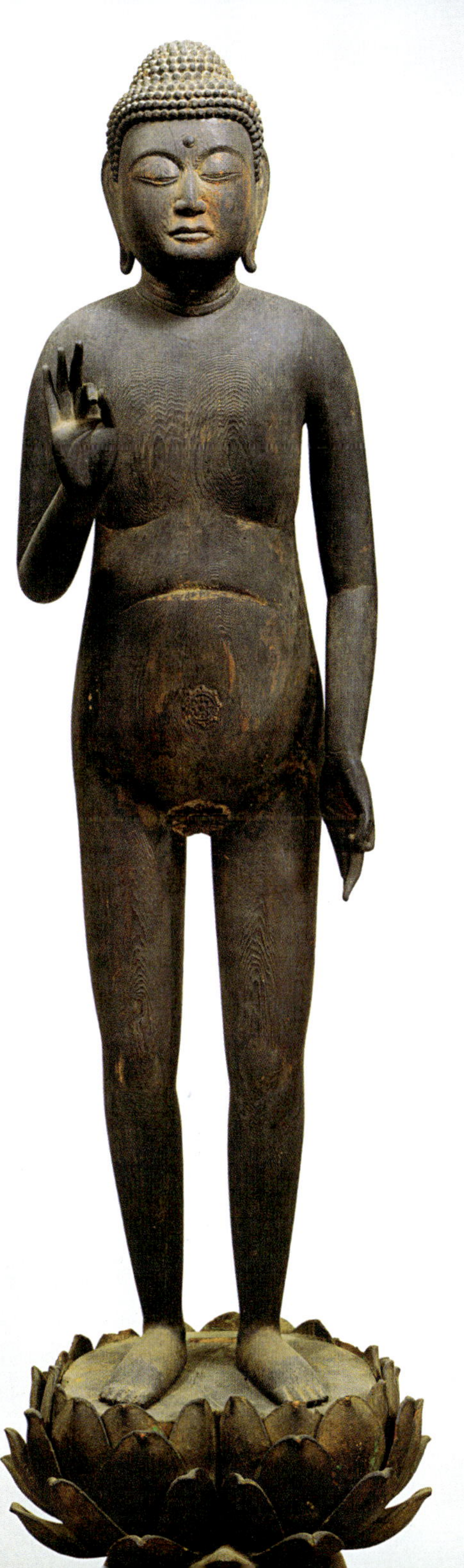

Fig. 24. Unclothed Buddha, 13th cent. This rare unclothed image of the Buddha Amida would never be displayed this way in a temple. It would first be dressed in actual Buddhist robes (fig. 71) and then enshrined on an altar. The figure, nonetheless, provides a glimpse into the Buddha's imagined body type. It includes several of the standard physical marks: a protuberance of the head, tight curls of hair, a dot between the eyebrows, long earlobes, three creases around the neck, and a retracted sexual organ, covered discreetly with a small lotus flower.

wheel-turning king. A prominent one found in most icons is large, elongated earlobes, sometimes attributed to the weight of the earrings worn by the Buddha during his previous incarnations as a prince. Another one is three rings (*sandō*) or folds of skin around the neck revealing the Buddha's fleshy fullness and perfect form.[4] Yet another, which is only occasionally depicted, is an insignia on the Buddha's chest that looks like an inverted swastika. This emblem was long treated as a sign denoting a specially endowed spiritual figure. A close comparison indicates that the features listed among the eighty minor characteristics overlap somewhat with those of the thirty-two marks, suggesting that the two lists evolved separately, not as a coordinated and systematized description of the Buddha's appearance. But together they provided a rich repertoire of physical characteristics for Buddhist icons, some of which have been used ubiquitously, others only occasionally, and still others almost never.

These various features, when displayed in a single icon, function as signifiers of the Buddha, or of a Buddha-to-be, since Bodhisattvas share the same destiny as the Buddha. According to tradition, the Buddha was endowed with these traits as a result of the virtuous acts he performed over innumerable past reincarnations. Some observers may find that certain features appear strange or even disfiguring, but in ancient India, and subsequently Japan, they were regarded as emblems of greatness, to be sure, and some as signs of beauty. The idea that the Buddha's body is a focal point for religious reflection is corroborated in a famous deathbed meditation that became popular in tenth-century Japan:

> You should reflect on the physical appearance of the . . . Buddha and allow that single image to reside in your mind. It is said that the physical body of the Buddha is gold like the riverbed in the Jambu forest. He is towering in his stateliness, like the golden mountain king, and his body is adorned with immeasurable features. Among them, the white tuft of hair between his eyebrows curls gracefully to the right, [as majestic] as five Sumeru mountains. Seven billion fifty-six million rays of light blaze out from it, as brilliant as thousands or millions of suns and moons.

This is the result of his manifold untainted virtues, flowing from his great meditation, wisdom, and compassion. If you reflect on this feature for even an instant, then the karmic effects of grave wrongdoings that would bind you for nine billion six-hundred million eons in Samsara—or for trillions, or for as many as [there are grains of] sand in the Ganges or as particles of dust—will be eradicated. Thus, you should now concentrate on this feature [of the Buddha], and you will eradicate the karmic effects of wrongdoings. You should generate the thought: "My aspiration is for the light from that feature, the [Buddha's] white tuft of hair, to eradicate all my wrongdoing."[5]

Hence, when devout Buddhists encountered an image with such features, they immediately realized they were in the presence of the Buddha in some guise or other, triggering a cascade of reflections as they beheld the Buddha.

HAND GESTURES

Beyond physical marks, the mudra (*inzō* or *ingei*) or hand gestures displayed by Buddhist icons further delineate their meaning.[6] These gestures function as coded or abbreviated messages in which the simple configuration of the fingers stands for entire events or phases in the Buddha's life or signify core themes in his teachings. Perhaps the most widely recognized mudra is that of the Buddha in a state of meditation. Seated in the cross-legged position known as the lotus, he holds his hands comfortably in his lap—one hand typically resting in the palm of the other, sometimes with the thumb tips touching lightly or with the fingers curled (fig. 22). This gesture, known as *jōin* or the meditation mudra, is one of the archetypal hand signs of the Buddha, and it is found in a great variety of other Buddhist images as well. What this pose communicates is not just the proper meditative posture or the Buddha in meditation; rather, it is a representation of the crowning event of the Buddha's story: his meditative quest under the bodhi tree resulting in wisdom and enlightenment.

Icons of a meditating figure therefore embody the quest and enlightenment dimensions of Buddhahood in the threefold pattern of his life. Occasionally, though rarely in Japan, images depicting this event show the Buddha's right hand touching the ground in front of his knee while the left hand remains in his lap. This gesture, known as the earth-touching mudra (*sokujiin*) or Māra-defeating mudra (*gōmain*), celebrates the moment when the Buddha called upon the earth to testify to his worthiness to attain enlightenment on that spot of land, thereby triumphing over his adversary Māra. While icons in the meditation pose seem to depict the Buddha in a state of equinimity, they also have an air of precision and energy in the configuration of the hands, suggesting that meditation is dynamic and not merely a passive mental state. And just as they recount visually the story of the Buddha's enlightenment, so every meditating figure, whether in iconic form or as an actual human practicing meditation, replicates that story and participates in its meaning.

Another common mudra found in Buddhist icons is the teaching gesture in which a hand is held in front of the chest with one finger touching the thumb lightly to form a circle, symbolizing the wheel of the Dharma (fig. 25). This gesture is known as the Dharma-preaching mudra (*seppōin*), and images are sometimes shown with both hands forming circles using the index, middle, or ring finger with the thumb. Occasionally a more complex version of this gesture is found in which one hand reaches across to touch the circle formed by the other hand. This more specific hand sign is typically referred to as the Dharma-wheel-turning mudra (*tenbōrin'in*). It signifies that the Buddha, whenever he expounds the Dharma, is figuratively turning the wheel of the Dharma, thereby rolling its liberating teaching out to the world. This hand gesture, found in both standing and sitting images of the Buddha, expresses succinctly the teaching dimension of the Buddha's identity and corresponds to the compassion phase of his life. From the time of his enlightenment the Buddha began proclaiming the Dharma to all living beings and continued to do so until his death. Icons in

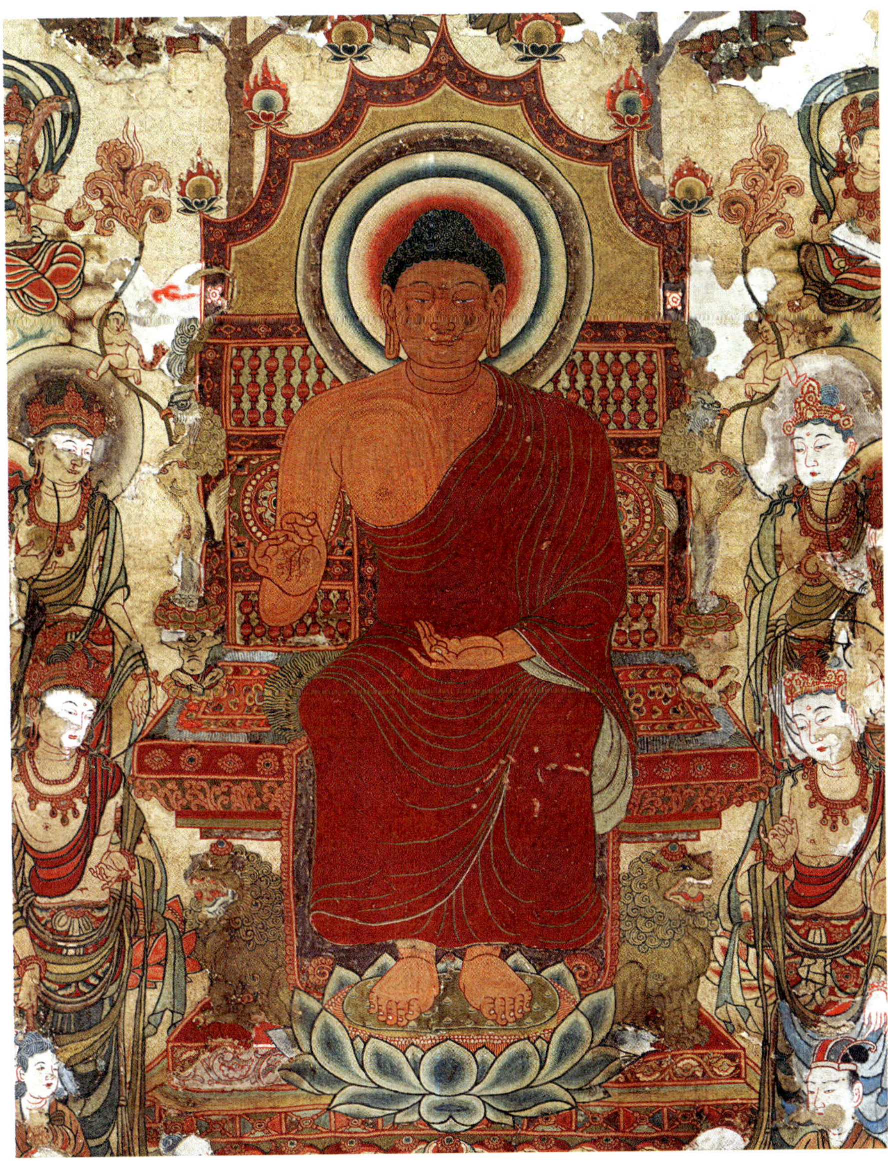

Fig. 25. Buddha with teaching gesture, 8th cent. In this detailed view from a silk embroidery the Buddha, seated on a lion throne, forms the Dharma-preaching mudra with his thumb and index finger. The circle symbolizes the wheel of the Dharma, which is also visible as a faint imprint in the palm of his right hand, one of the Buddha's thirty-two physical marks.

this configuration celebrate the Buddha's status as a teacher, but more particularly they hark back to the specific moment when he revealed the Dharma for the first time, the so-called Deer Park teaching. This event is considered especially significant, for it was from that moment that the Dharma became known in the world. Hence, Buddhist images displaying the teaching gesture simultaneously identify the Buddha as the supreme teacher and also allude to this celebrated episode in his life.

Another pose found widely in Japanese Buddhist icons is actually a combination of two hand gestures. The first one, in which the hand is held up with the palm outward and open, is known as the fearlessness-bestowing mudra (*semuiin*). The second, in which the other hand is extended downward with the palm out and the fingers uncurled, is known as the vow-granting mudra (*segan'in* or *yogan'in*). Together these two gestures proclaim the message, "Have no fear. I offer you aid," and present a classic pose of the Buddha conveying compassion (fig. 26). Like the teaching gesture, these mudras are found in both standing and sitting images of the Buddha. In presentation there can be considerable variation in how the fingers are arranged: extended completely, curled slightly, or with some folded into the palm of the hand. Rather than signifying a specific event in the Buddha's life, this pose reflects the phase of his life after his enlightenment when the Buddha sought to bring all sentient beings to enlightenment. These gestures bear a strong resemblance to another hand sign, known as the ease-and-comfort mudra (*an'iin*), which carries a similar compassionate message: to put sentient beings at ease and offer them comfort. In it one hand is held up and the other down, both open and with the palm turned outward, as in the fearlessness-bestowing and vow-granting mudra. But in this case each hand forms a circle by curling one finger to touch the thumb, similar to the circle in the teaching mudra (fig. 5). This might imply that the Dharma itself is a form of comfort bestowed on people.

The articulation of religious meanings through hand gestures is almost universal in Buddhist images. Besides the various mudras

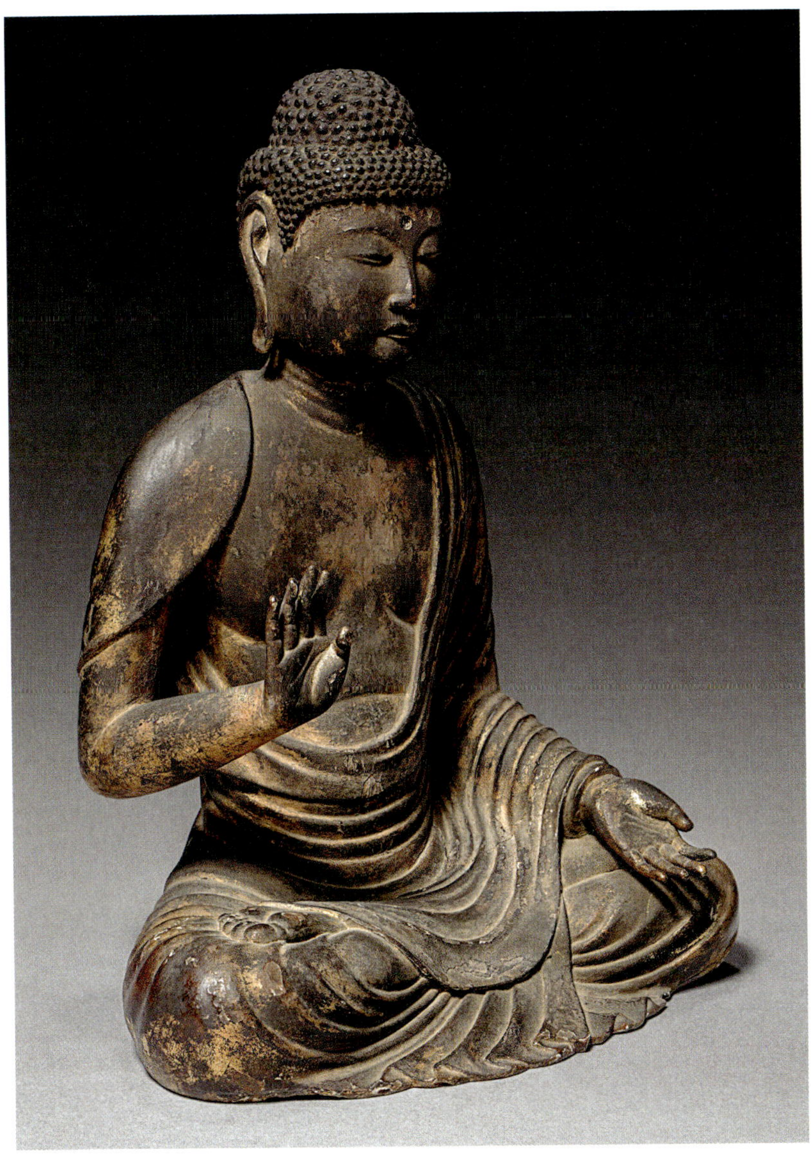

Fig. 26. **Buddha with compassionate gestures, 19th cent.** This classic pose combines two hand gestures to indicate the Buddha's compassion. The right hand signals assurance, expressing the idea "fear not," while the left hand denotes his commitment to aid all living beings.

presented here, there are many others described in iconographic guides for analyzing Buddhist images, some with wide application and others that pertain only to certain Buddhas or Bodhisattvas. The most common themes underlying this panoply of gestures are those elucidated above: enlightenment (associated with the meditation mudra), Dharma (associated with the teaching mudra), and compassion (associated with the fearlessness-bestowing and vow-granting mudras). These themes, as indicated, can be traced to events or stages in the life of Śākyamuni. Still, the story of the Buddha cannot be mapped too rigidly onto them, for variant uses of hand signs can give images a significance that extends beyond any particular episode in the Buddha's life. In some cases gestures themselves carry multiple meanings, such as the ease-and-comfort mudra, which seems to signify both teaching and compassion. In other cases particular icons mix or merge different hand signs so that separate themes become conjoined. In this way Buddhist images take on a life of their own that transcends specific moments or events in the Buddha's life, or rather meld these moments together in an instantaneous visual presentation of the Buddha in his various dimensions.

The face and hands of a Buddhist image, especially in juxtaposition to each other, are also the locus of complex messages. In virtually every depiction of the Buddha the face appears emotionless, placid, and even remote. The eyes are usually half-closed and seem to stare blankly ahead. This detached look suggests that the Buddha is in a meditative trance. He seems to gaze through the diverse objects of the world and see beyond their evanescence and insubstantial nature. This penetrating vision is part and parcel of his wisdom and enlightenment. Icons that portray the Buddha with such a countenance imply that he abides in a perpetual state of meditation and detached calm (fig. 27). Paradoxically, the Buddha is known to be engaged with the world simultaneously through boundless compassion that is aimed at bringing all living beings to enlightenment. This compassionate activity is represented by the various hand gestures found in Buddhist images, usually crisp, expressive, and strong. They

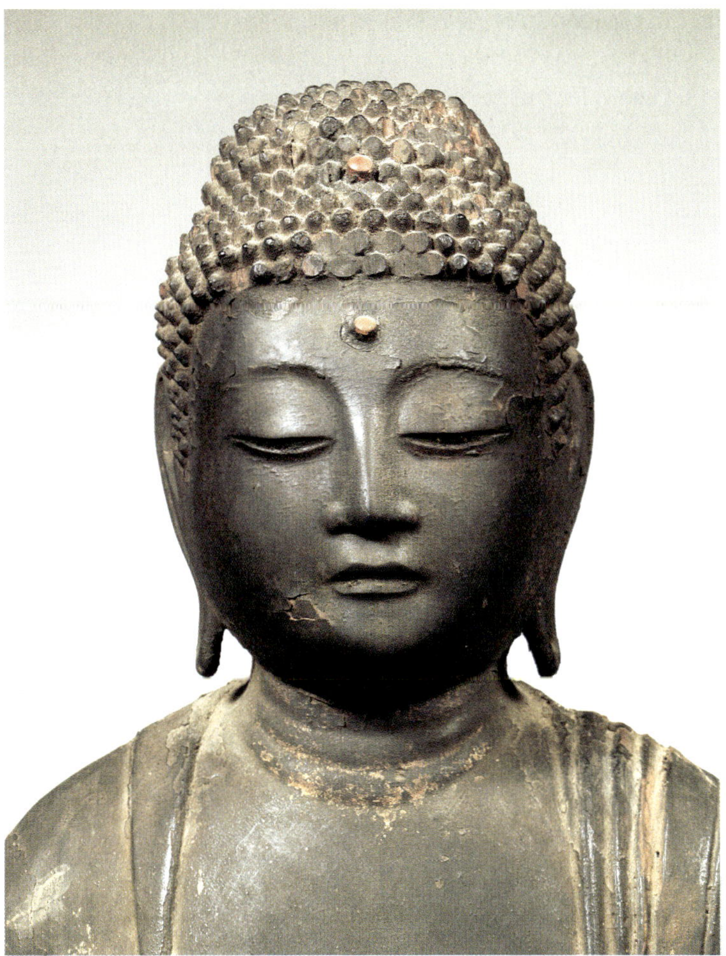

Fig. 27. Face of the Buddha (detail), 12th cent. The face of the Buddha Amida here typifies the calm, detachment, and equanimity found in most Buddhist icons. This expression suggests that the Buddha is in a continuous state of meditation and dwells in the quietude of wisdom.

signify that the Buddha, far from withdrawing into a solipsistic bliss, instead reaches out to others and skillfully guides them to wisdom. The power of the icon lies in the dual impact of the image's face and hands. The qualities they convey, detachment and engagement, are both defining characteristics of the Buddha, and they subtly reflect the enlightened and compassionate aspects of Buddhahood. Though the two may seem at odds, in Buddhism they are considered mutually engendering. In any particular icon, one must look to the Buddha's face to comprehend his wisdom and transcendence, and to his hands to discover his immanence and compassion. To neglect either is to overlook part of the Buddha's identity.

OTHER DISTINGUISHING CHARACTERISTICS

Beyond the bodily appearance of the Buddha, physical objects are sometimes presented as his possessions. Actually these items are more commonly associated with Bodhisattvas and Buddhist divinities than with Buddhas, whose hands typically hold nothing and are configured in various gestures. Nonetheless, when possessions do appear, they can likewise convey the meaning or activity of the Buddha. Examples include a multi-spoke wheel denoting the Dharma (*hōrin* or *rinbō*) and a magic wish-granting jewel (*hōjū* or *nyoijū*), both of which were originally counted among the seven precious possessions of a wheel-turning king. The use of regal symbols was fairly extensive in Buddhism. Other examples are objects normally associated with monks: a begging bowl (*hachi*), walking staff (*shakujō*), Buddhist rosary (*juzu* or *nenju*), insect whisk (*hossu*), water bottle (*suibyō*), or some other type of vessel. Yet another example is a lotus flower (*renge*), prized in Asian cultures for its beauty and purity and linked to Buddhism from an early period in India. In some cases these objects became attributes of particular Buddhist figures and hence function as signifiers of their identity (fig. 28).

Besides these elements Buddhist images are frequently displayed with other embellishments that emphasize their exalted nature. One is an ornate parasol (*sangai*) or canopy (*tengai*) situated over the icon to reflect the Buddha's regal pedigree and high spiritual status. In ancient India parasols were held over kings and high-ranking figures to protect them from the sun or rain. Once the parasol was incorporated into Buddhist imagery, it evolved into an elaborate, decorative canopy suspended over Buddhist icons (fig. 10). Another item is the

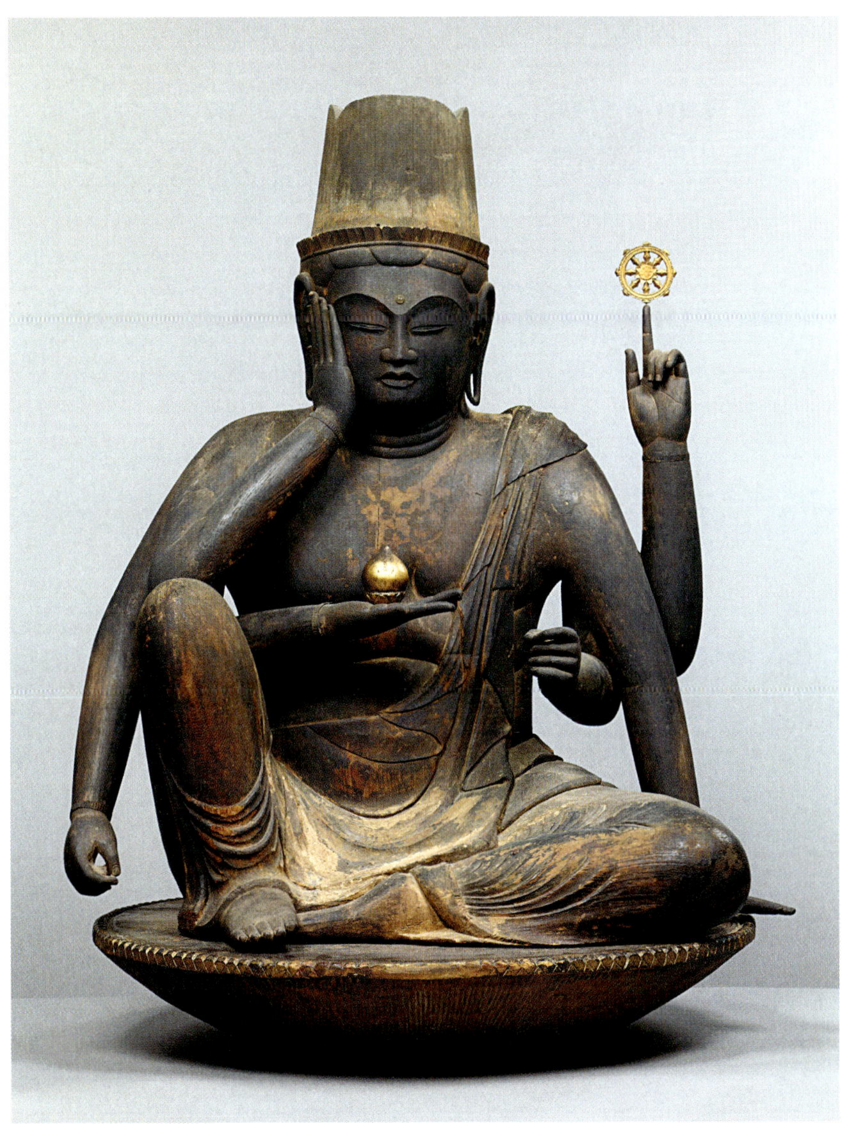

Fig. 28. Bodhisattva with Dharma wheel and wish-granting jewel, 9th–10th cent. This is an image of the Bodhisattva Kannon in a pensive pose, shown holding a Dharma wheel, representing the Buddha's teachings, in a left hand and a wish-granting jewel, that can magically fulfill one's highest aspirations, in a right. The six-armed figure may also have held a Buddhist rosary in the lower right hand and a lotus flower in the middle left, since these objects are typically found in similar images.

Fig. 29. Buddha on lotus flower pedestal, 9th cent. The Buddha Yakushi sits on a pedestal stylized as a giant lotus flower, a symbol of perfection and purity. Lotus-shaped bases appear frequently in Buddhist images, and also in the design of altar lamps, censers, sutra canisters, vases, and similar vessels.

platform or base on which the icon rests. It sometimes resembles a throne, befitting royalty. Other times it takes the form of a miniature and stylized Mt. Sumeru, the mythical mountain at the center of the world in Buddhist cosmology, whose flat summit coincides with the lower level of heaven. In fact, the central altar in Buddhist temples is frequently referred to as a Sumeru platform (*shumidan* or *shumiza*, fig. 10). Still another example of the base for an icon is a lotus-flower pedestal (*rengeza*). Images of the Buddha, whether standing or sitting, are often situated on a scallop-edged foundation depicting a giant lotus flower, bearing the Buddha upward (fig. 29). This motif derives in part from anecdotes outside the Buddha's standard biography that liken him to a lotus flower. Just as the lotus grows in murky, muddy water but stands above it as a pure and perfect blossom, so the Buddha appears in this defiled world and yet rises above it as a supreme and complete sage.[7] The lotus is thus a symbol of perfection, and by implication a signifier of enlightenment and the Buddha. To the extent that lotus pedestals are used not only for icons of the Buddha but also for other Buddhist images, these other figures are seen as a manifestation of the same perfection that the Buddha embodies.

MULTIVALENT RELIGIOUS MEANINGS

The multiplicity of poses, hand gestures, and symbolic objects that make up Buddhism's iconographic store—including many that have not been elucidated here—create a syntax and vocabulary of religious meaning in Buddhist icons. Based on them it is possible to reflect on the nature of icons and to propose various hypotheses about how they function. The first is that an icon of the Buddha is basically a commemorative representation. It is a physical likeness of the Buddha with particular attention to small details that attest to his extraordinary identity. The second is that the icon is a symbol of everything the Buddha embodies and thereby a source of inspiration for Buddhists. People attempt to model themselves on the Buddha

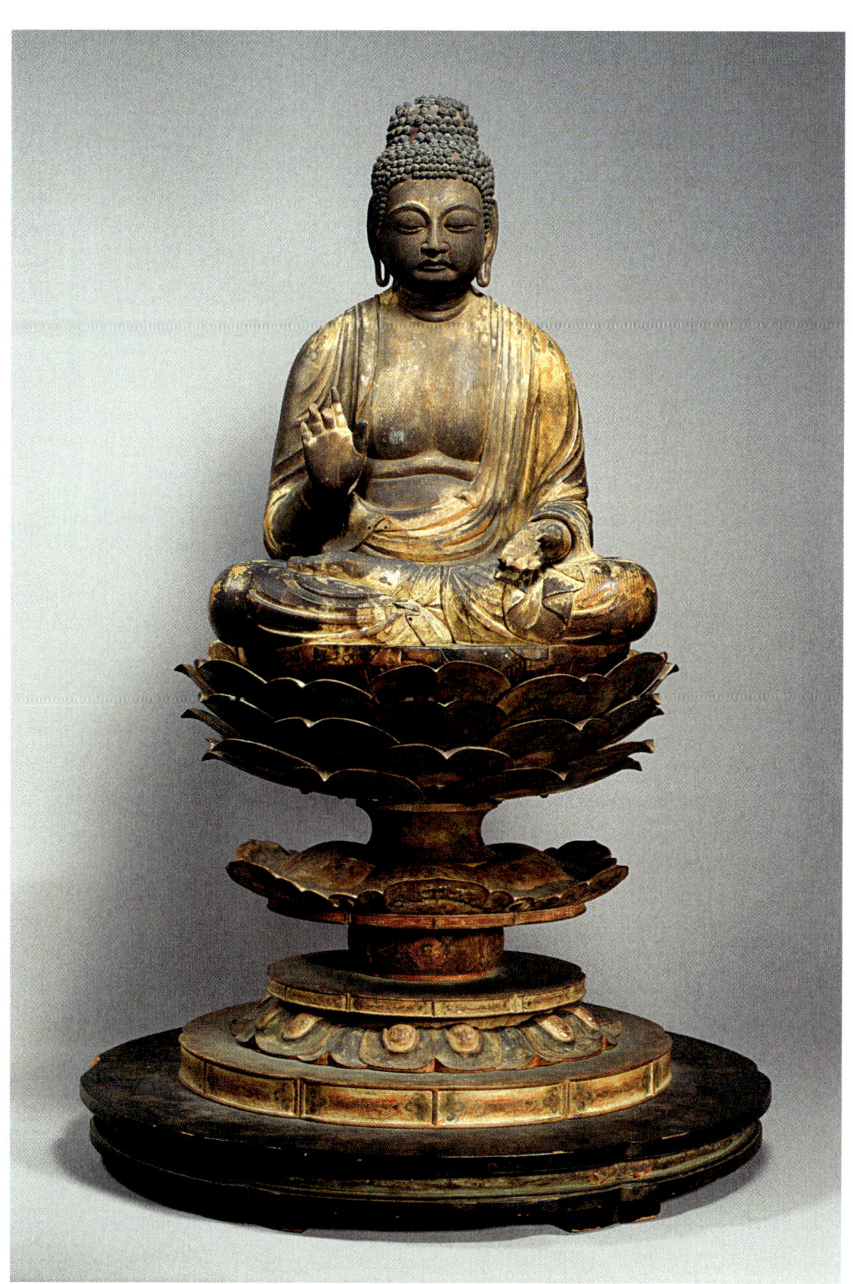

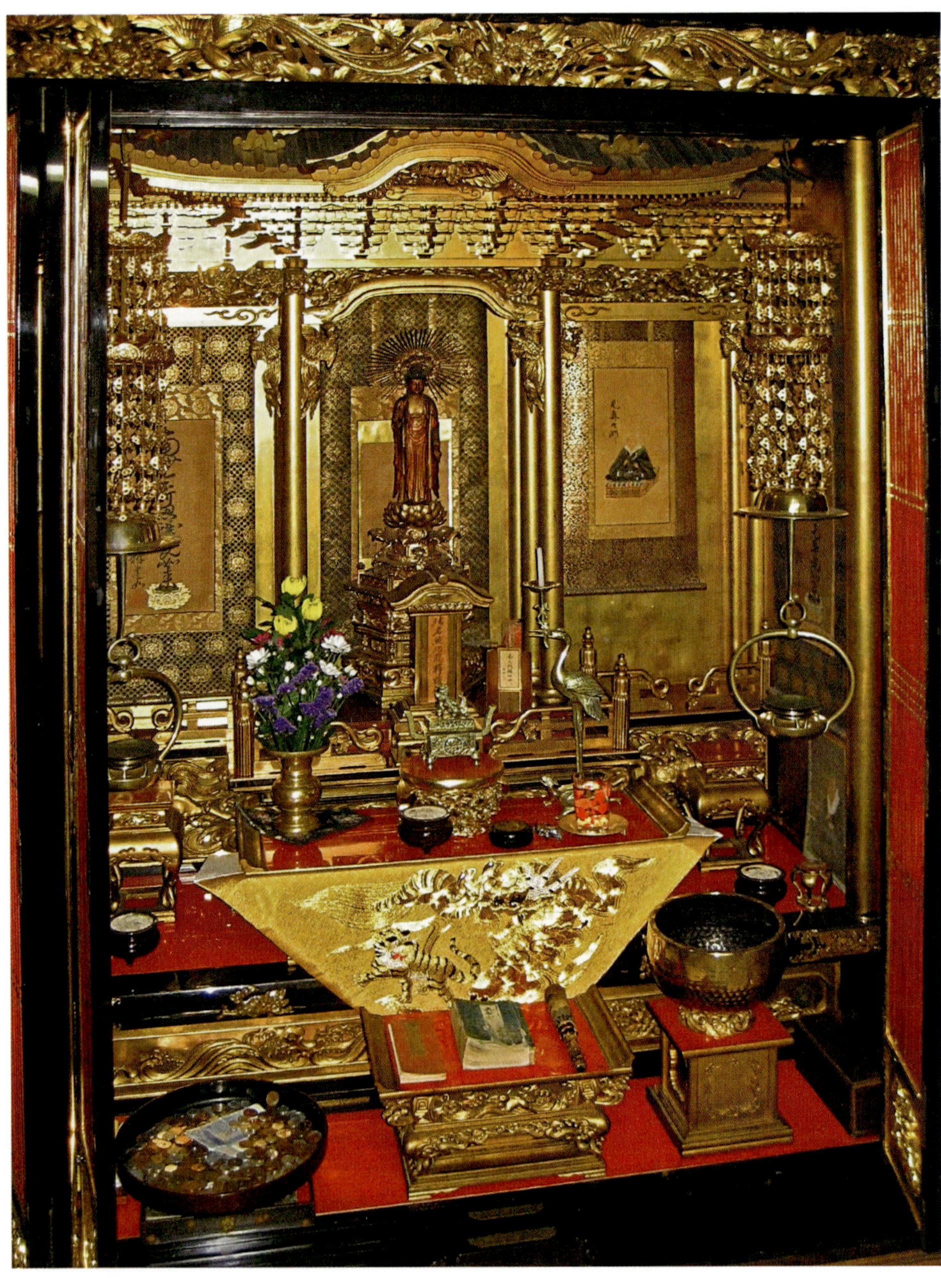

and aspire to his ideal. The third is that the icon is the Buddha himself, that is, the very instantiation of the Buddha in this world. His presence makes it possible for believers to interact and commune with the Buddha.[8] All three of these interpretations have been hinted at in previous chapters, and each has a clear-cut basis in the religion. The three dimensions of icons that they identify—(1) representation, (2) symbol, and (3) instantiation—operate alongside each other, giving icons a multifaceted significance in Buddhism.

The physical appearance of Buddhist icons, as indicated above, draws heavily from the Buddha's life story. Key themes, occurrences, and motifs of his life are expressed in the bodily characteristics of Buddhist images. To that extent icons have a commemorative function. They reenact for believers pivotal events and phases in the Buddha's life, such as his religious quest, enlightenment, first teaching, compassionate acts, and death. More generally, they express the character and qualities of the Buddha—his unsurpassed wisdom, his equanimity and detachment, his inexhaustible compassion, and his spiritual greatness—all of which are also conveyed in his life story. It is true that certain icons, especially of other figures than Śākyamuni, go beyond the traditional account of the Buddha's life and incorporate elements derived from other Buddhist stories or sources. Nonetheless, such images borrow at least some iconographic features from the Śākyamuni legend. In that respect, they too presuppose his story and are dependent on it for their appearance. The Buddha's life thus provides a narrative reference point for a wide range of commemorative representation, the first dimension of icons.

With the Buddha's story as a backdrop, icons function in a variety of ways. At most religious sites—whether a traditional temple, a wayside shrine, or a home altar—icons operate as the centerpiece of ritual activity. They are treated as special objects and are set apart from their surroundings by restricted areas, elevated stands, adornments, and elaborate enclosures (fig. 30). This treatment reflects the extraordinary status ascribed to the Buddha. He is perceived as an exalted figure, and the particular episodes in his life, expressed in

Fig. 30. **Buddhist home altar. Wada House, Shirakawa-gō village, Gifu prefecture.** An icon of the Buddha Amida is enshrined as the centerpiece of this ornate family altar. The icon stands on a pedestal beneath the roof of a miniature temple or palace, with space for ritual implements and offerings in front and below. The lavish ornamentation is considered to be splendors offered up to the Buddha and also ones that emanate from him. The entire altar is built within a shrine cabinet with doors that can be closed at night.

the gestures and poses of icons, are considered epic events for the religious destiny of living beings. These perceptions of the Buddha highlight his uniqueness and otherness, how he surpasses any other figure. The Buddha is thus invested with a sacredness and perfection that transcends the flawed world of humans, and this sacredness is by extension associated with the icons that portray him.

Beyond their exalted status in enshrinement, icons can also create a sense of closeness between the observer and the Buddha. Buddhism considers every living being, whether high or low, to have the capacity to achieve what the Buddha achieved and to be what the Buddha is. Hence, humans can view the Buddha as an idealized reflection of themselves. Seen in this light, the Buddha becomes a paradigm for religiosity and a spiritual role model. His life story offers not only an epic account of a savior sage but also a narrative guide for religious goals and action. When considered from this perspective, the icon symbolizes the ideals that humans aspire to and evokes from them a personal identification with the Buddha. Thus, an image of the meditating Buddha tacitly invites them to meditate; a teaching image invites them to teach; and a compassionate image invites them to be compassionate. This modeling power of Buddhist images, as symbols in the religion—the second dimension of icons—is as fundamental to their identity as their representational and commemorative function.

The standard response to icons from these two dimensions can be described as bimodal: a sense of sacredness and otherness on the one hand and a realization of shared spiritual identity on the other. These two reactions are in tension with each other, and certainly in any particular religious setting one or the other might dominate. But both are elemental to the religion. To neglect one in affirmation of the other is to fail to see the dynamism, versatility, and multidimensional character of Buddhist images. Ultimately, icons have the capacity to arouse awe—a recognition of the Buddha's wisdom and compassion. But they also have the ability to evoke identification—a feeling of common participation in the quest for enlightenment. These two responses are, in part, what it means to behold the Buddha.

Even while recognizing this bimodal power of icons, one must not lose sight of their autonomy as sacred objects in and of themselves. This point is often overlooked in modern-day considerations of icons, for the prevailing tendency is to treat them in the other two ways, as representations of the absolute and as symbols that inspire religious action. In premodern Japan, however, it seems clear that icons were also regarded as living entities in their own right, the very instantiation of the Buddha—the third dimension of icons. People, of course, were aware that icons were humanly constructed, composed of physical materials fashioned into distinct forms. But they approached them with the assumption that the Dharma could be expressed in the form of an icon just as surely as it was in Śākyamuni's body. What made this view possible was the idea of immanence found in Mahayana Buddhism, a branch of the religion that originated in India at the beginning of the Common Era and ultimately dominated East Asia, including Japan. Here I would like to outline the type of rationale and religious thinking that undergirded Mahayana's affirmation of icons.

Mahayana philosophy upholds the basic Buddhist premise that people are trapped in a cycle of attachments and desires arising from deluded perceptions of the world. Thus, the starting point for Mahayana, and for all of Buddhism, is a critique of human perceptions. This begins with the realization of the transient nature of things and the lack in people of any permanent or independent self. Mahayana, though, goes beyond these core Buddhist truths to declare that all things are empty (Skt. *śūnyatā,* J. *kū*). What this means is that nothing has an autonomous, distinct, and self-defining identity. The world is composed of interlocking and interdependent entities whose boundaries are difficult to delineate. What the mind may perceive as separate and discrete is in fact inextricably tied to and defined by the things around it. The idea of emptiness thus reveals a world of mutual dependence and overlapping identities. To that extent, it is not an expression of nihilism but a declaration of interrelatedness. To see things in this light—in their unfractured "suchness," as Buddhists might say—is to overcome illusion and manifest wisdom. In wisdom, attachments and desires fall away, for nothing can be cognized as separate, fixed, and distinct enough to cling to.

One important corollary to the concept of emptiness is that there is no such thing as Nirvana apart from this flawed world of Samsara. The Buddhist path has often been seen as a flight from impermanence and suffering toward the so-called other shore of Nirvana. Mahayana Buddhism asserts, however, that Nirvana and Samsara are not separate but identical. Viewed through a prism molded by one's deluded concepts and attachments, the world seems fraught with ills. But perceived in the luminescence of wisdom, it appears perfect just as it is. The flaw thus lies not in the world but in one's perception of it. That is what must be transformed. Hence, Nirvana is not attained by separating oneself from Samsara but by discovering it therein. Mahayana Buddhism, in short, begins with a vigorous critique of the world but ends with a thoroughgoing affirmation of it.

The immanence of Nirvana in all things, when carried to its logical conclusion, suggests that everything in the world is both the repository and the stimulus of enlightenment. But in most cases this is hardly apparent. People go through life oblivious to Nirvana's presence except for special moments or settings in which it unexpectedly erupts into their commonplace experience. In other words, people tend to encounter life as a vast field of Samsaric flatness in which Nirvana is occasionally and inexplicably disclosed. The appearance in the world of the historical Buddha propounding the Dharma is one such occurrence. The potency of icons is another. Far from lifeless objects, they are seen, like the Buddha, as dynamic religious agents, capturing attention and provoking spiritual realization. Their very presence exerts a power over humans. It is the authority of the Buddha, together with his Dharma and the presence of Nirvana, that inheres in and animates icons, which in turn constantly act to awaken sentient beings. Beheld in this way, Buddhist images become living instantiations of the Buddha at work in the world—the third dimension of icons.

PART II

THE PROLIFERATION OF THE SACRED

A Buddhist Gallery

CHAPTER 4

FULLY ENLIGHTENED BUDDHAS

More often than not, when people visit a Buddhist temple in Japan, the central icon on the altar is not Śākyamuni Buddha. Rather it is any one of a multitude of Buddhas, Bodhisattvas, or other divinities that comprise the teeming ranks of Buddhism's spiritual firmament. What made this proliferation of sacred figures possible was an expansion in the cosmological perspective of Buddhism, prompted in part by the sweeping reinterpretations of Mahayana. In addition to its dramatic claim that Nirvana is present in all things, Mahayana makes the equally provocative assertion that countless Buddhas and spiritual beings populate every sector and corner of the universe.

In early Buddhist thought Śākyamuni was recognized as the sole Buddha appearing in this world, although previous mythic Buddhas, commonly numbered as six before Śākyamuni, were thought to have appeared in earlier cycles of the world-system. The prevailing assumption was that only one Buddha would emerge in any cycle. Based on this notion, the future Buddha of this world was identified as Miroku (Skt. Maitreya), poised in one of the heavens to descend, attain enlightenment, and proclaim the Dharma anew once the world has passed through its cyclical collapse and regeneration. Mahayana Buddhism took these basic cosmological views and expanded them radically. It posited multiple world-systems in the ten directions (the eight points of the compass plus the zenith and nadir), each with its own heavens, land masses, populations, peaks, oceans, and underworlds. Some worlds are beset with sorrows, just as Śākyamuni's is, while others are identified as pure, radiant, and perfect. Most are spatially located, though many are considered miraculously constituted and not perceptible through ordinary human faculties—yet nonetheless real. The important point from the Mahayana perspective is that each has its own Buddha who, while residing apart from the humans inhabiting this world, is accessible to them through certain religious practices.

This cosmology may seem like a phantasmagoria from the standpoint of modern material science, but in Mahayana thought the recognition of countless Buddhas is simply a logical extension of the claim that Nirvana is inherent in all things. That is, the ubiquitous existence of multiple Buddhas in the universe is the cosmological analogue to the ubiquitous presence of Nirvana in Samsara. Although these Buddhas are treated as individual figures with their own life stories, they are not considered fundamentally separate. Mahayana offers various mechanisms for binding them together so that all are perceived as embodiments of Nirvana and wellsprings of the Dharma. One important strategy is to identify the different types of manifestations that a Buddha can have, as articulated in the Mahayana doctrine of the "three bodies" of the Buddha. The first type of manifestation is as a physically incarnated body (*ōjin*), like Śākyamuni appearing in this world. The second is as an ineffable, inconceivable, formless Dharma body (*hosshin*), identical with Nirvana itself and with the "suchness" of all things. The third, classified somewhere between the other two, is as a miraculous and radiant body (*hōjin*), the karmic outcome of a Buddha's infinite good works of the past, which has an ethereal form perceptible only through supernatural and spiritually cultivated vision. This doctrine creates a spectrum for explaining aspects of the Buddha that range from his physical appearance to his miraculous manifestations, and finally to his formless nature. The many Buddhas found in Mahayana are typically perceived as one or another of these "bodies," though virtually all have the capacity to cross over between them when necessary. This doctrine has given Mahayana the ability to recognize numerous Buddhas at the same time while asserting their common identity. Theoretically, any particular Buddha is regarded as an individualized expression of the universal character of Buddhahood, not as a rival to the others. The great variety of Buddhas depicted in Japanese iconography presupposes this philosophy of multiplicity amid shared identity.

In the abstract, the number of mythic Buddhas is immense. Mahayana sutras—core scriptures purportedly preached by Śākyamuni—sometimes list scores of Buddhas' names, though without much explanation or elaboration. In actuality, only a few Buddhas have captured the imagination of the Japanese, and it is these who appear regularly in their iconography. The historical Buddha Śākyamuni is of course one of them, as is the future Buddha Miroku. In addition, certain directional Buddhas have risen to prominence, as have cosmic Buddhas. The iconographic depiction of these Buddhas largely follows that of Śākyamuni, though some are given unique features, and all are thought to have their own sacred story. In some cases particular Buddhas have developed multiple reputations or identities based on divergent religious interpretations or localized traditions. Hence, variations occur not only in how different Buddhas are presented but also in how the same Buddha may be portrayed. Nonetheless, the archetypal themes of Buddhahood—quest, enlightenment, and compassion—persist amid this diversity and help define the identity of every Buddha.

ŚĀKYAMUNI BUDDHA

Śākyamuni is universally acknowledged as an incarnate form of the Buddha, the one who appeared in this world and opened the path to enlightenment for its sentient beings. In Japan the rudiments of Śākyamuni's life story are universally known and underlie any iconic representation of him. There has been, nonetheless, an assortment of narrative contexts and iconographic ensembles that have led to diversified portrayals of Śākyamuni. For instance, the famous sitting Śākyamuni enshrined in the main hall of Japan's ancient Hōryūji Temple is partly defined by the two principal figures who flank him:

the Buddha Yakushi on his left, whose realm lies in the remote eastern sector of the universe, according to Mahayana cosmology, and the Buddha Amida on his right, whose realm is located in the distant west (fig. 31). Art historians have debated when this ensemble of icons was first installed in the temple, since the Amida image dates from the thirteenth century, much later than the Śākyamuni and Yakushi images, which date from the seventh century. But once they were in place, the three together created a miniature cosmology of Buddhas within the confines of the temple hall.[1] In this configuration Śākyamuni's significance, over and above his life story, derives from his central position within this specific, site-defined universe of Buddhas.

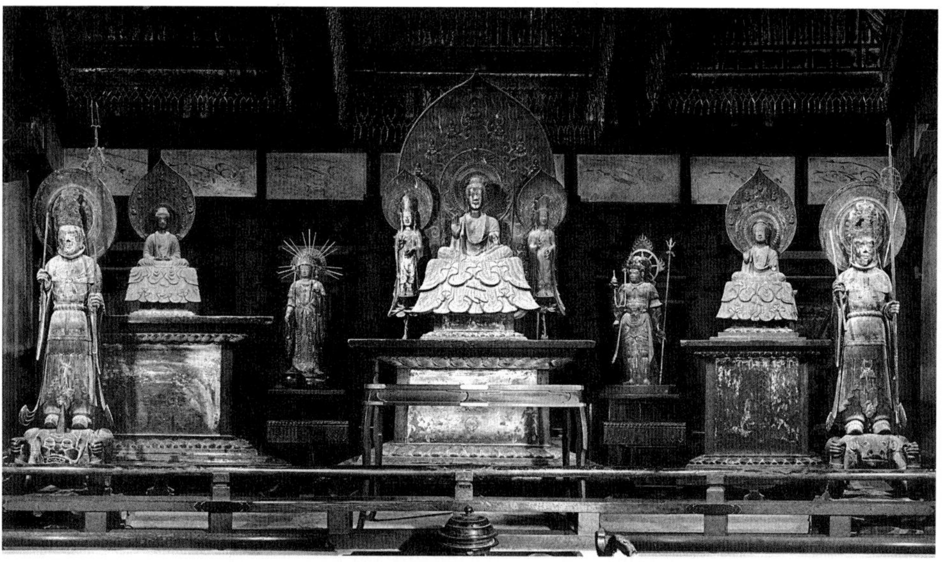

Fig. 31. Interior of Kondō Hall, 7th cent. Hōryūji Temple, Ikaruga. Śākyamuni (7th cent.), with two accompanying Bodhisattvas, is seated on the central "Sumeru" platform in the inner altar area. To his left (east) and right (west) are the directional Buddhas Yakushi (7th cent.) and Amida (13th cent.) respectively, suggesting the central importance of Śākyamuni in Buddhist cosmology. Art historians have pointed out that this configuration was not the original layout of the altar area but developed centuries later. (Note that this broad view of the temple's interior has been created digitally from three photos, so the spacing between images is compressed and inexact.)

Another example of diversification is found at the Seiryōji Temple in Kyoto, mentioned earlier. Its renowned standing image of Śākyamuni (fig. 21), which supposedly was an authentic likeness of the Buddha passed down from India, became the center of a local cult devoted to the icon. To its adherents, Śākyamuni actually manifests himself in the image (thus giving the Mahayana concept of an incarnate Buddha an added layer of meaning) and thereby becomes immediately accessible to devotees whatever their needs might be. As a result, the Seiryōji Buddha became famous as a localization of Śākyamuni's presence, and through it a belief in the miraculous powers of the icon itself was grafted onto the traditional account of the Buddha's life. In fact, the icon became so well known in premodern Japan that replicas of it circulated widely in the hope that its power, originating from the Seiryōji, could be transplanted elsewhere. Replicas of the Seiryōji Śākyamuni, bearing the unique physical characteristics of the original, were treated not simply as mementoes or souvenirs, but as surrogates of the temple's Buddha, imbued with the same capacity for miracles (fig. 32). Wherever they were enshrined—in other temples, private chapels, or home altars—these sites functioned as spiritual satellites of the Seiryōji and places where the Buddha's extended presence could be felt.[2]

Yet another specialized portrayal of Śākyamuni developed in Zen Buddhism. Because of Zen's focus on the practice of meditation, its monasteries typically enshrine a seated image of Śākyamuni in meditation in its main hall and also in the chapel on the second floor of its main gate. Sometimes this image is flanked by two Bodhisattvas—ordinarily Monju (Skt. Mañjuśrī), the Bodhisattva of wisdom and enlightenment, and Fugen (Skt. Samantabhadra), the Bodhisattva of practice and meditation—thereby situating the Buddha in an iconographic ensemble emphasizing the Zen themes of wisdom and meditation. In other configurations Śākyamuni is accompanied by an array of disciples, all enlightened arhats (often sixteen in number), or by a pair of eminent disciples,

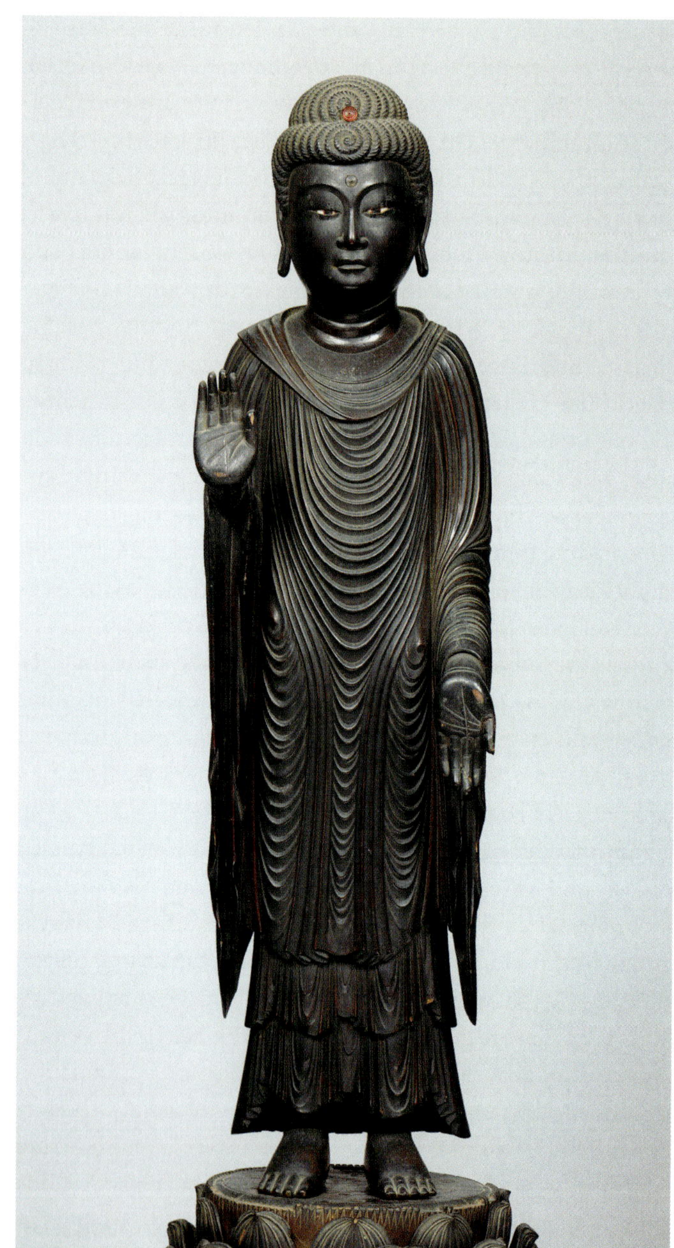

Fig. 32. Replica of the Seiryōji Buddha, 13th cent. The pose, draped garment, facial features, and hairstyle of this replica of the Seiryōji Buddha bear a strong resemblance to the original in Kyoto. Both were considered an exact likeness of Śākyamuni and a miraculous manifestation of his presence. An inscription on the base of the image indicates that it was sculpted in 1273 and revered by Buddhists associated with the priests Eison (1201–1290) and Ninshō (1217–1303), who promoted ceremonies of religious precepts and vows among common people.

Kāśyapa and Ānanda.[3] This ensemble, which was widespread in China, is, on the one hand, closer to the traditional story in which Śākyamuni's disciples are said to have traveled with the Buddha as he spread his teachings. On the other hand, the prominence given to Kāśyapa and Ānanda, the next two patriarchs after Śākyamuni in the Zen lineage, conveys an implicit Zen message not otherwise found in his life story. Specifically, it evokes the Zen legend of Śākyamuni's transmission of a wordless, mind-to-mind teaching to Kāśyapa, who then passed it on to Ānanda as the basis for a continuous Zen lineage. This placement shows how Zen has particularized Śākyamuni's identity to accommodate its own mythic heritage.

Another instance of diversification may be seen in Buddhist traditions that are rooted in the *Lotus Sutra*. This scripture was influential throughout East Asia, and in Japan it became the central text of the Tendai and Nichiren traditions. In it Śākyamuni is presented not merely as the historical Buddha but as an eternal Buddha who periodically appears in the world to bring all sentient beings to liberation. This revelation occurs in the sutra after a dramatic scene in which a stupa erupts out of the ground and its doors open to reveal another Buddha, Tahō (Skt. Prabhūtaratna), who invites Śākyamuni to sit alongside him. Tahō is identified as a primordial Buddha, and Śākyamuni is subsequently revealed to have a similar beginningless enlightenment and an everlasting presence.[4] The *Lotus Sutra* thus elevates Śākyamuni from merely the Buddha of this world to an undying Buddha of cosmic significance. Hence, whenever an image of Śākyamuni appears in a Tendai or Nichiren context, it is assumed to be the Śākyamuni of the *Lotus Sutra,* who on the surface plays the role of the Buddha of this present world-system, but in actuality spans all time and space. One interesting byproduct of this characterization is a distinctive iconic depiction in which Śākyamuni is presented side-by-side with Tahō as twin seated Buddhas either inside a stupa or pagoda, or enshrined on an altar (fig. 33).

Fig. 33. *Lotus Sutra* Mandala, 14th cent. This "mandala" depicts Śākyamuni preaching the *Lotus Sutra* on Vulture Peak. He and the primordial Buddha Tahō sit side-by-side in a pagoda-roofed stupa that has erupted out of the earth, while celestial beings float overhead to the sound of heavenly music. Seated below Śākyamuni and receiving his teaching are monks, Bodhisattvas, and laymen and laywomen (including, perhaps, the sponsor of the painting at the bottom). The young girl making an offering just below the two Buddhas is the pious eight-year-old dragon girl, featured in the sutra, who offers a precious jewel to the Buddha and instantaneously attains the highest enlightenment. Though Śākyamuni is the Buddha of a world of suffering, scenes that show him proclaiming the *Lotus Sutra* tend to depict it as an idealized and perfect world.

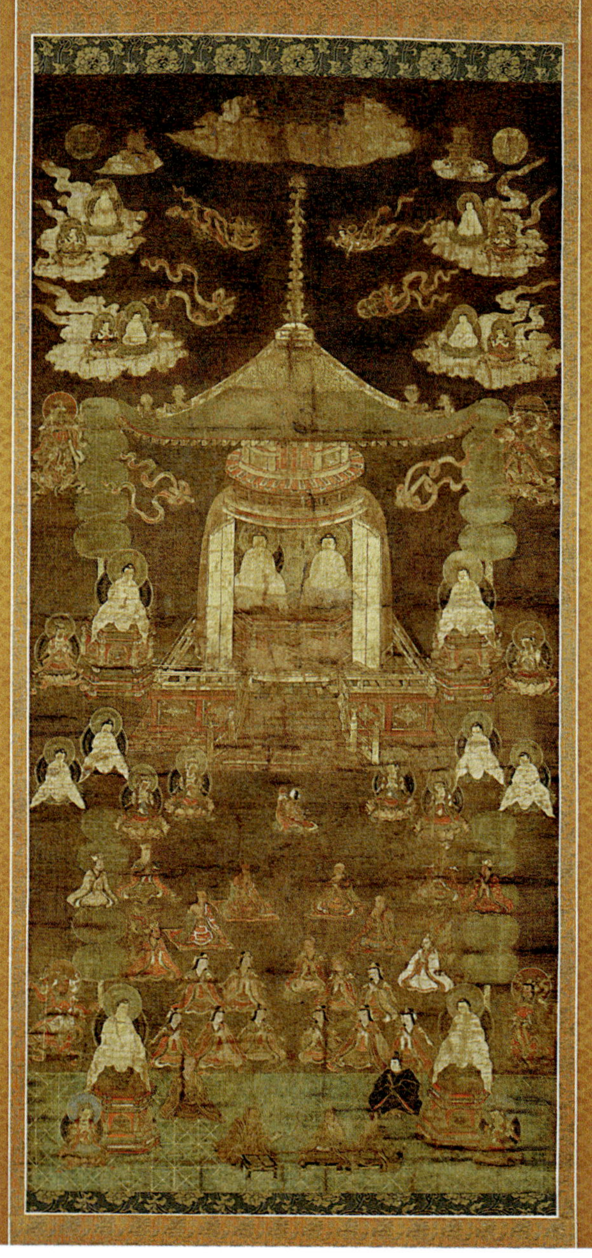

MIROKU BUDDHA

Miroku (Skt. Maitreya) is recognized in virtually every form of Buddhism as the future incarnate Buddha of this world. Strictly speaking, he is only a Buddha-to-be right now—that is, a Bodhisattva—but his spiritual advancement is considered so great and his renewal of the Dharma so anticipated that he is widely depicted in the guise of a fully realized Buddha—monk's robes, close-cropped hair, protruding cranial crown, long earlobes, and so forth. As a result, it is difficult to distinguish icons of the Buddha Miroku from Śākyamuni images unless explicitly identified. He nonetheless has his own religious story, propounded by Śākyamuni in several Buddhist sutras. It indicates that Miroku is currently residing in the Tuṣita (J. Tosotsu) heaven and that in 5.6 billion years when the world cycles into a new golden age he will descend to earth to become the next Buddha. As in the case of Śākyamuni, he will be born from his mother's right side and endowed with thirty-two auspicious marks and eighty secondary ones. He will leave lay life behind and take up a homeless life in pursuit of the Buddhist path. Then, sitting under a so-called dragon-flower tree he will attain unsurpassed enlightenment, to the great jubilation of the deities of heaven. Finally, he will proclaim the Dharma once again in three great assemblies at which billions of sentient beings, bereft after Śākyamuni's disappearance, will receive his teachings. Hence, an air of anticipation surrounds Miroku, with some believers aspiring to be reborn with him in that heaven and to linger there until he descends to earth so that they will be assured of encountering the Buddha's teachings (fig. 34).[5] The power of Miroku derives in part from his replication of the Śākyamuni paradigm. His birth and departure from home follow the pattern of Śākyamuni's life; his enlightenment reenacts Śākyamuni's meditative awakening; and his proclamation of the Dharma at the three assemblies echoes Śākyamuni's Deer Park teaching. In short, he passes through the same three phases—quest, enlightenment, and compassion—that Śākyamuni did.

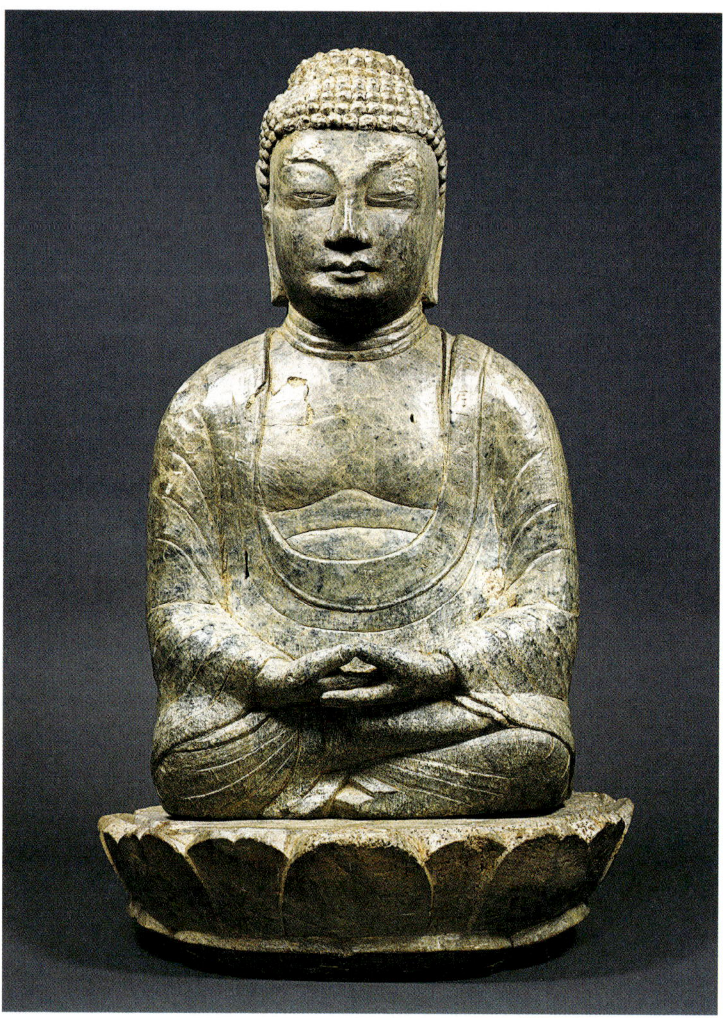

Fig. 34. **Seated Miroku Buddha, 11th cent.** This unusual stone statue of Miroku, dated 1071, appears virtually indistinguishable from images of Śākyamuni. What identifies it as Miroku is a long inscription on the back indicating that the sponsors of its sculpting expected Miroku to descend to earth and proclaim the Dharma. The image was originally buried in a sutra mound with a copy of the *Lotus Sutra* concealed in its inner cavity in order to preserve and safeguard the Dharma during its gradual disappearance in this world-cycle. Physically the image bears the standard marks of a Buddha—tight curls of hair, protuberance of the head, long earlobes, neck rings, and monk's robes—and is seated in the Buddha's archetypal meditation pose on a lotus-shaped base.

YAKUSHI BUDDHA

The healing Buddha Yakushi (Skt. Bhaiṣajyaguru) was a common figure in early Japanese iconography but became less prominent over time. He is regarded as a fully actualized Buddha replete with the thirty-two auspicious marks and the eighty secondary ones, but not an incarnate Buddha of this world-system. Rather he is a transcendent Buddha located in an untainted realm of his own making in the distant eastern region of the universe. This realm is as much an emanation from the Buddha as it is a domain where he resides. The appeal of Yakushi, which literally means master of medicine, is that he offers aid to those suffering from afflictions. In Japanese history Yakushi became the center of a Buddhist healing cult, and many icons of him were produced in the hope that he would assist people recovering from illness. As part of Yakushi's story, recounted in the *Sutra on the Merits of the Fundamental Vows of Yakushi, the Lapis Lazuli Radiance Buddha*, he is said to have made twelve vows as a Bodhisattva during his quest for enlightenment. The seventh among them was:

> I vow that when I attain enlightenment in a future age, if there are any sentient beings who are ill and oppressed, who have nowhere to go and nothing to return to, who have neither doctor nor medicine, neither relatives nor immediate family, who are destitute and whose sufferings are acute—as soon as my name passes through their ears, they will be cured of all their diseases and they will be peaceful and joyous in body and mind. They will have plentiful families and property, and they will personally experience supreme enlightenment.[6]

Thus, simply hearing the sound of Yakushi's name is thought to trigger a cure. But his particular identity as a healer has always merged with his broader identity as a Buddha who aids sentient beings in their quest for enlightenment. Thus, physical well-being and spiritual awakening, which were never considered at odds in Mahayana Buddhism, are both dimensions of Yakushi's all-encompassing compassion as a Buddha. It is not surprising, then, that images of Yakushi, hardly distinguishable in pose and physical marks from other Buddhas, commonly display the "Have no fear, I offer you aid" hand gestures. Iconographically, the one specific feature differentiating Yakushi from Śākyamuni is a medicine vessel or container resting in the palm of his left hand. This attribute does not appear in Japan's earliest images of Yakushi, nor is it mentioned in the scriptures about him, but it became a standard iconographic marker of Yakushi from around the tenth century (fig. 35).[7]

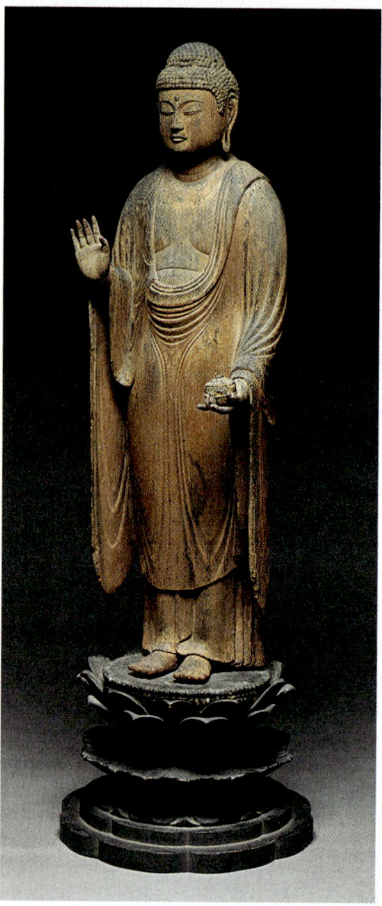

Fig. 35. Healing Buddha Yakushi, 12th cent. Images of Yakushi, the transcendent Buddha of healing, largely resemble those of other Buddhas in hairstyle, physical attributes, and clothing. Many Yakushi icons from the tenth century and later, however, are distinguished by a variant of the usual hand gestures of compassion. In these images Yakushi holds a medicine container, as here in the palm of his left hand.

VAIROCANA AND DAINICHI BUDDHA

Another prominent Buddha—famous in part because he is enshrined as the Great Buddha at Nara's Tōdaiji Temple, described earlier—is Vairocana (J. Birushana or Rushana). In physical appearance the Great Buddha is difficult to distinguish from Śākyamuni. One hint of his separate identity is his enormous size, many times larger than even the towering "life-size" icons of Śākyamuni (fig. 36). Another telling feature is the etchings of Buddhas and world-systems on the lotus petals surrounding the Great Buddha's pedestal. This feature is based on a passage in the *Brahma's Net Sutra* describing the thousand petals of Vairocana's lotus platform, each of which manifests yet another Buddha under whom there are numerous world-systems with their own Buddhas of Śākyamuni's stature (fig. 37).[8] Vairocana is thus a cosmic Buddha from whom emerges the countless other Buddhas of the universe. This identity is conveyed iconographically in yet another feature of the Great Buddha of Nara: tiny radiant Buddhas surrounding his body on the huge mandorla behind him. These are known as apparitional Buddhas (*kebutsu*), miraculously emanated figures that can skillfully lead sentient beings to enlightenment. Virtually any Buddha is thought to have the capacity to generate them. But they are especially associated with Vairocana, as intimated by a passage in the *Flower Garland Sutra* describing their emergence out of his body.[9] In short, Vairocana is portrayed as a Buddha of cosmic proportions responsible for all the worlds and Buddhas in the universe.

The Shingon tradition of esoteric Buddhism in Japan also recognizes Vairocana as the foremost Buddha but commonly uses the East Asian version of his name, Dainichi (Skt. Mahāvairocana, meaning Great Vairocana), and relies on different religious texts from those that inspired the Great Buddha of Nara. Shingon makes the claim that Dainichi is the very Dharma body of the Buddha—sublime, inexpressible, and without form—though it unabashedly depicts this "formless" Buddha in iconic form. Shingon images of Dainichi are an exception, however, to the standard depiction of a Buddha. Specifically, their appearance bears a greater resemblance to a Bodhisattva than a Buddha. Dainichi is commonly shown wearing

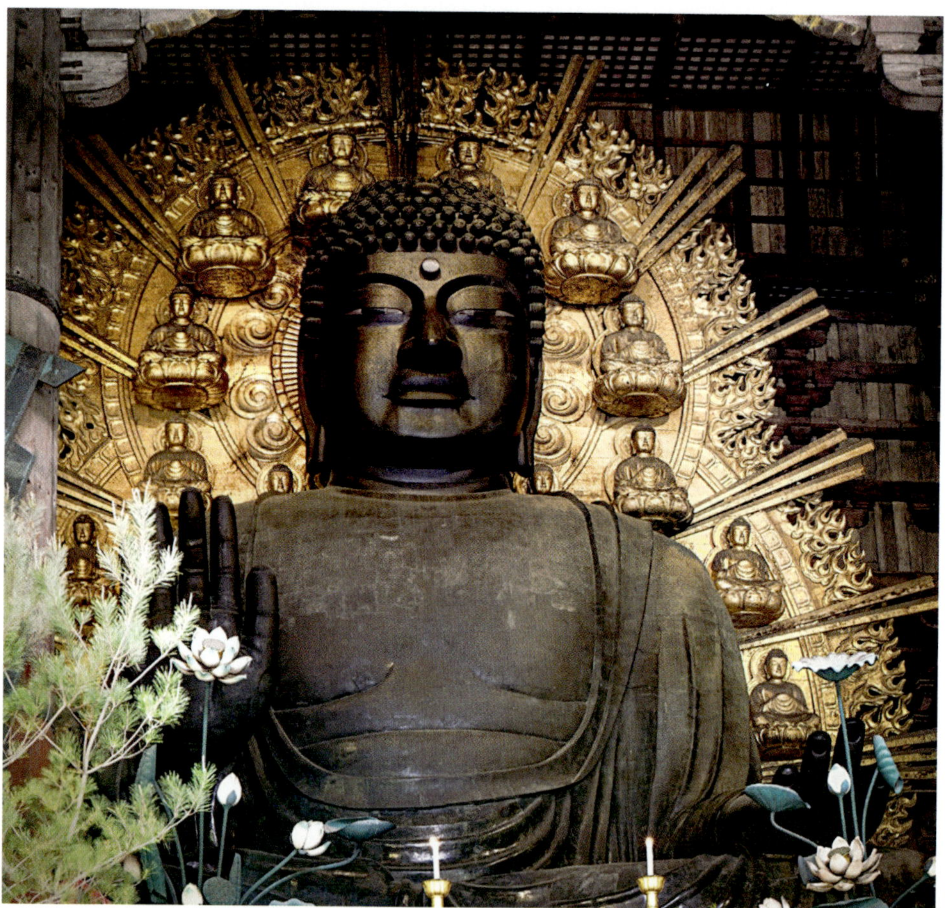

Fig. 36. Apparitional Buddhas around the Great Buddha. Tōdaiji Temple, Nara. The Great Buddha is an icon of the cosmic Buddha Vairocana. Scriptures assert that countless "apparitional Buddhas," seen here as smaller Buddhas around him, emerge out of his body and serve as Buddhas of world-systems throughout the universe. Each world has its own distinct Buddha, though all of them are simultaneously extensions and manifestations of Vairocana. The golden backdrop consisting of a halo, mandorla, and light beams represents one of the Buddha's thirty-two physical attributes—the golden light streaming from every pore of his body.

various jeweled adornments and an elaborate crown or headdress. These are used perhaps to suggest his kingly eminence, since kingship is a motif found in other Buddhist contexts. Ordinarily Dainichi is presented in two poses, each associated with one of Shingon's two principal sutras. The first is a meditative sitting position with his hands in his lap, one resting in the other with the thumb tips touching lightly, producing the so-called Dharma-world meditation mudra (*hokkai jōin*). The second is Dainichi, again in a cross-legged sitting position, displaying a hand gesture unique to him, the so-called wisdom-fist mudra (*chiken'in*), in which his right hand

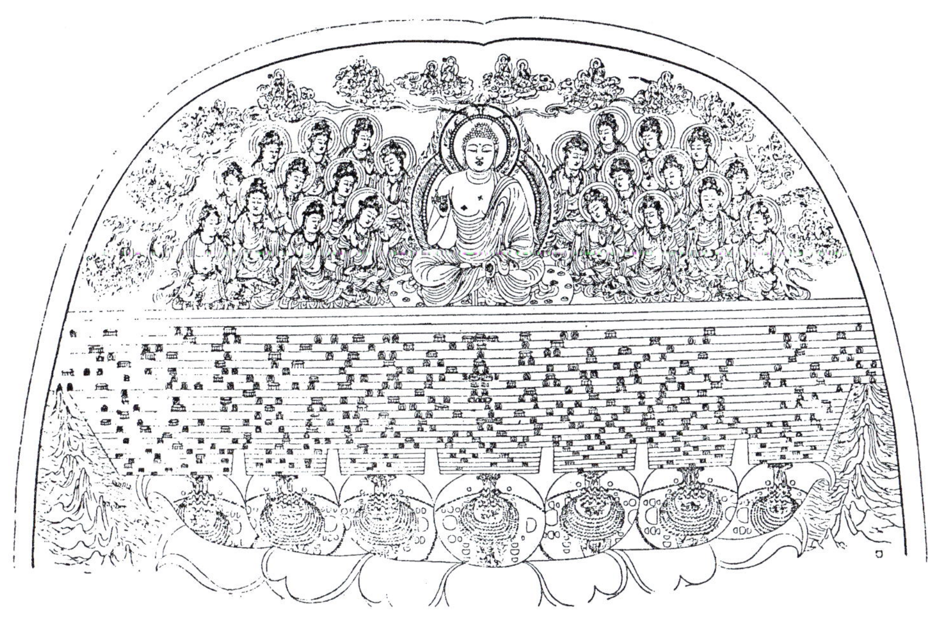

Fig. 37. Etching on lotus petal of the Great Buddha. Tōdaiji Temple, Nara. The etching on each petal of the giant lotus flower surrounding the pedestal of the Great Buddha of Nara depicts a Buddha and his attendant host presiding over a world-system. Immediately below are multiple layers of heaven in which hundreds of palaces appear, and beneath them are circles containing individual worlds with their own towering Mt. Sumeru at the center and oceans and continents arrayed all around. The message conveyed by this imagery is that there are countless worlds emanating from Vairocana, each with its own Buddha. Śākyamuni and this present world are only one, and are dwarfed by the cosmic scale of Vairocana.

clutches the index finger of his left (fig. 38). This gesture signifies the Buddha's enlightened activity—grasping wisdom—and also the cosmic unity of mind and matter, of Buddha and living beings, and of womb and diamond motifs—gender imagery conveying Dainichi's nature, mentioned again below.[10] These two poses thus express the awakening power of wisdom and the interpenetration of all things, and they highlight the enlightenment dimension of Buddhahood more than the quest and compassion dimensions (though all three are encompassed in Dainichi's cosmic identity). As the embodiment of enlightenment Dainichi offers a powerful image to adherents who seek ritually to "actualize Buddhahood in their very body" (*sokushin jōbutsu*), a core theme of Shingon Buddhism.

Iconographically, Shingon is well known for its dual mandalas. Each in its own way conveys the message of the centrality, emanational capacity, and all-pervasiveness of Dainichi. The first, called the womb-world (*taizōkai*) mandala (fig. 39), consists of a square central panel enclosed by concentric rectangular compartments several layers deep. In the central panel is a lotus flower with eight red petals, in which are arrayed a central Buddha encircled by eight other figures. Dainichi, posing with the Dharma-world meditation mudra, is the pivotal figure, surrounded by four Buddhas in the cardinal directions and four Bodhisattvas in the ordinal directions. On the four sides around this panel are compartments known as halls (*in*) containing rows and columns of Buddhist figures: Buddhas, Bodhisattvas, ferocious divinities, celestial spirits, and others. These compartments seem to cascade out from the center four or five layers deep and display over four hundred figures arrayed around Dainichi in the middle.[11]

The second mandala, gendered male and called the diamond-world (*kongōkai*) mandala, consists of nine square panels known as assemblies (*e*)—three across the top, three in the middle, and three at the bottom—in a tic-tac-toe pattern (fig. 40). Each of the nine is a miniature mandala in its own right, and each has Dainichi at its center in either anthropomorphic, symbolic, or substitutionary form. The panel in the very middle contains five moon disks—top, bottom, left,

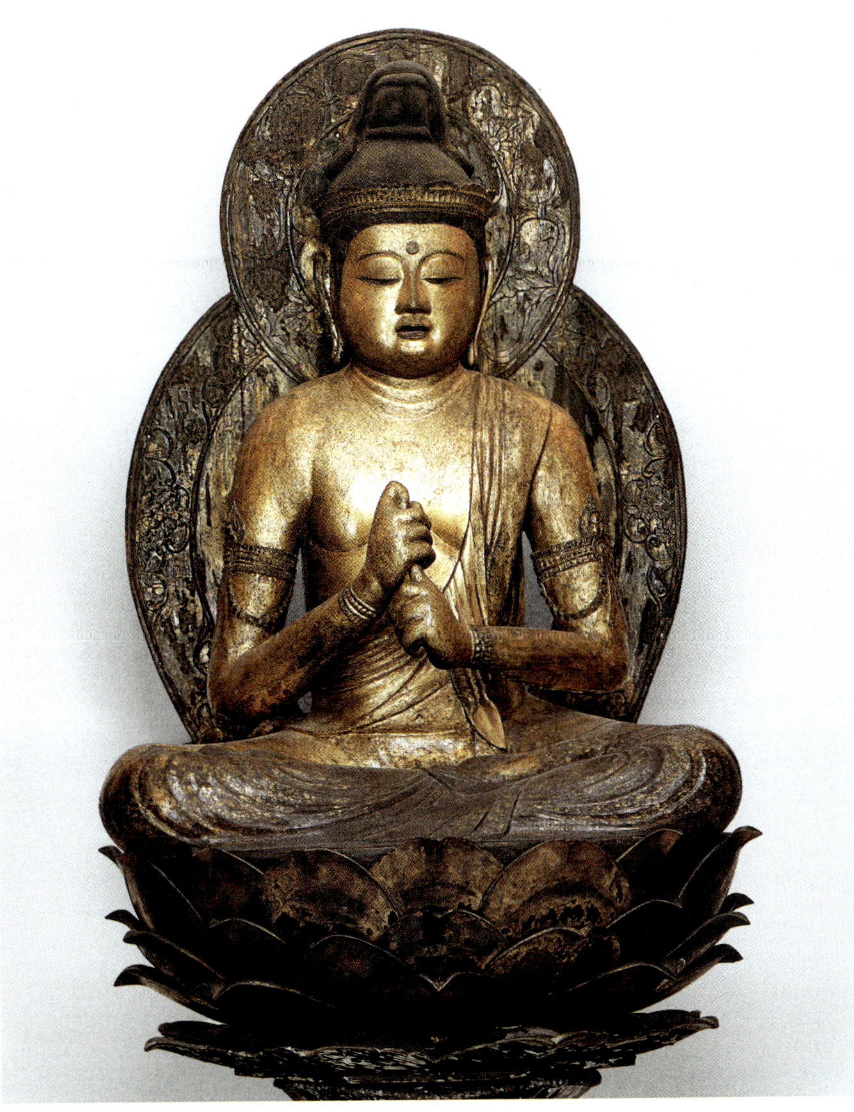

Fig. 38. Dainichi Buddha, 12th cent. The wisdom-fist mudra expresses Dainichi's grasp of wisdom as well as the interpenetrating unity of all things. He is identified as the very Dharma body of the Buddha. Iconographically, Dainichi's bracelets, armbands, long hair, and crown are more characteristic of a Bodhisattva than a Buddha. Photo © 2020 Museum of Fine Arts, Boston.

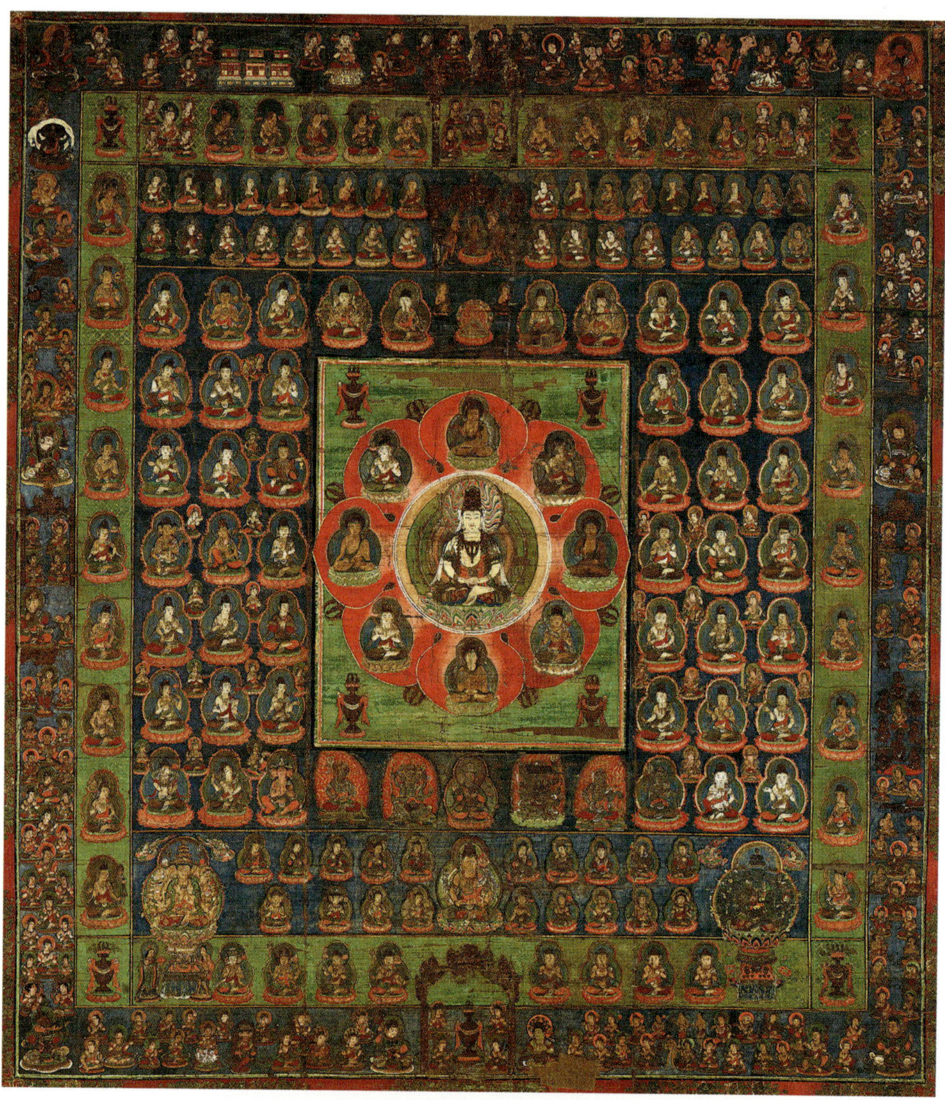

Fig. 39. **Womb-world mandala, 13th cent.** The mandala offers a graphic representation of the spiritual universe. The eight-petal lotus flower in the central panel shows Dainichi displaying the Dharma-world meditation mudra, with four directional Buddhas around him interspersed with four Bodhisattvas. The concentric rectangles contain a host of other figures—Buddhas, Bodhisattvas, celestial spirits, ferocious divinities, monks, lay people, sentient beings in various rebirths, and symbolic objects—all regarded as emanations of Dainichi.

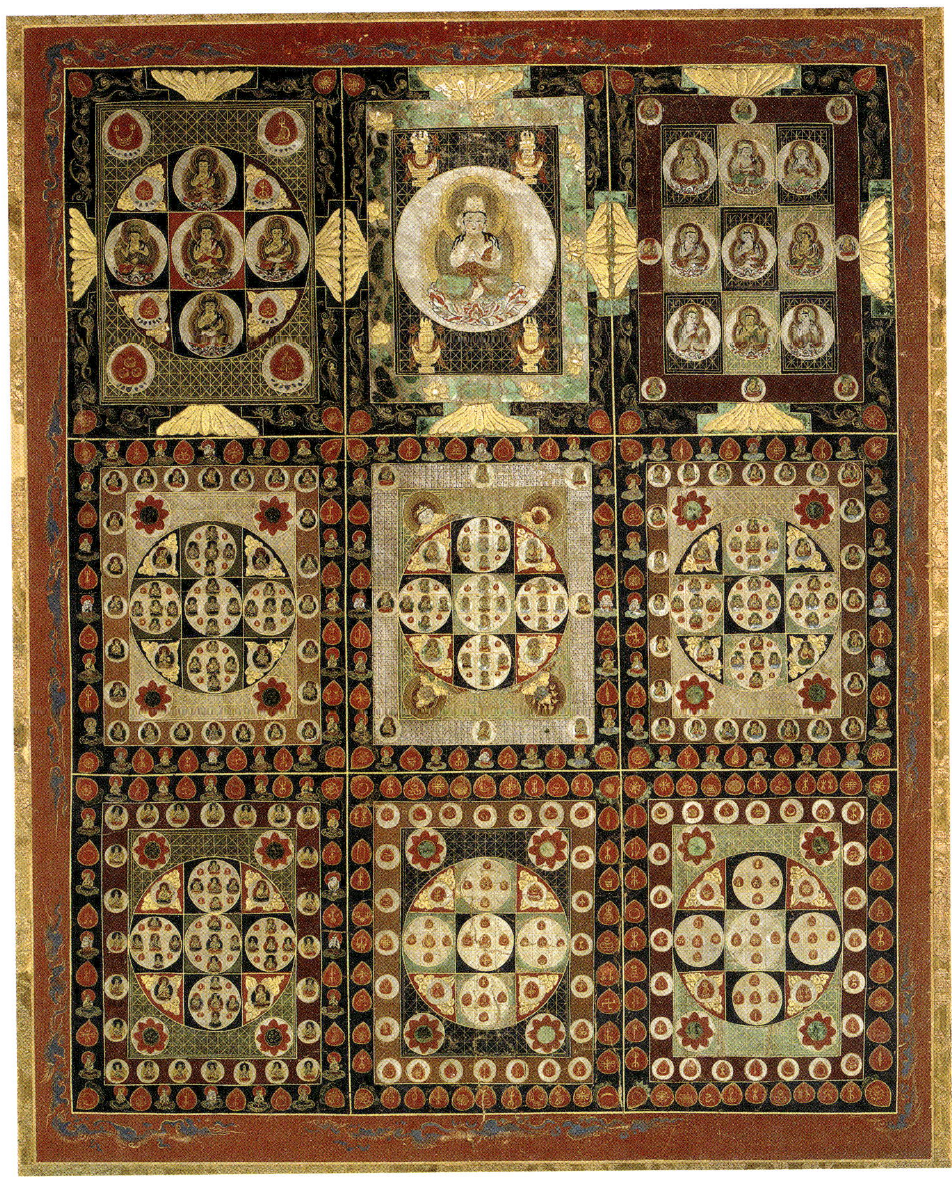

Fig. 40. **Diamond-world mandala, 14th–16th cent.** This mandala consists of nine panels, each with Dainichi in one guise or another as its central figure. The lower six panels are all configured with five moon disks, each containing a central Buddha and four Bodhisattvas, whereas the top three panels vary in configuration. The wisdom-fist mudra is Dainichi's primary hand gesture at the center of the mandala. When installed in a temple, the two mandalas provide a physical space where the Buddha and other figures can be ritually engaged.

Fig. 41. **Seated Amida Buddha, 11th cent. Byōdōin Temple, Kyoto.** This renowned image of Amida Buddha is a "life-size" figure over nine feet tall. The mudra, with two index fingers curled inward, indicates that Amida is meditating on the highest category of sentient beings whose rebirth in his Pure Land is assured. Two curled fingers—whether the index, middle, or ring fingers—are an important marker of Amida images.

right, and center—each with a tiny Buddha in the middle and four surrounding Bodhisattvas. The central Buddha in the central disk is Dainichi displaying the wisdom-fist mudra. The other four disks contain directional Buddhas, each with its own four Bodhisattvas. Around this central panel, five of the remaining eight have the same basic configuration: five moon disks with five figures in each, creating a structure analogous to the central panel. The other three panels, all across the top, vary somewhat: the left one with five main figures, the center one with a single figure, and the right one with nine main figures. In each case Dainichi or his surrogate is situated in the middle.[12]

Inside Shingon ritual halls the two mandalas are installed facing each other on opposite walls, the womb-world on the east end and the diamond-world on the west. In front of them is a low square altar platform on which a variety of ritual implements, containers, and offerings are placed.[13] Religious interaction with the mandalas in this setting is complex—for instance, in the case of the diamond-world mandala it involves ritually coursing through the nine panels either in a counterclockwise spiral ending at the center or in a clockwise spiral beginning at the center. Some interpreters hold that the function of the two mandalas is to inspire visualizations of the Buddha, Bodhisattvas, or deities in these rituals, although analysis of actual ritual texts and performances suggests that visualization may not be the mandalas' purpose. Rather it is to provide a ritual location for the embodiment or palpable presence of the Buddha.[14] Whatever the case, the layout of the two mandalas testifies to the centrality and primacy of Dainichi, to his role as the source and substance of all things, and to a reality that emanates entirely from him.

AMIDA BUDDHA

Amida (Skt. Amitābha or Amitāyus) is another widely known Buddha who inspired an abundance of iconographic expression (fig. 41). Technically, he is a transcendent directional Buddha originating

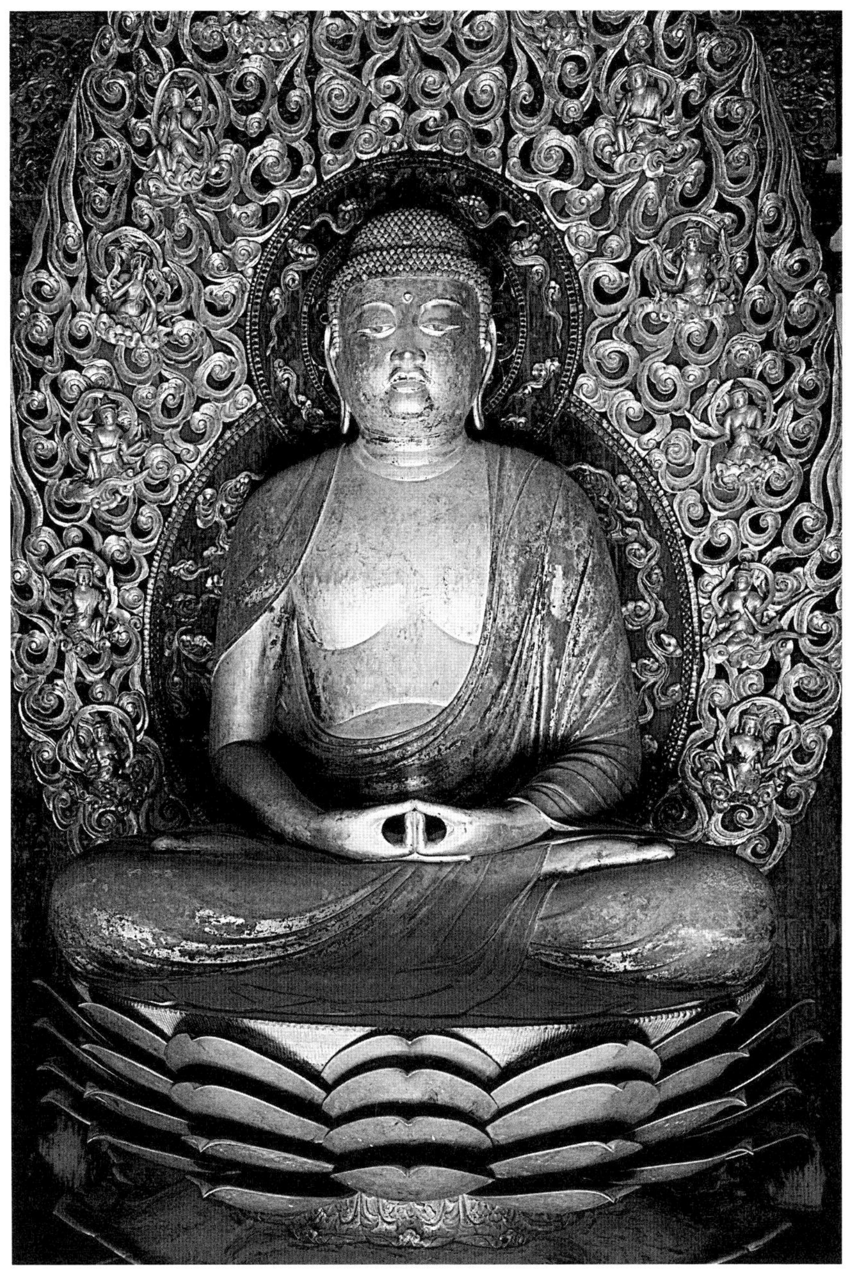

from the same Mahayana cosmology that gave rise to Yakushi. He is thought to reside in the western region of the universe and to preside over a resplendent and blissful realm commonly known as the Pure Land (Jōdo). The two Shingon mandalas described above include Amida as the directional Buddha of the west. But historically his appeal outstripped that of most other Buddhas and he came to be perceived more as a universal and all-encompassing Buddha. As the name Amida is meant to convey, he is a Buddha of unlimited light and life, suggesting his ubiquitous presence in all space and time. Moreover, his Pure Land represents not merely a locale where he resides, but a perfect world generated out of himself that bears all his miraculous qualities. People born there during their next life are assured of complete enlightenment. The Pure Land tradition has thus engendered both a sense of the pervasiveness of the Buddha and an otherworldly aspiration to attain enlightenment in his Pure Land.

Amida, like many transcendent Buddhas, has his own sacred story, recounted in the *Larger Pure Land Sutra*. According to it, in the remote past he was inspired by the Buddha of his mythic age to embark on his own quest for Buddhahood. He subsequently practiced meditation for five eons, contemplating the ideal characteristics for his Buddhahood and for the miraculous world he would generate. The product of this meditation was a series of forty-eight Bodhisattva vows describing what Amida, his Pure Land, and its inhabitants would be like once he became a Buddha. He vowed, for instance, that there would be no religious retrogression for those born in the Pure Land and all would achieve Nirvana without fail; that all other Buddhas in the universe would proclaim his name; that anyone who is sincere, has faith, aspires to be born in the Pure Land, and reflects on Amida even ten times would be assured of birth there; and that he would appear with a celestial entourage at the deathbed of such people to usher them into the Pure Land. According to the story, Amida went on to attain Buddhahood and is now working compassionately to bring all sentient beings to enlightenment via the Pure Land. Those born there fall into three categories, ranging from spiritually advanced Bodhisattvas down to lowly wrongdoers who call Amida's name at death. Religious reflection (*nen*), the primary practice advanced in Amida's eighteenth vow, is sometimes interpreted as meditative visions of the Buddha and his Pure Land, but more often as the chanting of Amida's name with faith, known as the Nenbutsu.[15] This story of Amida's Buddhahood is a classic example of a later religious narrative rising to prominence in certain Buddhist circles and overshadowing Śākyamuni's original story. Far from disavowing Śākyamuni, however, Pure Land Buddhism portrays him as the great, compassionate teacher who has revealed Amida to people and as the foremost proponent in this world of the Pure Land path. Thus, Śākyamuni's sacred story is folded into the Pure Land tradition as an ancillary one to Amida's.

Pure Land Buddhism's beliefs and practices have stimulated a variety of iconographic forms. There are, of course, standard images of Amida that closely resemble those of Śākyamuni. They are found in both standing and sitting poses, and they bear the typical physical marks of a Buddha. One difference, however, is that Amida images show a slight variation in their hand gestures. In the meditating, teaching, and compassionate mudras, Amida's index, middle, or ring fingers are curled touching the thumb to indicate the highest, middle, or lowest category of those born in the Pure Land as the focus of his attention at that moment (fig. 41). This subtle difference is sufficient to set Amida images apart as a distinct iconographic genre.

In addition, there are certain presentations of Amida that are unique to the Pure Land tradition. One is a large-scale, landscape-like depiction of the Pure Land known as the Taima Mandala. It presents an all-encompassing view of Amida's luminous and opulent paradise: the Buddha is situated on a lotus pedestal in the center flanked by his attendant Bodhisattvas Kannon and Seishi, with a celestial retinue gathered round, a giant lotus pond in front, musicians and dancers performing nearby, jeweled trees on either side, imperial palaces in the background, and the skies filled with

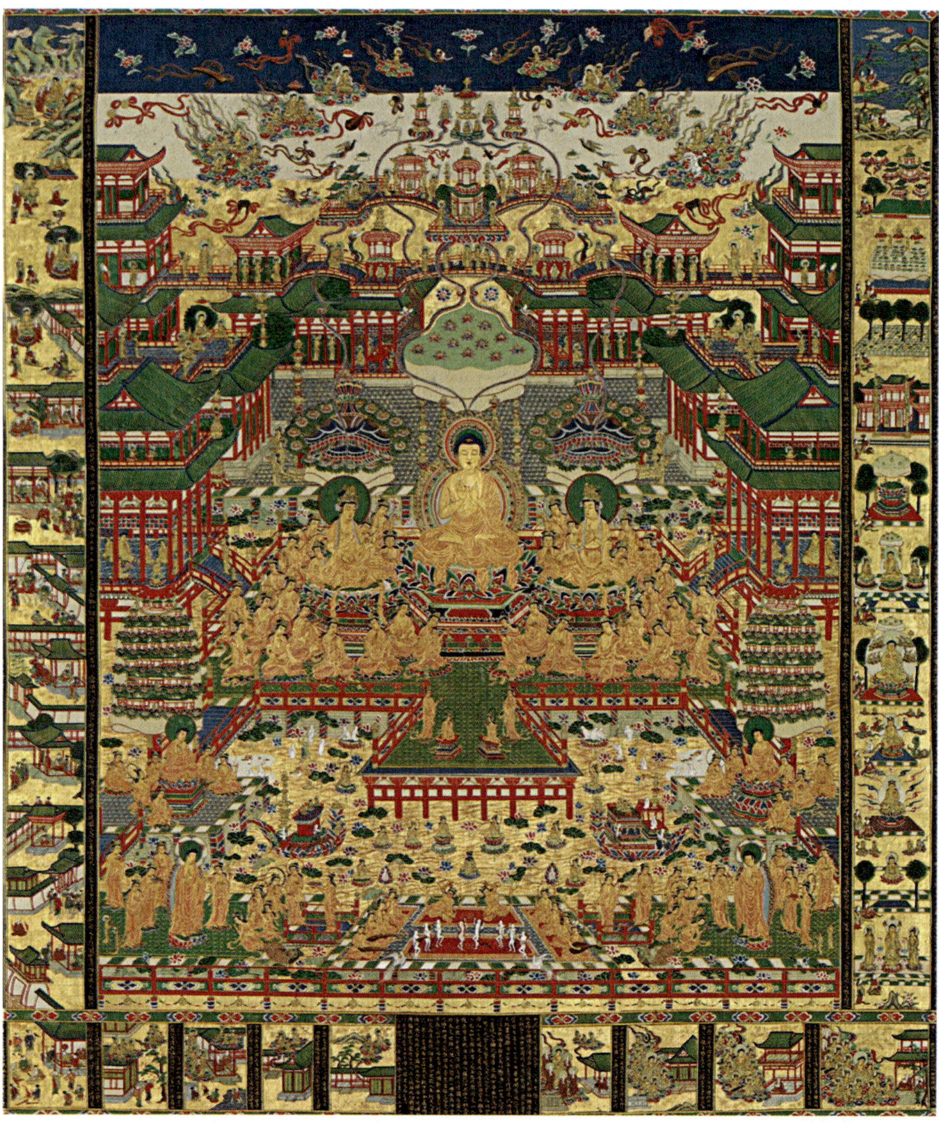

Fig. 42. Taima Mandala, 18th cent. A panoramic view of Amida's Pure Land shows the Buddha sitting on a lotus pedestal with his hands in the Dharma-wheel-turning mudra, indicating that he is preaching the Dharma. The paradisal imagery replete with celestial deities, palaces, jeweled trees, hosts of Bodhisattvas, and a lotus pond where believers are reborn on giant lotus flowers is based on the *Pure Land Meditation Sutra,* episodes of which are presented in frames along the left edge. On the right are depicted the stages of meditation for visualizing the Pure Land, while the nine levels of rebirth in the Pure Land are arrayed across the bottom. Though the icon is sometimes characterized as an aid to visualization meditation, for most Buddhists it is simply a vicarious way of encountering Amida in his miraculous and perfected realm.

heavenly spirits, apparitional Buddhas, falling flowers, and floating musical instruments that play spontaneously (fig. 42). Paintings like this one were produced both as revelations of the Pure Land's appearance and as artistic inspirations for visualizing it. In content and layout they follow closely the *Pure Land Meditation Sutra*, which

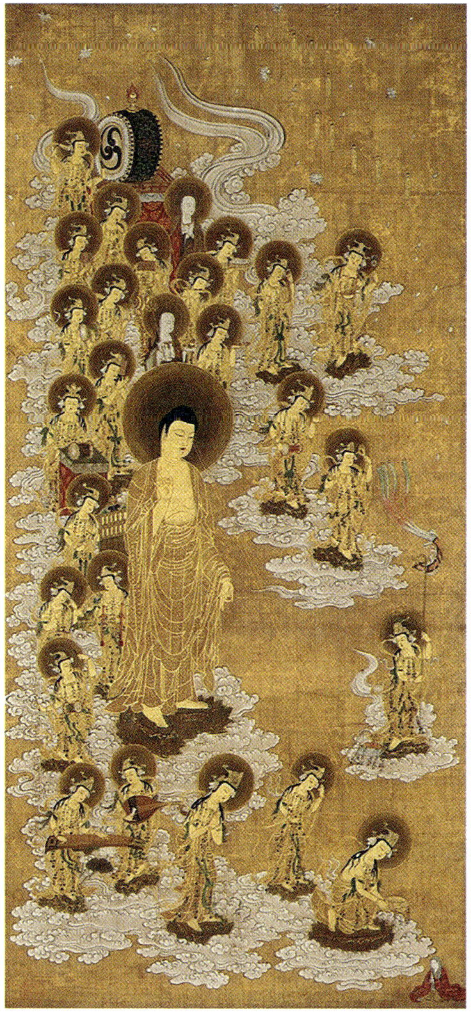

Fig. 43. **Amida Buddha welcoming the dying believer, 17th cent.** Based on the Pure Land sutras, there emerged a common belief that the Buddha would appear before dying believers to welcome them into his Pure Land. Amida, depicted here with an entourage of twenty-five Bodhisattvas waving banners and playing celestial music, beckons with gestures of compassion. The dying person is shown in miniature in the lower right corner with hands held prayerfully in reverence. The Bodhisattva in the lower right, Kannon, extends a lotus pedestal on which the dying person will be reborn in the lotus pond of Pure Land.

guides aspirants through a series of meditative visions until the entire Pure Land is perceived in all its splendor. These meditative stages are in fact depicted in small frames along the right edge of the Taima Mandala.[16] The gripping vision of this radiant world, which makes objects of desire in this world pale by comparison, is thought to propel one throughout life toward birth in the Pure Land.

Another visual motif distinctive to the Pure Land tradition is the image of Amida coming to greet faithful adherents at death. Paintings of this type are sometimes composed from a diagonal, third-person perspective, showing Amida descending with his entourage toward the dying person (fig. 43). Other times they are constructed from the first-person perspective of the dying, displaying Amida and his host approaching head-on, perhaps appearing over the horizon. These images are linked to a deathbed ritual that became common in some forms of Pure Land Buddhism. A dying believer would be moved to a quiet place and, facing the west (just as Śākyamuni did at death), would be encouraged to chant Amida's name and to watch for his arrival. Sometimes an icon of Amida would be placed in front of the person, and a five-colored cord draped from the image to the person's hand. This ritual is aimed at focusing the dying person's last thoughts on Amida and the next world.[17] Pure Land, more than many types of Buddhism, makes eloquent use of form—visual, verbal, meditative, and iconographic—to engender a Buddhist frame of mind, while simultaneously affirming Mahayana themes of formlessness—emptiness, suchness, Dharma body, and Nirvana—which are considered congruent and implicit in these Pure Land forms.

CHAPTER 5

MIRACULOUS BODHISATTVAS

The influence of Mahayana on the development of Japanese Buddhist iconography was far reaching, especially in the idealization of the Bodhisattva. A Bodhisattva is someone on the path to Buddhahood, and the term originally referred to Śākyamuni prior to his enlightenment. But Mahayana expanded its meaning exponentially by recognizing many more beings working toward Buddhahood. In fact, it assumes that the universe is populated with an incalculable number of Bodhisattvas, just as it is with Buddhas. Some Bodhisattvas are on the brink of Buddhahood, while others are just at the starting point. Some are well known throughout all world-systems, while others pursue their religious practices in anonymity. Hence, the Bodhisattva figure is as pervasive and prominent in Japanese Buddhism as the Buddha.

In Mahayana the Bodhisattva ideal arose in large part as a critique of the arhat model in earlier Buddhism. Generally, Mahayana denigrates the arhat—admittedly, rather unfairly—as an example of a selfish form of religious liberation—that is, an attempt to extricate oneself from the throes of Samsara without concern for others. This is considered contrary to the example of the Buddha and symptomatic of a subtle form of attachment: obsession with one's own religious fate. Mahayana claims that true enlightenment entails not only individual enlightenment but also enlightenment for all living beings. Thus, emulating the Buddha in all his dimensions is perceived as the correct approach to religious practice.

The Bodhisattva path, strictly speaking, corresponds to the quest phase of the Buddha's paradigm. The compassion phase, by contrast, characterizes the Buddha's life after the attainment of enlightenment, when he begins to spread the Dharma. What is noteworthy is that in the Mahayana tradition compassion plays just as prominent a role in the Bodhisattva's life before full enlightenment as in the Buddha's life after it. Specifically, the Bodhisattva integrates compassion into the quest for wisdom. The cultivation of wisdom allows the Bodhisattva to break worldly attachments and illusions just as arhats do. But compassion prevents the Bodhisattva from becoming attached to non-attachment itself, as arhats are accused of doing. These two, wisdom and compassion, represent the twin virtues of the Bodhisattva in the path to enlightenment. They reflect the Bodhisattva's aspiration to transcend the things of the world on the one hand and to identify with everyone in the world on the other. These dialectical pairs—wisdom and compassion, otherworldly transcendence and this-worldly identification—also are the defining characteristics of the Buddha, who is the role model for the Bodhisattva.

Through the impact of Mahayana's Bodhisattva ideal, the iconographic repertoire of Buddhism has increased significantly. In addition to all the Buddhas, a host of Bodhisattvas, illustrious Buddhas-in-the-making, are recognized as well. Theoretically, anyone who has made a vow to attain Buddhahood is a Bodhisattva. But the path is considered indescribably long, and most ordinary individuals stand near the beginning. A few Bodhisattvas, however, are thought to be on the brink of full enlightenment, and they are treated as religious models and objects of great reverence and devotion. Because they can attain Buddhahood any moment they choose, they are considered virtual Buddhas. In appearance Bodhisattvas are commonly depicted as highborn lay people rather than monks, the typical guise of a Buddha. But in bodily characteristics they bear some of the same physical marks that Buddhas do, suggesting that the two belong to a common spiritual genus.

MIROKU BODHISATTVA

Of all the Bodhisattvas revered in Japanese Buddhism, Miroku (Skt. Maitreya), the next Buddha of this world, should be considered first.

Strictly speaking, Miroku, who is thought to have been a disciple of Śākyamuni in a previous lifetime, is not yet a Buddha. Nonetheless, he is sometimes depicted as a Buddha (fig. 34), and other times as a Bodhisattva. Clearly he was a figure of widespread appeal in early Japanese history, for numerous images of him survive from the seventh and eighth centuries. One distinctive pose seen in Miroku icons is believed to have been inherited from Korea. It portrays Miroku in a previous incarnation as the beautiful young prince Aitta (Skt. Ajita), sitting in a half cross-legged and pensive pose, contemplating his future enlightenment (fig. 44). Besides this striking pose, Miroku is frequently depicted in the standard guise of a Bodhisattva with ornate jewelry and headdress, sumptuous clothing, and long hair. While these features in themselves render him indistinguishable from other Bodhisattvas, certain physical objects sometime appear either in his hand or in his headdress that are considered identifying markers. One such object in Indian images of Miroku is a water bottle, symbolizing his ability to quench the spiritual thirst of sentient beings or to nourish them with the nectar of the Dharma. In Japan, it is more common to find a small stupa or its East Asian equivalent, a pagoda or a "five-element stupa" (*gorintō*), as the defining feature of Miroku. This object is a symbol of Śākyamuni's death, since the stupa is where his relics were enshrined after cremation. Miroku's display of it reflects his status as the next Buddha in this world, who is to succeed Śākyamuni after his passing (fig. 45).[1]

A number of cults emerged around Miroku of adherents seeking to participate in his future renewal of the Dharma. In China groups of this type occasionally provoked millenarian or revolutionary uprisings to usher in Miroku's new age. In Japan the Miroku beliefs found other forms of religious expression. One was the desire for rebirth in Miroku's assembly in the Tuṣita heaven to await his descent to the world to reestablish the Dharma. Another was to sustain existence in this world in order to await Miroku's arrival. For instance, Kūkai (773–832), the great founder of Shingon Buddhism in Japan (fig. 86), is said to reside in an eternal state of meditation in

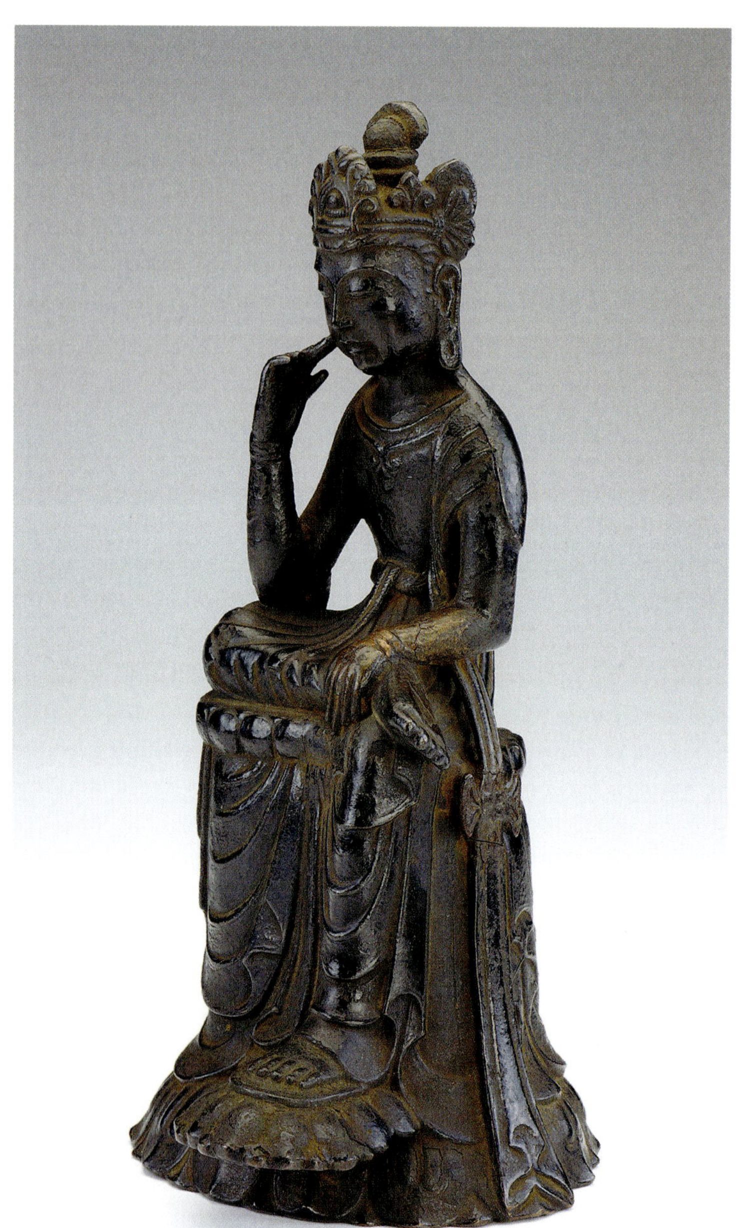

Fig. 44. Miroku in pensive pose, 7th cent. This pose, with the hand touching the cheek lightly, captures the look of Miroku as a young prince, dressed in flowing robes and a crown, reflecting on his future enlightenment. One of the earliest depictions of Miroku in Japan, it is said to have been inspired by Korean models.

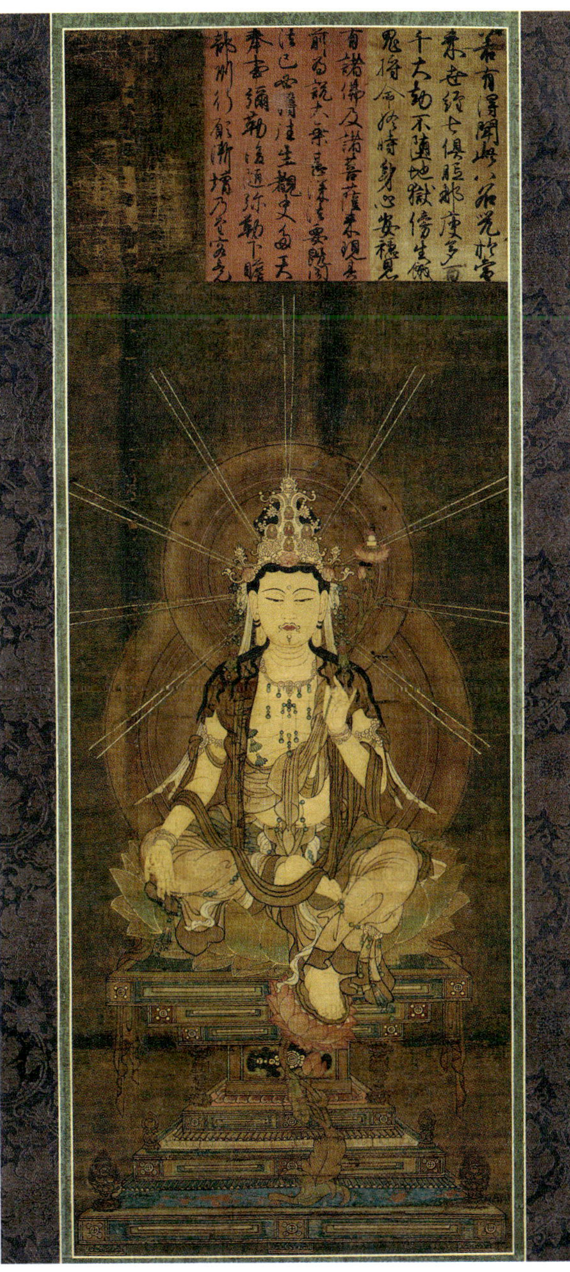

Fig. 45. Miroku Bodhisattva, 14th cent. This image of Miroku, in a comfortable sitting pose with one leg pendant, displays the standard attributes of a Bodhisattva: elegant clothing, jeweled necklace and bracelets, cascading hair, and a regal crown (adorned with five Buddhas). He also bears some of the physical marks of a Buddha: dot between the eyebrows, long earlobes, three neck creases, rays of radiant light, and a halo. Seated on a lotus pedestal atop a Sumeru platform, he holds in his left hand a long-stemmed lotus flower with a small five-element stupa resting on the blossom, symbolizing Śākyamuni's death and his own succession as the next Buddha in this world.

his mausoleum on Mt. Kōya awaiting Miroku's appearance. Such an example on rare occasion inspired later Buddhists to sit in continuous meditation until they starved to death, resulting in the mummification of their body and its enshrinement as an icon for the reverence and inspiration of others. The cult of Miroku never dominated Japan, however, and was largely eclipsed by the Pure Land movement with its aspiration for birth in Amida's Pure Land after death.

JIZŌ BODHISATTVA

Jizō (Skt. Kṣitigarbha) is another Bodhisattva who gained widespread recognition and popular appeal. His name literally means earth storehouse. There is some speculation that Jizō evolved from an ancient Indian earth deity who was integrated into the Buddhist pantheon. It is noteworthy that another figure in Japanese Buddhism is a conceptual counterpoint to Jizō—the Bodhisattva Kokūzō, meaning empty space or sky storehouse. Kokūzō is closely linked to the Buddhist virtue of wisdom whereas Jizō is associated with compassion. Hence, the two Bodhisattvas represent a dyadic pairing of sky and earth and of wisdom and compassion. However, the two seldom appear together, and of the two Jizō has emerged as the more widely recognized and revered Bodhisattva. The reason for his popularity derives from traditions inherited from the Asian continent, but also from ideas and associations that emerged in Japan.

The Mahayana sutras containing Jizō's story, principally the *Sutra of the Past Vows of Earth Storehouse Bodhisattva,* depict him as a Bodhisattva devoted to rescuing sentient beings from any of the six types of rebirth during the period after Śākyamuni Buddha's death and before Miroku's appearance. According to the text, Jizō declared in a series of Bodhisattva vows that, among other things, he will duplicate himself multiple times in order to lead others to enlightenment, that he will descend into the hells to retrieve those who have fallen there, and that he will complete his own enlightenment only after all unfortunate beings have been liberated. Jizō is seen as especially dedicated to those who are suffering in the hells. According to Buddhist cosmology, the hells are subterranean realms of torment where wicked beings fall after death in karmic recompense for their evil deeds. The fallen, however, are not doomed to stay there eternally but can be reborn out of the hells if they are brought into the Buddhist path and expiate their past karma. Jizō has committed himself to this task. There seems to be a connection between his name, Earth Storehouse, and the fact that he willingly descends deep into the earth to liberate sentient beings from the hells. Among those that Jizō explicitly rescues are women, who, based on ancient biases in Buddhism, were often stereotyped as ill equipped to attain enlightenment and therefore vulnerable to falling into the hells. In fact, a number of scriptures indicate several connections between Jizō and women, including previous incarnations as a woman and concrete efforts made in behalf of women. These texts encourage believers to take refuge in Jizō through a variety of devotional practices, such as singing his praises, presenting offerings, reciting his sutra, and making painted or sculpted images of him.[2]

One distinctive aspect of Jizō is his appearance in icons. Instead of assuming the typical lay guise of a Bodhisattva, he usually appears as a monk with a shaved head and clerical robes (fig. 46). Unless identified otherwise, he might be mistaken for a Buddha, though he is most often presented without the cranial protuberance characteristic of a Buddha. Jizō's example shows that there are exceptions to the standard iconography of Bodhisattvas as laypeople and that the Mahayana virtue of compassion can be expressed by monks as well. Two objects that frequently appear as Jizō's possessions are a walking staff and a magical wish-granting jewel. The monk's staff suggests that Jizō will journey anywhere to rescue sentient beings, and the jewel signifies his miraculous ability to come to the aid of those in dire straits.

Popular beliefs about Jizō can be found in Japan's tale literature. One representative story from the *Record of Miracles of the Bodhisattva Jizō* is about a Shinto shrine priest named Koretaka, who was a devotee of Jizō:

Koretaka was suddenly taken ill in bed. Seventeen days later he was seized by a sudden convulsion and passed away. While crossing a desolate wasteland alone on his journey to the Land After Death, he lost his way and cried out tearfully as he looked here and there. He then saw six handsome boys slowly approaching him in a line. One held a staff; another carried an incense burner; another clasped a rosary in his hands as he pressed his palms together in prayer; and another had a *maṇi* ball [or wish-granting jewel]. They were all slightly different from each other—for example, one bore a jeweled banner, while another gripped a branch of a *tāla* tree.

As they came closer to Koretaka, they said to him, "Do you know that we are the Six Jizō whom you worshipped while still alive? Just as all sentient beings in the Six Realms [of reincarnation] have different roots and potentials, so also their behavior and their sufferings vary. In our unsparing efforts to save them, we manifest ourselves in a hundred thousand forms according to the hundred thousand suffering sentient beings. Each of our manifested forms benefits an individual sentient being according to his suffering. Since you have such deep faith in us, even though you are from a Shinto family, we have come here to help you. Go back home, make six statues of Jizō, and offer suitable services to them. Your residence is just south of here." As they spoke, the six Jizō pointed to the south.

Koretaka thereupon came back to life and learned that three days had already passed. When he told his story to the members of his family, they were all moved to tears. Koretaka soon had a temple built and statues made just like each of the Six Jizō he had seen on the way to the Land After Death; he then placed them in the temple as the principal images.[3]

The story reveals the standard lore on Jizō in premodern Japan and the way that reverence for his image fits into the religious life and practice of ordinary believers.

Jizō's identity developed well beyond his portrayal as a liberator from the hells. In certain settings he is also characterized as a

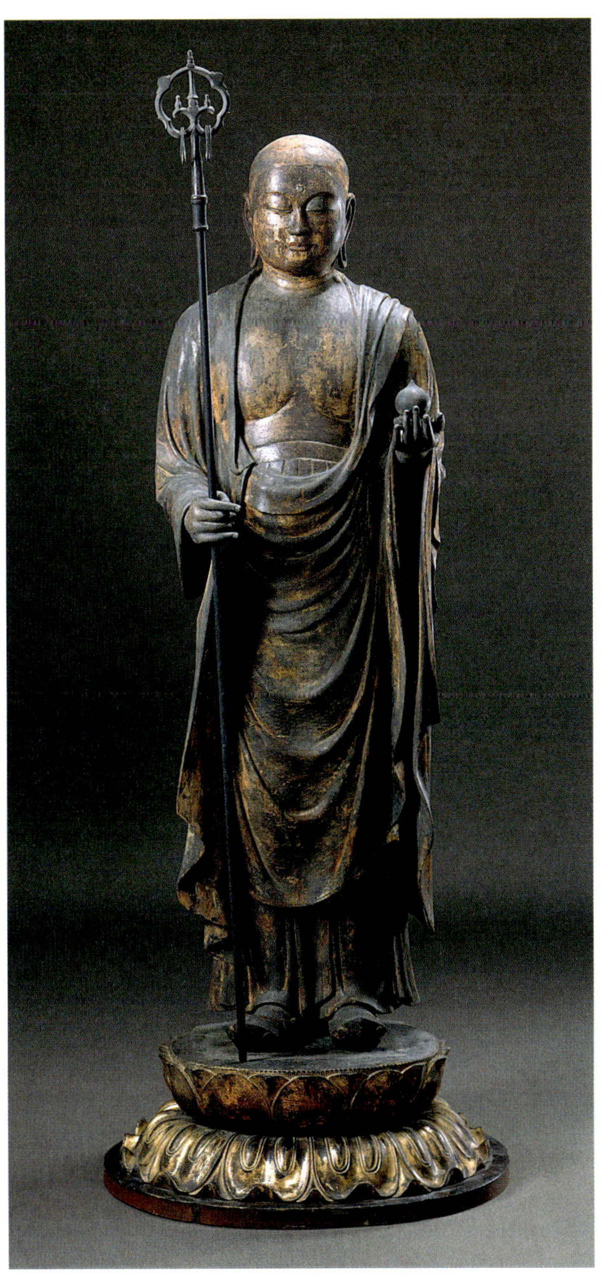

Fig. 46. Jizō Bodhisattva, 12th–13th cent. Jizō, unlike most Bodhisattvas, typically appears not as a layperson but as a monk. In addition to the tonsured head, clerical robes, and lack of jewelry or ornamentation, he bears some of the physical marks of a Buddha—the dot between the eyebrows, elongated earlobes, and neck creases. The walking staff in his right hand and the wish-granting jewel in his left are two common markers of a Jizō figure. The head of the monk's staff has six very thin rings attached, symbolizing the six realms of rebirth (including the hells) where Jizō labors tirelessly to save sentient beings and deliver them to enlightenment.

deliverer into Miroku's heaven or into Amida's Pure Land. In addition, he is closely associated with the *Lotus Sutra,* either encouraging people to practice it or watching over those who do. In Japan Jizō is also recognized as a protector of travelers. To this day small stone images of Jizō are found along roads throughout the country. This role may represent an extension of his earlier identity as a savior of the vulnerable, since travelers are at the mercy of others. From early modern times he has also been identified in Japan as the guardian of children. Images of Jizō actually bear childlike features—an innocent face and a bald head resembling an infant's—and are frequently

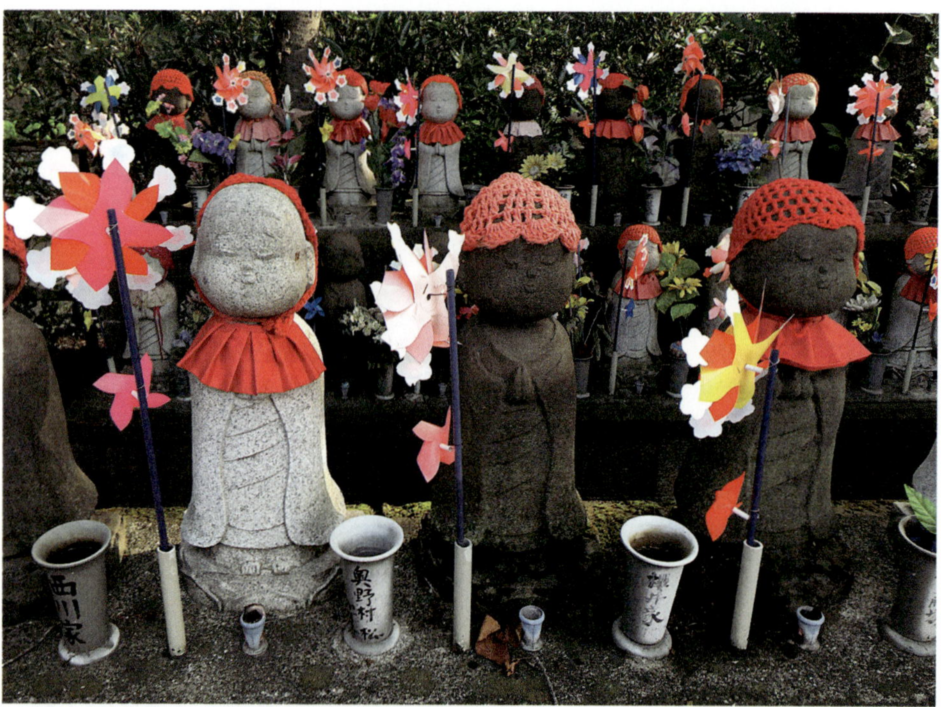

Fig. 47. Child-saving Jizō Bodhisattvas. Zōjōji Temple, Tokyo. During the last half century Jizō has been integrated into Buddhist rites held for deceased, stillborn, miscarried, and aborted infants. Parents dedicate small images of Jizō such as these to their lost child. The images are dressed in hand-knitted or hand-sewn caps and bibs as worn by small children, and are equipped with a pinwheel as a substitute for a walking staff. In this role Jizō is both a protector and a surrogate who takes on the child's sufferings and burdens.

dressed in a child's cap and bib, as if he were their surrogate. Since the mid-twentieth century Jizō has been integrated into so-called *mizuko kūyō* ceremonies—Buddhist rites for deceased, stillborn, miscarried, or aborted infants—and revered as their guide to enlightenment in future rebirths. Temples performing these rites allow (or sometimes insist) people to set up an image of Jizō as the personal protector of their deceased child (fig. 47). Such icons represent only the latest expression of Jizō's compassionate character aimed at leading the lowest and the weakest to enlightenment. The diversification of Jizō's identity over the centuries is testimony to the capacity of Buddhist figures to evolve far beyond their original sacred stories in canonical texts.[4]

MONJU BODHISATTVA AND FUGEN BODHISATTVA

Monju (Skt. Mañjuśrī) and Fugen (Skt. Samantabhadra), two widely recognized Bodhisattvas in Japanese Buddhism, are frequently presented together as the flanking Bodhisattvas of Śākyamuni Buddha, notably in Zen monasteries but also in other temples as well. Monju is considered the Bodhisattva of wisdom and is presented as an interlocutor of Śākyamuni in many Buddhist sutras, including the *Vimalakīrti Sutra*, in which he famously debates the wise layman Vimalakīrti on the nonduality of things.[5] Fugen, identified as the Bodhisattva of practice, is renowned for a series of ten vows, recounted in the *Flower Garland Sutra*, made in praise of the Buddha and dedicated to pious and compassionate activity.[6] As attendants of Śākyamuni, the two symbolize his wisdom and compassion respectively. In addition, Monju and Fugen are part of Dainichi Buddha's entourage in the central lotus panel of the womb-world mandala of Shingon Buddhism (fig. 39), though they share pride of place with several other Buddhas and Bodhisattvas. Also, in a famous story from the *Flower Garland Sutra* the two Bodhisattvas are included in a sequence of fifty-three wise teachers from whom the boy pilgrim

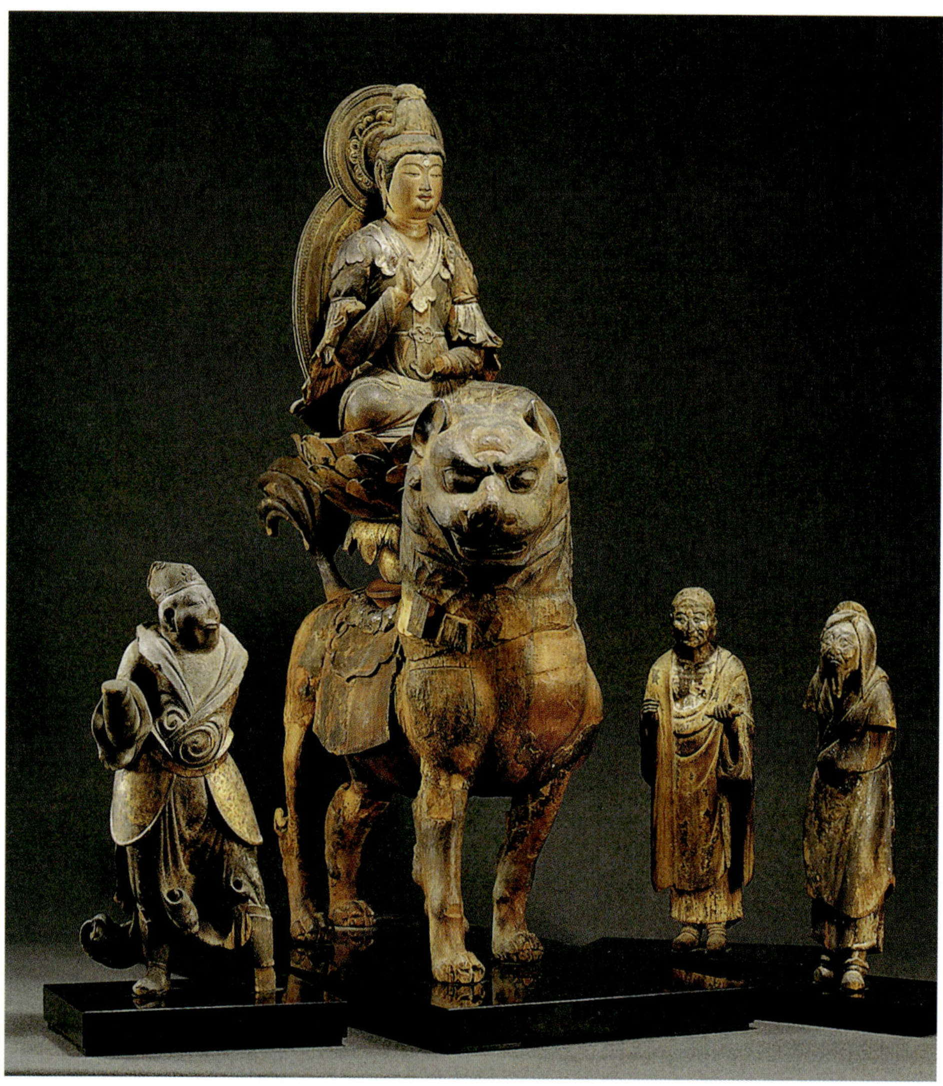

Fig. 48. **Monju Bodhisattva riding a lion, ca. 12th cent. Jionji Temple, Yamagata.** In this set of figures Monju wears the characteristic dress and hairstyle of a Bodhisattva, and his lotus base is mounted on the back of a lion. King Udayana (*left*) serves as a lead to the lion while the priest Buddhapāli (*near right*) and the wise old man Saishō (*far right*) attend. The boy Zenzai, who sought Monju's advice in his quest for enlightenment, is ordinarily included with these attendants, but he has been lost from this set.

Zenzai (Skt. Sudhana) seeks instruction in his pursuit of enlightenment, beginning with Monju and ending with Fugen.[7] This fifty-three-stage spiritual journey was later imitated in Japan's popular culture with the fifty-three-station Tōkaidō highway between premodern Tokyo and Kyoto.

The two Bodhisattvas also developed their own separate iconographic identity and cultic following. Monju is frequently presented in standard Bodhisattva guise, sitting in a cross-legged position on a lotus-flower dais. Many images, however, have his lotus base balanced on the back of a lion, an iconographic feature distinctive to Monju. The lion, a symbol of regal authority, is perhaps associated with the so-called lion's roar of the Buddha, whereby the Dharma is proclaimed to the world. The most common objects shown in Monju's hands are a sword, emblematic of wisdom's ability to cut through ignorance, and a sutra scroll, in which the wisdom of the Dharma is preserved. His image is sometimes enshrined with other figures as attendants (fig. 48)—typically, the boy pilgrim Zenzai, King Udayana of India, the Buddhist scripture master Buddhapāli (J. Butsudahari), and a wise old man named Saishō (sometimes identified as the layman Vimalakīrti instead). All have associations with Monju based on stories and vignettes in various texts.[8]

The veneration of Monju had an early base at the Japanese Tendai monastic center on Mt. Hiei outside Kyoto. It was influenced by practices from Mt. Wutai in China, the cultic center dedicated to Monju where the great Japanese Tendai master Ennin (794–864) traveled. Also, iconic representations of Monju are enshrined in the meditation hall of Zen monasteries to personify the wisdom actualized in Zen meditation. Additionally, Monju assumes a special place in the ordination ceremonies of the so-called Bodhisattva vows found in various schools of Buddhism. Traditionally, three masters are required to conduct ordinations. But in the case of the Bodhisattva vows it became customary to symbolically assign these roles to images of Śākyamuni, Miroku, and Monju. In short, Monju is integrated into diverse and distinctly different religious settings throughout Japanese Buddhism.

Images of Fugen, like Monju, have the appearance of a traditional Bodhisattva seated on a lotus throne, but in his case the figure is depicted riding a white elephant, an auspicious creature that is counted among the seven precious possessions of the archetypal wheel-turning king. Typically Fugen is shown with "joined palms" (*gasshō*), a hand gesture of gratitude and reverence that looks like a sign of prayer, perhaps associated with his ten vows to praise the Buddha and perform devotional acts. As a Bodhisattva he is also popular among adherents of the *Lotus Sutra,* for according to its last chapter Fugen has declared that he will protect practitioners of the sutra. Iconographically, Fugen is sometimes paired with ten female figures who are identified in the *Lotus* as demons who turned into defenders of the sutra and protectors of its adherents. Though there is no narrative tradition connecting Fugen to these women, the proximity of their stories in different chapters of the sutra, as well as a heightened focus on the religious piety of women in twelfth-century Japan, may have resulted in this iconographic ensemble (fig. 49). Additionally, in Shingon Buddhism Fugen is sometimes conflated with Kongōsatta, a Bodhisattva symbolizing unshakable aspiration for enlightenment, and he is also identified as a bestower of long life.[9] Hence, beyond his connection to Monju, Fugen has several separate and distinct associations of his own.

From the examples of Monju and Fugen, it is possible to surmise that the sacred story of a particular Buddha, Bodhisattva, or Buddhist divinity does not always derive from a single text but may emerge from a diversity of vignettes and textual references, and even from nontextual sources. These disparate pieces blend together to form a general sacred identity, one that sometimes results in iconic representations that do not conform completely to any one text. Nonetheless, the broad Buddhist themes of religious quest, enlightenment, and compassion are usually expressed in these religious images and narratives, and people who encounter them enshrined in temples comprehend them within that framework. This is certainly true of the Bodhisattvas Monju and Fugen.

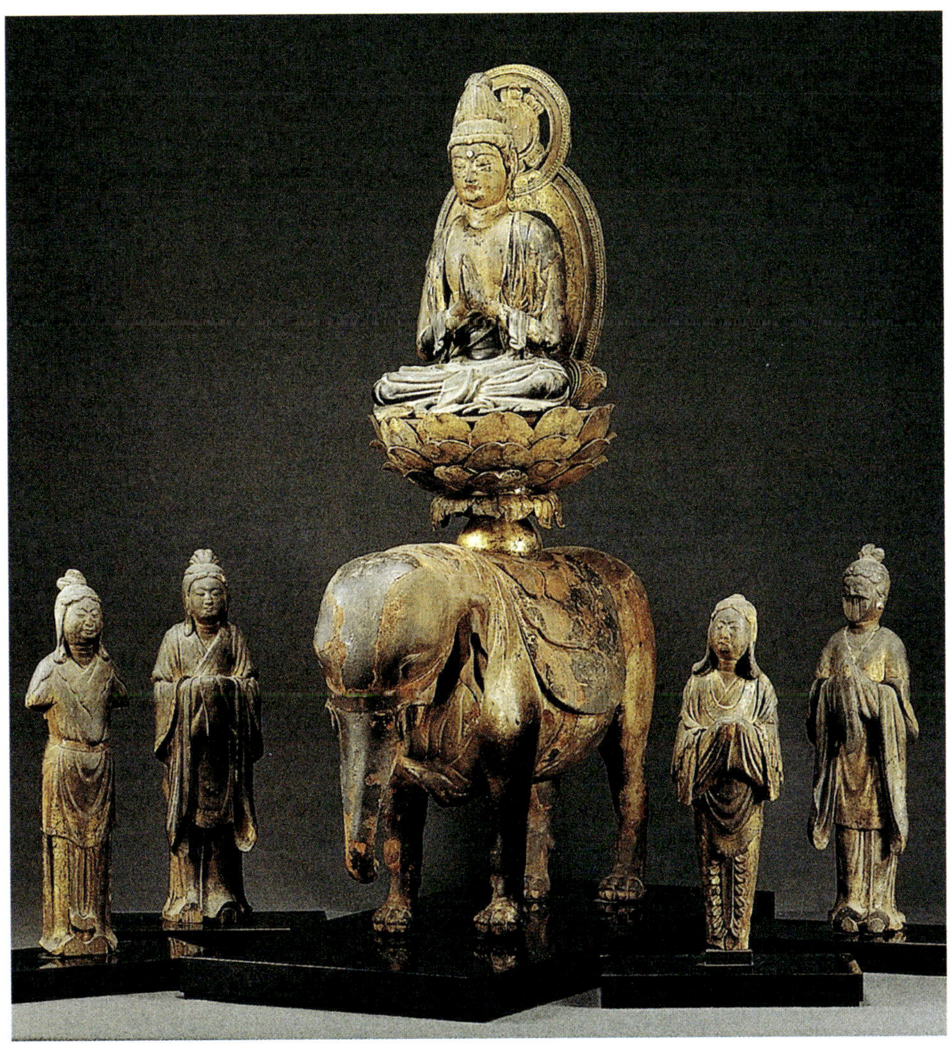

Fig. 49. **Fugen Bodhisattva riding an elephant, ca. 12th cent. Jionji Temple, Yamagata.** In this companion set, Fugen's lotus base is carried on the back of an elephant. In contrast to Monju's hand gestures, his joined palms convey reverence and perhaps allude to his ten vows declaring his devotion to the Buddha and commitment to pious practice. He is attended by four of the ten female demons identified in the *Lotus Sutra* as defenders of those who revere the sutra; the other six are missing from the set.

KANNON BODHISATTVA

Of all the revered figures in Buddhism, Kannon—or, more fully, Kanzeon (Skt. Avalokiteśvara) or sometimes Kanjizai—emerged very early as the most prominent and widely venerated Bodhisattva in East Asia. He (or sometimes she) is commonly identified as the Bodhisattva of compassion (fig. 50). This virtue is attributed to many other Buddhist figures as well, but in Kannon's case compassion is considered such a dominant and overriding characteristic that the Bodhisattva is treated as a virtual personification of compassion. The name Kanzeon literally means the one who "sees the sounds of the world," signifying that the Bodhisattva is fully attuned to those living beings in the world calling for help, and constantly comes to their aid. He thus makes compassion the very content of his quest for enlightenment, thereby collapsing the three dimensions of Buddhahood into this single virtue. Over the centuries, people have looked to Kannon for so many different needs that it is only natural that his identity and iconographic characteristics have diversified considerably.

The textual foundations of Kannon's identity are several and varied. Perhaps the most famous account is found in the twenty-fifth chapter of the *Lotus Sutra,* which asserts that Kannon will come to the aid of people in dire circumstances, such as fires, floods, storms at sea, precipitous heights, imprisonment, and attacks by foes, bandits, beasts, and demons. He will also assist people in overcoming the primary obstacles to enlightenment: attachment, anger, and ignorance. And he will answer the prayers of women longing for the birth of a child. The sutra enumerates some thirty-three different miraculous guises that Kannon will assume in order to assist humans: as a Buddha, an enlightened disciple, a deity, a king, a priest, a nun, a householder, a wife, a boy, a girl, a dragon, and a variety of other creatures. This chapter is interpreted by *Lotus Sutra* adherents as an assurance of Kannon's protection, but it has also assumed a life of its own and circulated separately under the title *Kannon Sutra,* thereby supporting an independent Kannon cult.[10]

A second textual source on Kannon is the Pure Land sutras. They depict him, along with the Bodhisattva Seishi (Skt. Mahāsthāmaprāpta),

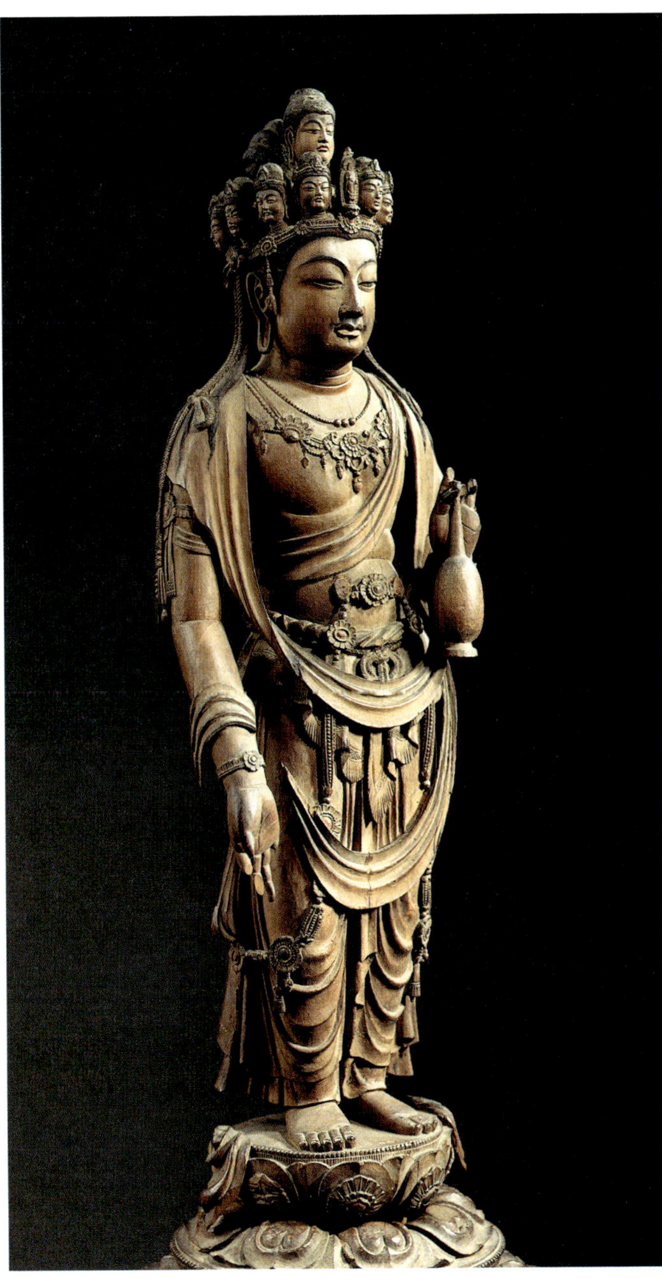

Fig. 50. **Eleven-headed Kannon Bodhisattva, 8th–9th cent.** In this image Kannon appears in the classical guise of a Bodhisattva wearing an elegant garment, jewelry, long hair, and a crown. His right hand displays the mudra of offering aid, and his left holds a water vessel, both common attributes of the Bodhisattva. The eleven heads on his crown symbolize the various manifestations the Bodhisattva takes to aid sentient beings, while among them, at the front center of the crown, is a tiny standing image of Amida Buddha, a sign of Kannon's close tie to Amida.

who represents wisdom, as the twin attendants of Amida Buddha who act as his agents to deliver sentient beings into his Pure Land, where they will attain enlightenment. Kannon is specifically identified as the figure offering a lotus-flower pedestal to dying believers when Amida's host appears at their deathbed (fig. 43). Kannon's close link to Pure Land Buddhism is reflected in the fact that the small Buddha displayed in the headdress of most Kannon images is said to be Amida, who serves as a role model of compassion and for whom Kannon serves as an extension of his compassion.[11]

A third textual source on Kannon is a host of short sutras typically associated with esoteric Buddhism, particularly Shingon and Tendai, which were composed several centuries after the *Lotus* and the Pure Land sutras. These texts treat Kannon as an independent object of devotion apart from Amida and the *Lotus* tradition, and each text focuses on a particular iconic representation of Kannon or a specific ritual chant that devotees should adopt. These sutras presuppose the importance of icons in religious life and reflect the diversity of Kannon images that emerged. They inspired some of the principal icons found in the Kannon cult in Japan.[12] What is noteworthy about all these sources is that none present a well-developed story of Kannon's quest for Buddhahood. Instead, they simply allow Śākyamuni's life story, and the Bodhisattva ideal in general, to function as a subliminal archetype, and concentrate instead on Kannon's miraculous efforts to aid living beings.

Popular images of Kannon in Japan span a wide variety. The most basic one, known as Saintly or True (Shō) Kannon, appears in the conventional form of a Bodhisattva replete with long hair, elegant garment, crown or headdress, and jewelry (fig. 23). In many cases a small figure of Amida Buddha is situated in the crown. Common objects held in Kannon's hands include a lotus flower, a water vessel, and a wish-granting jewel, symbols of purity, sustenance, and beneficence, respectively. Or the hands might display one or another gesture of compassion, such as the mudra offering aid or allaying fear or conveying ease and comfort. Images of Kannon may be posed in either a standing or a sitting position and can range in size from miniature to colossal. Kannon is also widely portrayed with a feminine or androgynous appearance, a characteristic sometimes found in other Bodhisattvas as well. In Kannon's case the reason for this depiction may be the passages in the *Lotus Sutra* indicating that the Bodhisattva will take on various guises, including female ones, in order to aid sentient beings. Or it may be the result of stereotyping compassion as a feminine quality. In China many images of Kannon are overtly female, but in Japan they usually seem more androgynous, feminine at first glance but sometimes sporting a faint moustache or appearing with the chest exposed. This androgynous identity is typical of many styles and poses of Kannon images.[13]

Beyond more conventional portrayals, Kannon is also depicted in a variety of unusual configurations, typically with multiple heads or arms. Some scholars speculate that these representations arose partly from ancient Indian iconographic influences.[14] Examples of this genre that became prevalent in Japan are the eleven-headed and the thousand-armed Kannon. In fact, these two features are often combined in the same figure. The eleven heads, along with the small image of Amida Buddha, are arranged in various groupings on Kannon's headdress—some in front, others on the sides, and perhaps one in back (fig. 50). The expression on their faces ranges from kind to fierce, but they are all considered miraculous apparitions of Kannon that can aid sentient beings. Images of Kannon bearing a thousand arms (frequently abbreviated to forty-two) are even more striking. The arms are distributed evenly on the left and right, creating a fanlike array on each side of the body (fig. 51). Certain hands hold symbolic objects: water vessel, lotus flower, wish-granting jewel, Dharma wheel, apparitional Buddha, sutra, rosary, mirror, ritual implements, bow, arrow, skull, rope, willow branch, grapes, sun and moon disks, and so forth. All are considered instruments to bring sentient beings closer to enlightenment, either gently or by force. In some images each hand has an eye in the palm, in accordance with sutra descriptions indicating that the hands also "see the cries of the world."[15] The profusion of hands in the thousand-armed Kannon conveys in hyperbolic form the same message of engagement with the world found in the expressive hands of all Buddha icons.

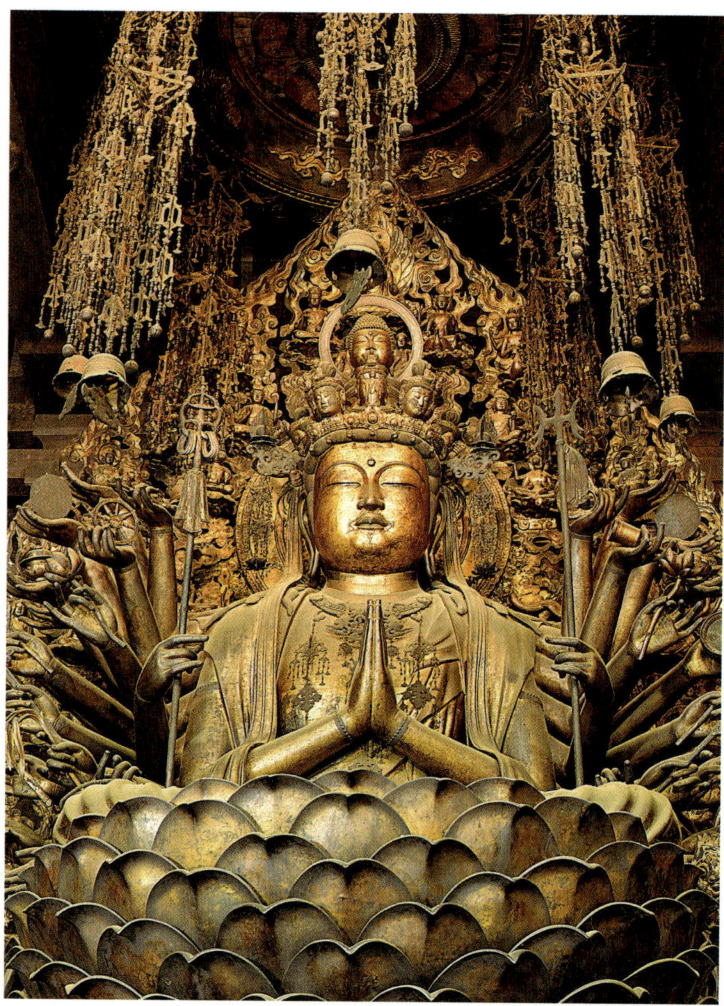

Fig. 51. **Eleven-headed thousand-armed Kannon Bodhisattva, 12th cent. Sanjūsangendō Temple, Kyoto.** This eleven-foot image of Kannon is the central icon of the famous Sanjūsangendō Temple in Kyoto. The Bodhisattva is seated on a multilayered lotus pedestal with an ornate canopy overhead, and his crown is adorned with eleven heads representing his diverse manifestations in aid of sentient beings. Although the figure is described as thousand-armed, fewer actual arms are displayed. His hands in front form the mudra of devotion, whereas others hold an array of objects that can summon beings to enlightenment, including a Dharma wheel, lotus flower, sun and moon disks, walking staff, trident, bell, water vessel, mirror, rosary, hatchet, willow branch, skull, fly whisk, and so forth.

Kannon is depicted in numerous other poses that have become formulaic in Buddhist iconography. A common one is the Wish-Granting Dharma-Wheel (Nyoirin) Kannon, usually with six arms and sitting in an informal, pensive pose (fig. 28). Another is the Inescapable Snare (Fukūkenjaku) Kannon who appears with multiple arms and holds a rope in one hand to grab desperate sentient beings. Yet another is the Horse Head (Batō) Kannon, displaying multiple arms and three faces, all with ferocious expressions, and typically crowned with a horse head—a guise meant to intimidate foes of enlightenment. Still another is the Pure (Skt. Cundī; J. Juntei) Kannon, a multi-armed female figure with a beneficent face who is thought to be the mother of past Buddhas. These figures, along with the previously mentioned ones, are often included in the so-called Six Kannon, a standard iconographic set recognized in Japan. Beyond them, other identities are also attributed to the Bodhisattva—for instance, the White-robed (Byakue) Kannon (fig. 52), the Willow Branch (Yōryū) Kannon, and the Fish Basket (Gyoran) Kannon, all of whom bear distinctly feminine characteristics and are listed in a larger iconographic classification of thirty-three Kannon, emulating the *Lotus Sutra*'s list but diverging from it in actual content.[16] In addition, Kannon is sometimes shown holding an infant, a composition that was occasionally conflated with icons of the Madonna and child after Christianity came into Japan in the sixteenth century.[17]

This profusion of images reflects the pervasive influence and diversity of identities that the Bodhisattva has assumed. Kannon's reputation as an all-compassionate and ever-responsive Bodhisattva has resulted in an abundance of miracle stories in Japanese tale literature describing aid to people in one unfortunate situation after another. The Bodhisattva's omnipresence is also conveyed by the famous hall of one thousand and one images of Kannon at the Sanjūsangendō Temple in Kyoto (fig. 53). Ultimately, the popularity of the Bodhisattva inspired a pilgrimage route of thirty-three temples in western Japan (Saikoku Sanjūsankasho) enshrining icons of great renown, many following the styles of the Six Kannon classification.[18]

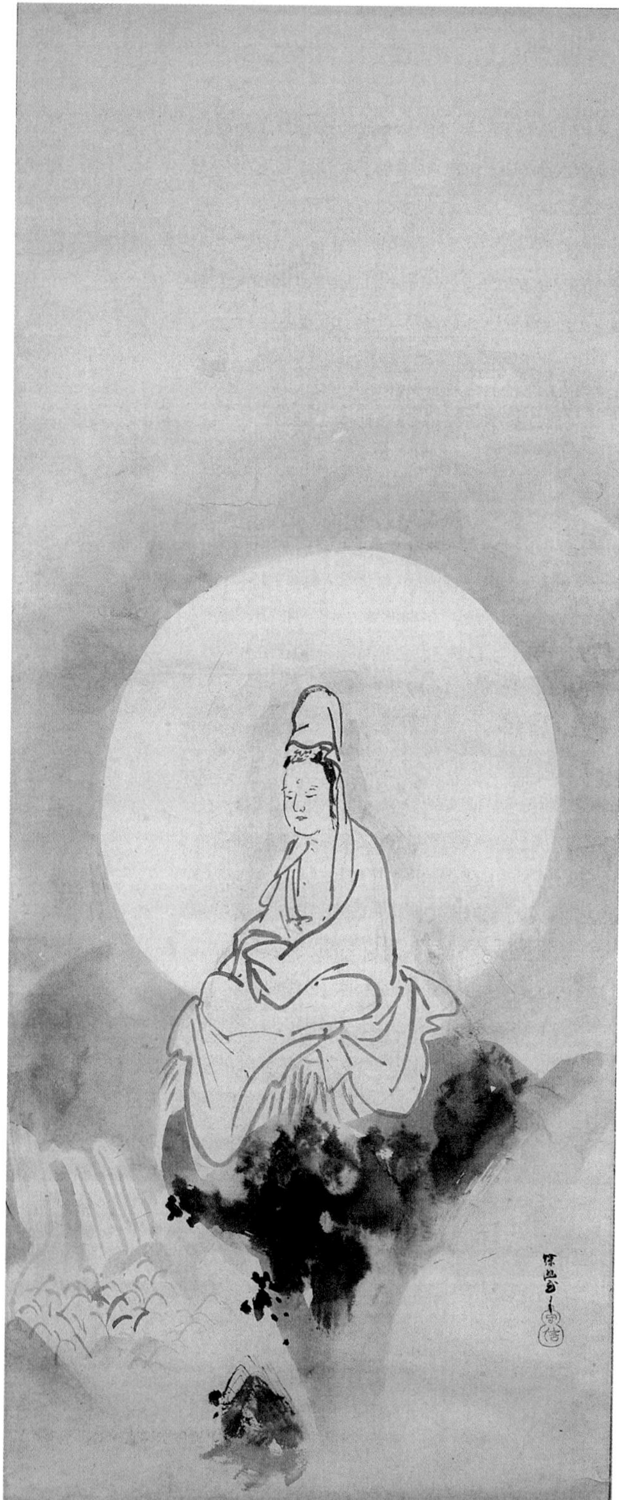

Fig. 52. White-robed Kannon, 17th cent. In a characteristic pose for this genre, Kannon is presented sitting in meditation on a rock promontory overlooking water and silhouetted by the moon. With head covered, the Bodhisattva appears in feminine or at least androgynous guise. She is without jewelry or crown, although an auspicious dot does appear between her eyebrows. The White-robed Kannon, one of thirty-three iconographic identities attributed to the Bodhisattva, is particularly celebrated in Zen Buddhism.

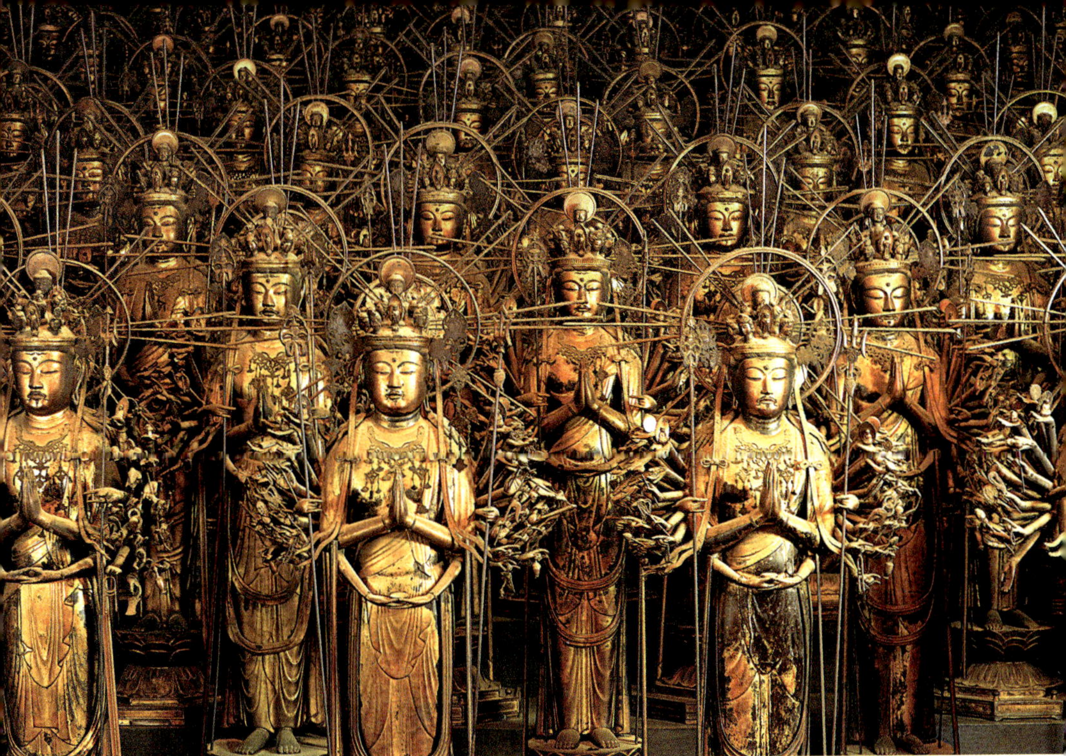

Fig. 53. **Hall of 1001 Kannon Bodhisattvas, 12th–13th cent. Sanjūsangendō Temple, Kyoto.** Sanjūsangendō, or the Hall of Thirty-three Bays, is the popular name for the temple in Kyoto officially known as the Rengeōin, which is dedicated to Kannon. The hall is extremely wide, measuring almost four hundred feet, with thirty-three bays or divisions between pillars. (The number thirty-three may allude to the different manifestations of the Bodhisattva enumerated in the *Lotus Sutra*.) In the middle of this wide space is the central icon of the temple, a large seated image of Kannon (fig. 51), and on both sides are an additional thousand images standing in rows and phalanxes, all of the eleven-headed thousand-armed Bodhisattva. Every image is five and a half feet tall, approximately life-size, and at first sight they all look identical, although there are minute variations. The overwhelming effect of this ocean of Bodhisattvas is to express the vastness of Kannon's compassionate vow to bring all beings to enlightenment.

It is hard to overstate Kannon's prominence and impact in Japan. The Bodhisattva is found in virtually all forms of Buddhism and also in an independent movement of its own. The predominance of compassion in Kannon's identity has inspired innumerable interpretations of the Bodhisattva, channeling devotion to Kannon into otherwise disparate Buddhist discourses and pathways to enlightenment. As a result, Kannon has become a Bodhisattva for virtually all times and places and people. Perhaps more than Śākyamuni Buddha, Kannon epitomizes and embodies for the Japanese the Buddhist ideal of compassion.

CHAPTER 6

OTHER MYTHIC BUDDHIST FIGURES

The cast of characters found in Japanese Buddhism extends well beyond Buddhas and Bodhisattvas. It also includes a variety of figures that are largely secondary to Buddhas and Bodhisattvas but stand out in particular religious settings or have developed their own religious cult. These figures exert both spiritual and worldly influence, so people are cognizant of them and engage them through various ritual means. What has made this broad and diverse spirit world possible is the open-ended cosmology of Mahayana Buddhism. It recognizes not only multiple Buddhas and Bodhisattvas but also countless spirits and deities, some fully integrated into Buddhism's soteriology of enlightenment and others peripheral to it. Historically, Buddhism accepted many of the common deities that ancient India recognized, and popularized them throughout East Asia. Moreover, it accommodated itself to the local cultures it encountered in other parts of Asia and incorporated their domestic pantheons into its religious path. For the most part these other deities are treated as allies and protectors of Buddhism or as extensions of the Buddhas and Bodhisattvas working to aid sentient beings and to bring them to enlightenment.

MYŌŌ

Myōō are Buddhist divinities parallel in some ways to Buddhas and Bodhisattvas but not as widely recognized. They are primarily seen in esoteric Buddhism, chiefly Shingon and Tendai. The word Myōō, sometimes translated as "wisdom king," literally means king (*ō*) of knowledge or light (*myō*), but the syllable *myō* may actually be an abbreviation for *myōju,* denoting an incantation in the form of a mantra or dharani that banishes the darkness of ignorance and ushers in enlightenment. Incantations are one of the principal religious practices of esoteric Buddhism. Myōō are mostly depicted as frightening, militant figures that can conquer opponents of enlightenment and destroy obstacles to it. Shingon Buddhism considers Myōō agents or emanations of the Buddhas who use forceful means to implement their teachings. One sector of the womb-world mandala in Shingon is actually dedicated to the five great Myōō, thus reflecting their importance in its array of spiritual figures. Most Myōō are intimidating in appearance—showing ferocious expressions, baring fangs, brandishing weapons, and emitting flames from their body. And many have multiple heads and arms. In short, Myōō may be conceptually analogous to Bodhisattvas in that both use their power and insight to lead beings to enlightenment, but most Bodhisattvas do so gently, whereas Myōō use aggressive or coercive means.[1] If Bodhisattvas take a palliative approach to alleviating the sufferings of sentient beings, Myōō take a surgical approach, excising impediments by force.

Perhaps the best known and most widely revered figure in this group is Fudō, whose name means immovable (fig. 54). He is the classic example of a Myōō. Commonly presented in a standing or sitting position, Fudō exudes belligerence and foreboding: frightful face, bared fangs, wrinkled brow, and bulging eyes (with the left sometimes ominously half closed, looking earthward). In his left hand he holds a rope, used to restrain ignorance and attachments, and in his right he holds the "beneficial sword" of wisdom used to slay them. His body emits a nimbus of fire, and a twisted pigtail hangs down onto his left shoulder, supposedly signifying his compassionate reach downward. The popular perception of Fudō as a potent spiritual ally is reflected in a story from the thirteenth-century collection of tales *Sand and Pebbles:*

After many years of discipline at a mountain temple in Shinano province, an old monk began having hallucinations and was no longer his usual self. So his many disciples recited the Spell [or Incantation] of Compassionate Help in order that he might meet death in the proper frame of mind. Among those present was a man from whose head issued black smoke. When the others later questioned him, the man related that he had seen many obstacles on the old monk's path; but, as he persisted in the spell, he was aware of Fudō's sword sweeping them away. The old monk calmly prepared for death, and, in appreciation of

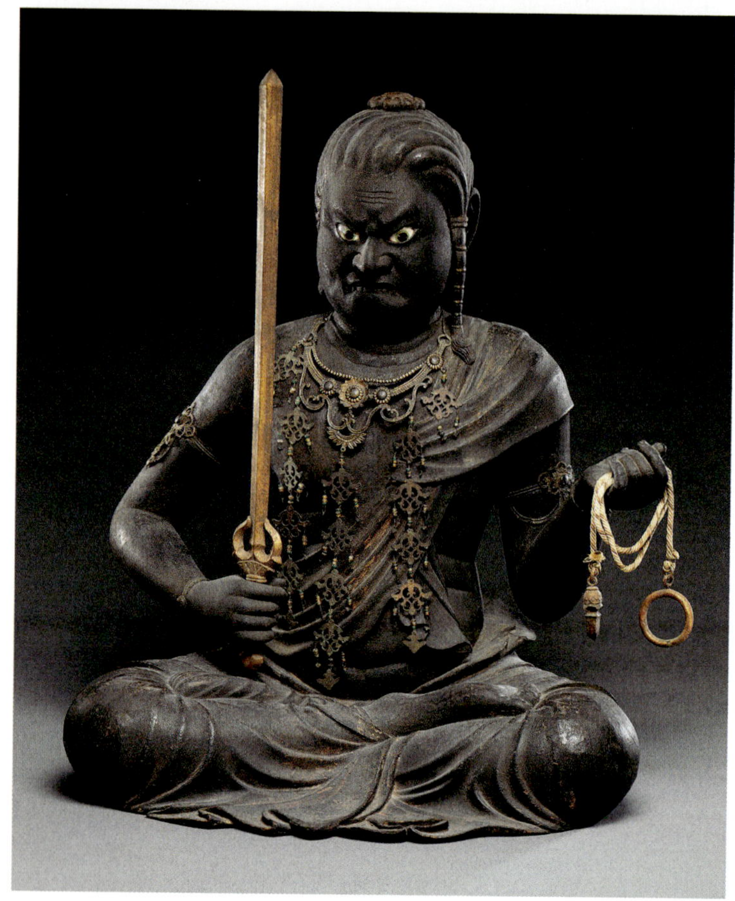

Fig. 54. Fudō Myōō, 13th cent. The best known of the Myōō, or kings of enlightenment, Fudō exudes a formidable and ominous air. His sword of wisdom severs ignorance, and his restraining rope harnesses obstacles to enlightenment. This image bears some of the characteristic marks of other Buddhist figures, combining the three neck creases of a Buddha with the jeweled adornments of a Bodhisattva. The small lotus flower on the crown of his head, representing the Dharma, is also a common feature of Fudō images.

> the man's help, bequeathed to him, rather than to his close disciples, a relic of the Buddha which was the principal object of worship at the temple. He then passed on peacefully.
>
> The following day a lay priest who had been the monk's benefactor rode up to the temple and related a dream of the previous night. He had seen the hindrances to the holy man's enlightenment swept away by Fudō Myōō, and observed that he came to a happy end.
>
> A sutra says that we should pray to Fudō because of the severity of the Three Hindrances to enlightenment. Jizō [Bodhisattva] is the ultimate of Mahāvairocana's [i.e., Dainichi's] compassion; Fudō, of his wisdom.[2]

The assumption of this story is that deeply rooted obstacles to religious advancement require radical solutions. Fudō is seen as the perfect, fearsome agent to clear them away.

In Shingon Buddhism Fudō is identified as the most important of the five great Myōō, who are each associated with a Buddha in the central panel of Shingon's two sacred mandalas (figs. 39 and 40). Fudō is considered an extension of the highest Buddha, Dainichi, exercising stern compassion in his behalf to exterminate ignorance and attachments. Fudō has also been the object of veneration in an independent cult apart from the five Myōō, attracting clerical and lay Buddhists alike to his awesome powers, which, they pray, may be deployed for both spiritual and worldly benefit.[3]

Another prominent Myōō is Aizen, who, like Fudō, has a terrifying and ferocious appearance. If Fudō's identity is characterized by anger and fury, Aizen's is associated with passions and physical attachments, especially sexual. In appearance, Aizen is usually depicted with six arms sitting in a cross-legged position atop a giant lotus flower sprouting from a narrow-neck vase (fig. 55). His hair is swept upward like flames and he wears a crown in the shape of a lion's head. His face is frightening and crazed—eyes crossed, mouth half-open showing fangs, and an ominous third eye in the middle of his forehead. In two of his hands are a bow and arrow, and in two more are the twin ritual implements

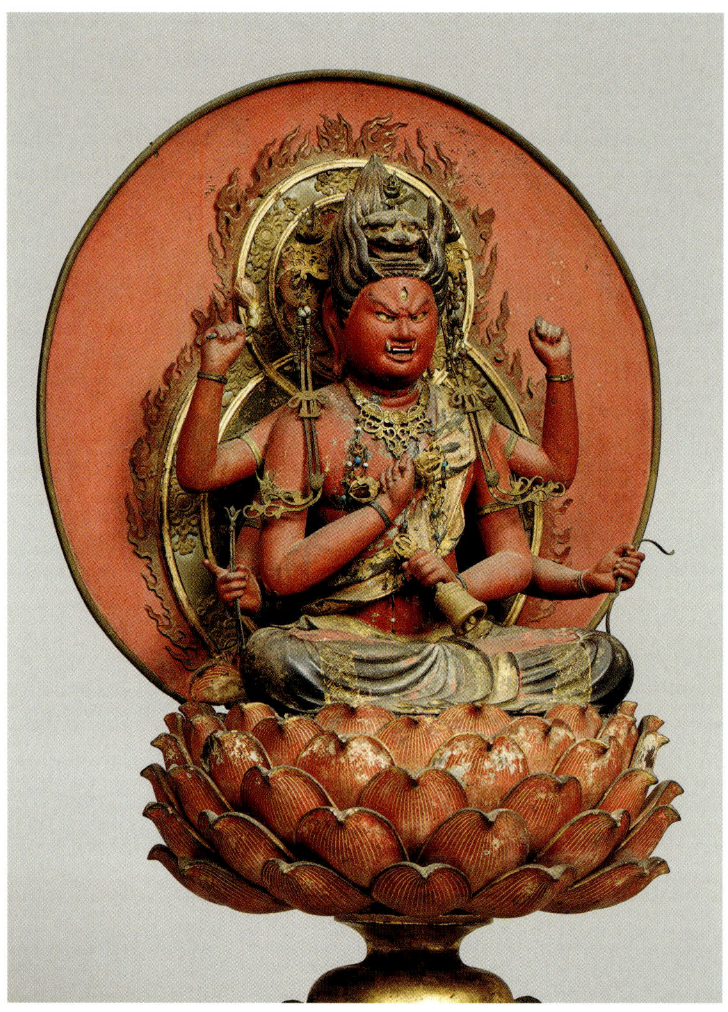

Fig. 55. Aizen Myōō, 13th cent. This six-armed Myōō with a bow and arrow, bell and thunderbolt, and lotus flower and empty fist personifies the transmutation of lustful passions into the aspiration for enlightenment. His name, Aizen, literally means "taint of lust." Like other Myōō, he has a frightening appearance, extending to the flaming halo and nimbus around his body. He also combines the physical marks of a Buddha with the adornments of a Bodhisattva. Characteristically, he sits on a giant lotus pedestal colored bright red.

of a five-pronged vajra thunderbolt and a vajra bell, symbolizing male and female. One remaining hand holds a lotus flower, and the final one holds nothing. He has a flaming halo behind his head and a disk-shaped nimbus around his body, and the entire icon is passionate red in color. Aizen signifies the craze of physical desires and lust, which are ordinarily seen as an obstruction to enlightenment. But instead of trying to destroy them Aizen seeks to redirect and transform them into a force for enlightenment. The Mahayana belief that the perfection of Nirvana is inseparable from the cravings of Samsara makes possible this logic and imagery.[4]

A third noteworthy Myōō is Kujaku, primarily because he is an exception to the rule. Instead of adopting a ferocious guise, he has the gentle and beneficent appearance of a Bodhisattva, albeit one with four arms (fig. 56). The distinguishing feature of Kujaku is that he rides on the back of a large peacock, and in fact the name Kujaku means peacock. In India this deity was originally identified as female, sometimes as the mother of the Buddhas, but in Japan the female identity is obscured, or at least submerged in a more androgynous appearance. Kujaku is depicted with a lustrous complexion sitting cross-legged on a lotus flower atop the peacock. Typically, his four hands hold a lotus flower, a pomegranate, a peacock feather, and a citrus-like "liberating karma fruit" (*guenka*). The peacock's fanned tail feathers form a halo-like circular backdrop to the body of Kujaku, creating a subliminal aura. Though gentle in appearance, Kujaku, like other Myōō, can proactively transform evil into good, based on the Indian belief that peacocks can eat poisonous snakes and digest them without harm. Thus Kujaku is revered for his ability to allay misfortune and bestow blessings.[5]

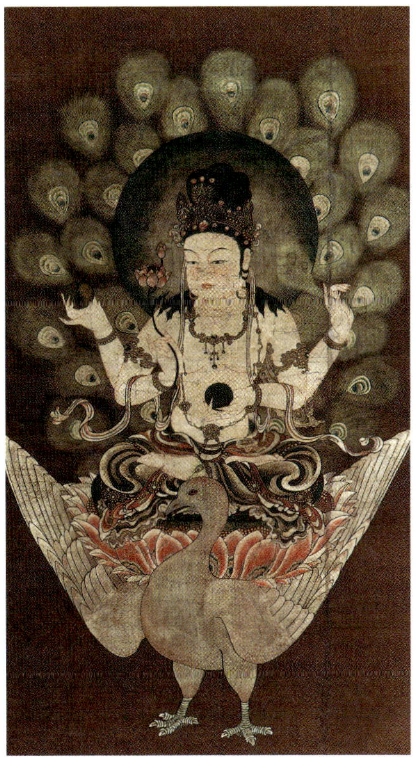

Fig. 56. **Kujaku Myōō, 14th cent.** Although classified as a Myōō, Kujaku has the gentle and comely appearance of a Bodhisattva. Since the name Kujaku means peacock, the most distinctive feature of Kujaku images is the peacock on which his lotus dais rests. His four hands hold a lotus flower, a pomegranate, a citrus-like fruit, and a peacock feather, all tokens for warding off misfortune and sickness. Traditionally, devotees would appeal to Kujaku to cure illness, break a drought, and avoid calamity.

Myōō, unlike most Buddhas and Bodhisattvas, are rarely defined by a well-developed sacred story. At most, they may be associated with simple narratives explaining their appearance or with miracle tales describing how they can come to the rescue of believers in distress and vanquish their adversaries. This is definitely true of Fudō, the most popular of the Myōō. Nonetheless, all Myōō participate in the archetypal story of the Buddha if only vicariously or symbolically. That is, they too operate within the framework of the Buddhist ideas of quest, enlightenment, and compassion to the extent that they exercise compassion, though admittedly through forceful means, to advance people toward enlightenment. Like Bodhisattvas, their reason for existence is shaped by these themes, though manifested in aggressive rather than gentle actions.

GUARDIAN FIGURES

Although Mahayana proclaimed a philosophy that ideally recognizes the entire world as suffused with Nirvana, it did not always look upon the conventional world as benign but instead considered it fraught with dangers. As a result, a variety of protective figures emerged alongside Buddhas and Bodhisattvas. Some of them can be traced back to external or pre-existing deities that were absorbed into Buddhism as it spread. Technically, they are classified as *ten* (a term often attached to their name as a suffix), meaning deity or divinity or heavenly spirit, one of the five or six types of rebirth recognized in Buddhism. Soteriologically, the task assigned to guardian figures is to protect the teachings and the adherents of Buddhism from threats and dangers. Hence, they are frequently depicted in militant or martial guise, similar to Myōō.[6] It is rare, however, for guardians to function as the centerpiece of a temple in Japan. Instead, they tend to play a subservient role to other Buddhist figures.

Perhaps the best known of the guardians are the Shitennō, or Four Heavenly Kings. In ancient Buddhist cosmology Mt. Sumeru, the mythical mountain at the center of the world, was thought to be protected by four kings located in the cardinal directions: Jikokuten (Deity Guarding the Country) in the east, holding a sword;

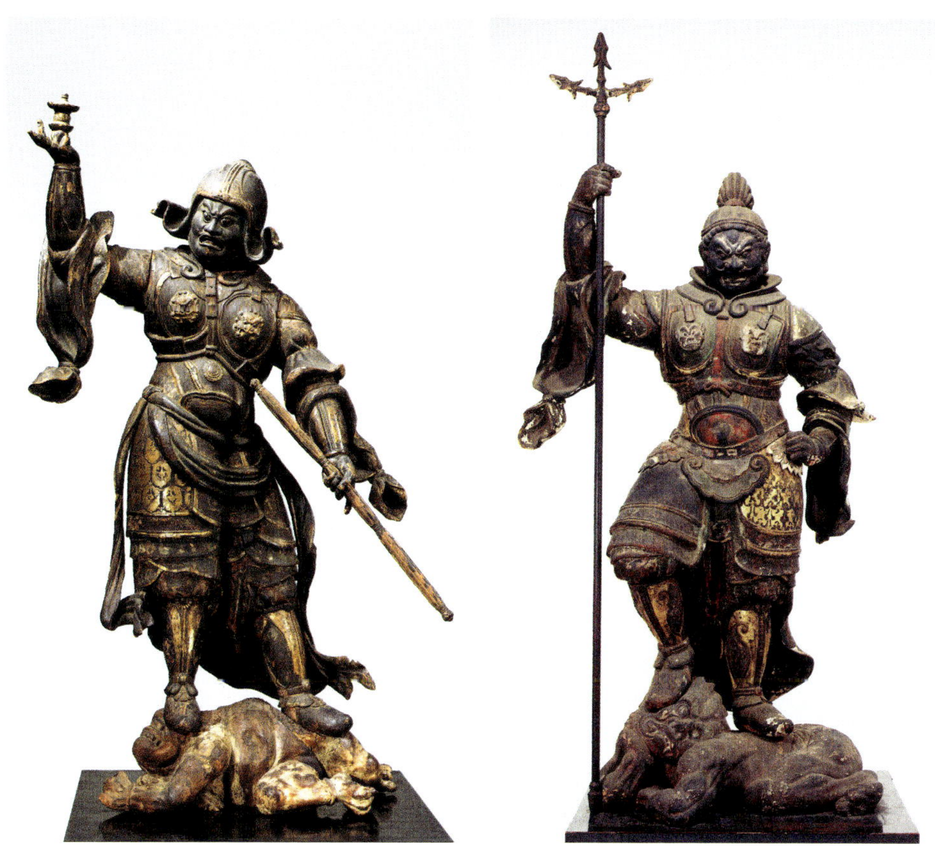

Fig. 57. **Two of the Four Heavenly Kings, 11th–13th cent.** These ominous figures, originally installed at the Kōfukuji Temple in Nara, are Tamonten, king of the north (11th–12th cent., *left*), and Zōchōten, king of the south (13th cent., *right*). They are two of the Four Heavenly Kings who are thought to guard Buddhism on the summit of Mt. Sumeru, the highest point in the world. Images of the kings are typically presented dressed in armor, carrying weapons, and trampling demons underfoot.

Zōchōten (Deity of Expansion and Growth) in the south, holding a spear; Kōmokuten (Deity of Wide-ranging Vision) in the west, holding a writing brush and scroll; and the foremost king, Tamonten (Deity Who Hears Everything) in the north, holding a miniature reliquary for treasures in one hand and a sword, rod, or spear in the other (fig. 57). Images of the four are commonly presented in a hip-swung standing position, clad in armor, ferocious in countenance with bulging or squinting eyes, and subduing small demons or creatures underfoot. In Buddhist temples these images are usually displayed in sculpted form and may be positioned at the four corners of an altar area or ritual site, demarking it as a cosmologically guarded space. Hence, the four tend to revolve around some other Buddhist icon or ritual activity but are nonetheless integral to it as protectors at the periphery.[7]

Of the Four Heavenly Kings, only the chief among them, Tamonten, became an independent object of devotion. Under his alternate name Bishamonten (fig. 58), he is usually associated with success in warfare and protection of the capital, linked in part to legends that he once manifested himself as a great warrior in Central Asia who defended his kingdom against foreign invasion. Thus, he is commonly depicted in armor, sometimes with the face of a ferocious animal shown on the front. Subsequently, Bishamonten became one of the so-called Seven Gods of Good Fortune (Shichifukujin), a group popularized around the sixteenth or seventeenth century. In that capacity, he came to be seen not only as a patron saint of warriors but also a source of benefits and blessings. All these characterizations were extrapolations from his original role as a guardian of Buddhism and Buddhists.[8]

Another set of protective divinities is the Niō or Twin Benevolent Kings installed inside the front gate, to the left and right, at many temples (fig. 59). Again, like the Myōō and the Four Heavenly Kings, they assume a fierce and menacing pose. Sometimes classified as vajra-possessing deities (*shūkongōjin*) or earth spirits (*yashashin*), they too project terrifying power to support Buddhism. Displaying bare-chested muscular physiques and crazed facial expressions, they prevent enemies and opponents of Buddhism from entering the temple's gate. The breadth of their influence is intimated by the syllables being formed in their mouth—one is open forming the letter A (pronounced "aah") and the other is closed sounding the letter N (pronounced "mmm"), the first and last letters of the Japanese

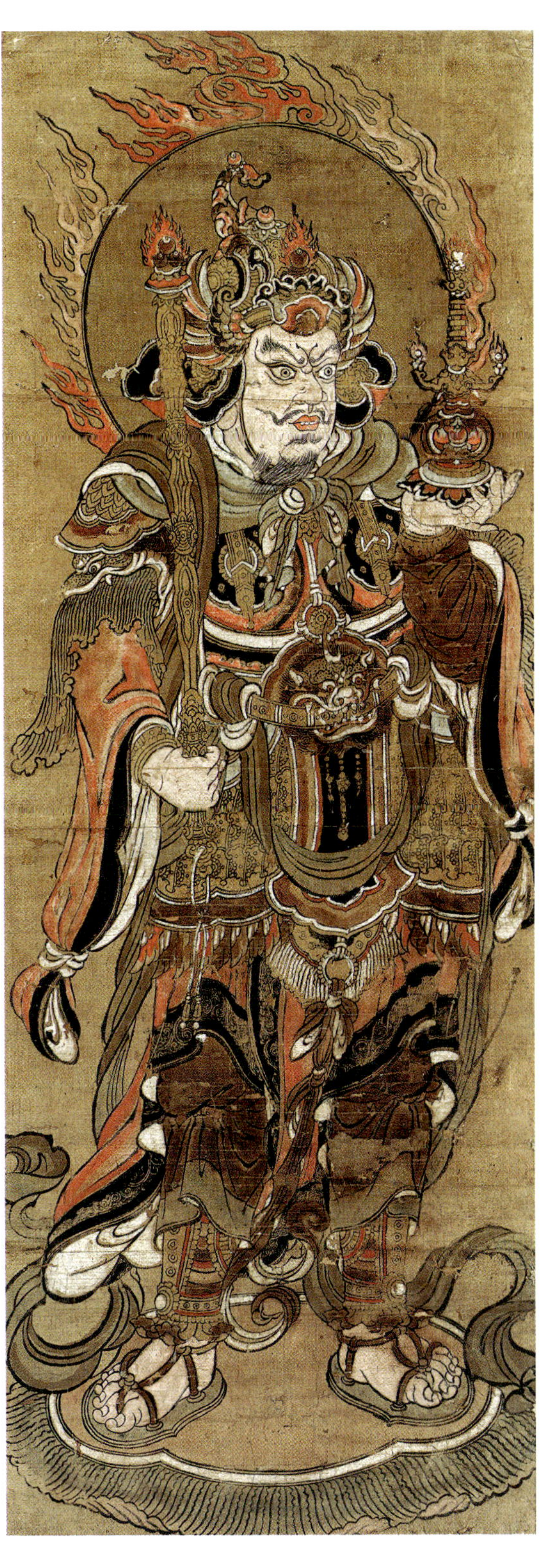

Fig. 58. Bishamonten, 15th cent.
Bishamonten evolved from Tamonten, the foremost of the Four Heavenly Kings, to inspire a cult of his own. This hand-colored woodblock print shows him wearing armor decorated with the face of an animal and wielding his trademark rod and reliquary. Bishamonten eventually became one of Japan's Seven Gods of Good Fortune, from whom devotees would seek both benefits and protection. Photo © 2020 Museum of Fine Arts, Boston.

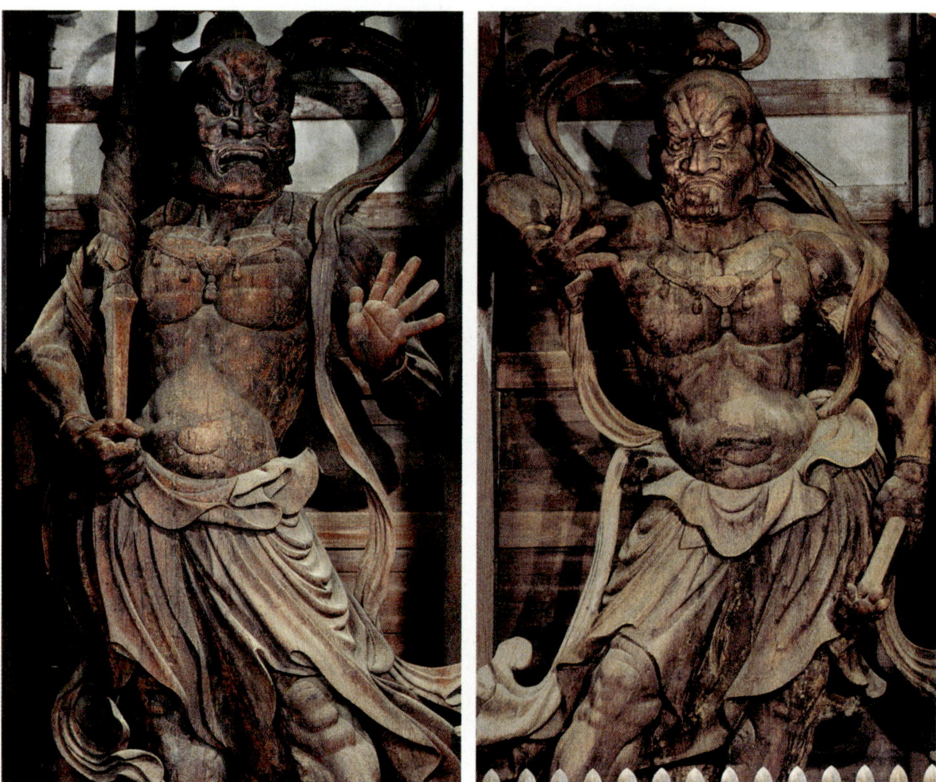

Fig. 59. Twin Benevolent Kings, 13th cent. Tōdaiji Temple, Nara. Installed on each side of the main gate of many temples in Japan are two intimidating guardian figures, the so-called Benevolent Kings. The two here, looming more than twenty-seven feet tall in the Great South Gate of the Tōdaiji Temple, are thought to protect its precincts from the foes of Buddhism.

(and Sanskrit) syllabary—suggesting that their power extends to all things, from alpha to omega, or A to Z. The presence of these two figures sets the temple apart as a protected space where adversaries of Buddhism dare not enter.[9]

One more set of guardian figures is the Jūni Shinshō or Twelve Divine Generals (fig. 60). They are presented in military guise—brandishing weapons, wearing helmets and armor, and striking intimidating poses—and they too are usually classified as earth

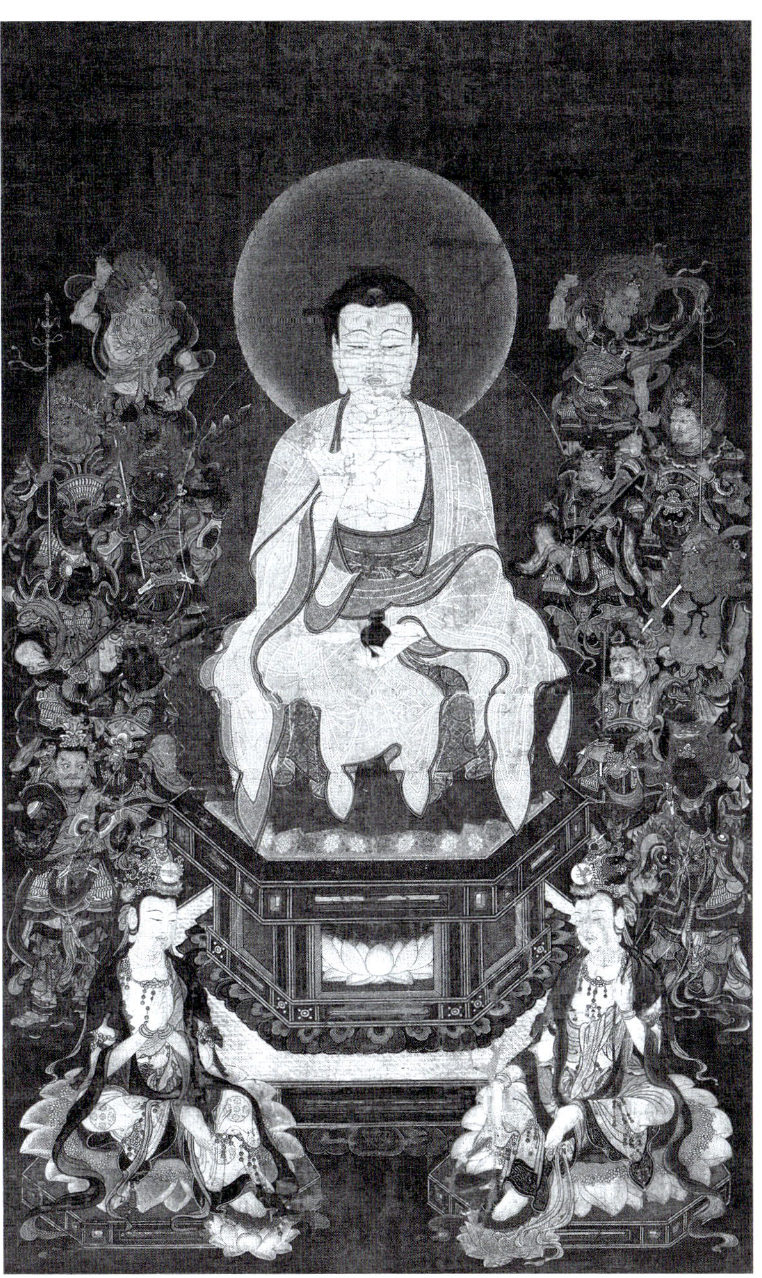

Fig. 60. **Twelve Divine Generals with Yakushi Buddha, 16th cent.** This scene presents the Buddha Yakushi and his two attendant Bodhisattvas accompanied by the Twelve Divine Generals who surround his lotus throne, six on each side. The generals are dressed in armor and carry spears, swords, and other weapons. Assuming menacing stances, they act as both defenders and proponents of the Buddha's teachings. Photo © 2020 Museum of Fine Arts, Boston.

spirits in the service of Buddhism. They are, however, not as common as the Four Heavenly Kings or the Twin Benevolent Kings. The temples displaying the twelve generals are usually dedicated to the healing Buddha Yakushi, as they are mentioned in the *Sutra on the Merits of the Fundamental Vows of Yakushi, the Lapis Lazuli Radiance Buddha* as converts and proponents of Yakushi and as benefactors of those who embrace his teachings.[10] The number of generals, twelve, is thought to correspond to the twelve vows that Yakushi made as a Bodhisattva to come to the aid of sentient beings. In time, the twelve were also associated with the twelve Asian zodiac signs and the twelve hour-markers of the day. In the layout of some temples, such as the Shin'yakushiji in Nara, statues of the Divine Generals are arranged in a circular pattern around the central altar enshrining Yakushi Buddha. As protectors of this sacred space, they contribute in their own way to the ascendancy of Buddhism just as other guardian figures do.[11]

OTHER BUDDHIST DIVINITIES

In addition to these figures, a variety of other divinities in the Buddhist pantheon have sundry origins and functions. Among them are two female divinities, Kichijōten and Benzaiten, who emerged separately. Unlike Buddhist figures with androgynous or oscillating gender identity, these two have consistently been identified as female. Both had origins in India antedating Buddhism but were transmitted to Japan in association with Buddhism. Kichijōten commonly appears as a highborn and elegantly dressed woman of classical Chinese beauty, usually holding a wish-granting jewel in her left hand. In India she was sometimes considered the consort of the god Vishnu, and in Japan she is occasionally shown alongside Bishamonten, the most prominent of the Four Heavenly Kings. But more often she is treated as an independent deity who bestows happiness and prosperity.[12] According to tale literature, the beauty of her image has sometimes provoked unchaste thoughts in virtuous Buddhists.[13] Benzaiten likewise had Indian origins, first as a formidable river goddess and then as a deity of music and literature named Saraswati. In Japan these associations with water-nourishing abundance and with learning, culture, and the arts have persisted and diversified. Benzaiten is commonly depicted in one of two guises. The first is as a powerful and protective eight-armed divinity holding symbolic objects standard to Buddhism as well as weapons common to guardian deities. The second is as a beautiful woman playing music on a stringed instrument (fig. 61). Over the centuries Benzaiten has gradually overshadowed Kichijōten as a popular female divinity in Japan and is prayed to for all manner of blessings and benefits. In fact, her appeal diversified to such an extent that she came to be identified as a Shinto deity and as one of the Seven Gods of Good Fortune as well.[14]

Another widely recognized figure is Enma (Skt. Yama), king of the Buddhist hells (fig. 62). He is designated a king and holds the same status as the Four Heavenly Kings, but the domain under his jurisdiction is the underworld. Buddhism has a complex cosmology of the afterlife that includes eight subterranean hells, each with a distinctive torture reserved for the sentient beings reborn there. According to the doctrine of karma, a person's next rebirth is the just deserts of acts done in this life and previous ones. Hence, those who have committed an abundance of wrongdoing are destined to an unfortunate rebirth in one of the hells. But their life of torment, though unimaginably long, is not eternal, for they can eventually be reborn out of the hells and even as a human again. Enma is the most eminent of ten kings who serve as the administrators of these hells. In appearance, he is often blood red in complexion, posed with a menacing facial expression, and dressed in the traditional attire of an imperial magistrate or judge in China. According to popular accounts, people at death appear before King Enma and are shown their wrongdoings in a magical crystal mirror. If on balance the good they have done outweighs the bad, they can avoid rebirth in the hells. If not, Enma will sentence them to the particular hell that best

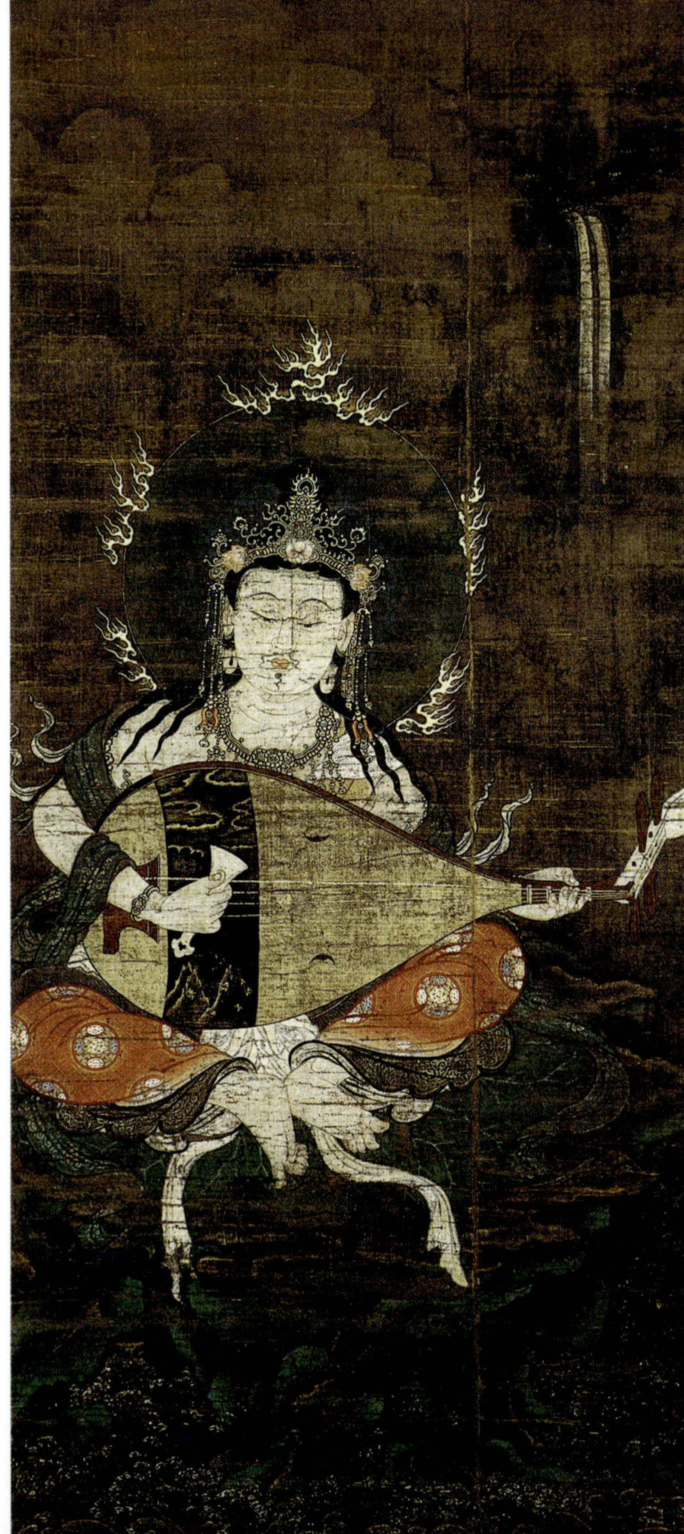

Fig. 61. **Benzaiten, 14th cent.** Benzaiten is a female divinity with roots in India. Originally identified as a goddess of waterways, she came to be associated with learning and the arts, especially music. In this painting she is shown playing the lute in a setting that bears a strong resemblance to compositions of the Bodhisattva Kannon sitting on a rocky promontory above flowing water (fig. 52). Here the appearance of Benzaiten with a faint moustache is more characteristic of the iconography of an androgynous Bodhisattva, such as Kannon, than of a female divinity.

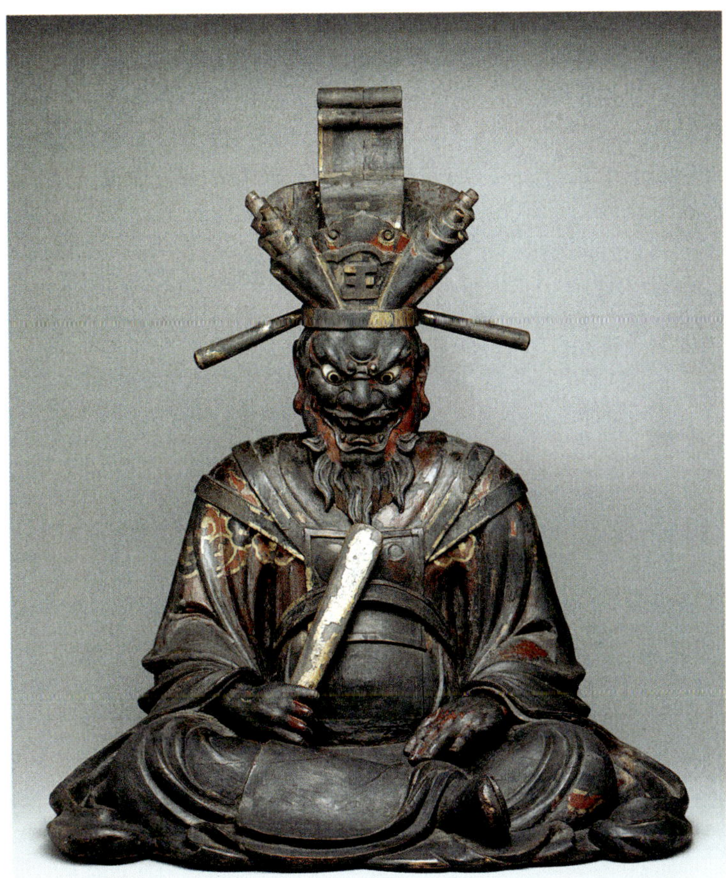

Fig. 62. King Enma, 16th–17th cent. Enma is the head administrator of the Buddhist hells, underground domains where people may be required to suffer for long periods in the afterlife because of their evil deeds, but not permanently. He is usually depicted with a menacing scowl on his face and in the garb of a Chinese magistrate. If Enma personifies the harsh justice of karma, Jizō Bodhisattva (fig. 46), who rescues sentient beings from the hells, personifies Buddhist compassion.

suits their evil deeds. Thus, Enma and the other magistrates function as an infernal bureaucracy of the hells, which a person can escape permanently through Buddhist liberation and enlightenment.[15]

A special category of divinities that became prominent in Japanese Buddhism consists of manifestations or miraculous appearances in the form of Shinto kami. The word kami refers to spirits or deities that inhabit specific places in the world, whether in nature or among humans. Historically, such spirits were thought to populate

Japan at countless locations. In the modern period the religious ideas and practices surrounding these spirits have been systematically classified as Shinto, in contrast to the religion of Buddhism. But in premodern times it is less clear whether there was ever a well-defined bifurcation of the Buddhas from the kami. Rather, they all seemed to belong to a broad and variegated field of spiritual beings, across which people could pick and choose those that they found most spiritually captivating. Among kami, some have become closely associated with Buddhism and are even identified as Japan-specific embodiments of Buddhist figures. A good example is the primary kami of Kumano Shrine, who is considered a so-called Gongen, or worldly manifestation, of Amida Buddha. The idea behind this manifestation—as articulated in the medieval Honji Suijaku doctrine—is that Buddhas and Bodhisattvas willingly take on the appearance of particular kami in Japan to adapt themselves to the spiritual proclivities of the Japanese people. Hence, Buddhists have oftentimes treated religious interaction with the Kumano Gongen as an encounter with Amida Buddha himself.[16]

Another idea linking Buddhism to the kami is the belief that certain kami actually adopt a Buddhist identity to embark on the path to enlightenment. The kami Hachiman, for instance, who was widely recognized as a powerful martial deity, is sometimes depicted in the guise of a Buddhist monk, known as Sōgyō Hachiman.[17] Yet another elision of Buddhism with a localized kami is Zaō Gongen, the central deity of the Mt. Kinpu religious complex in Yoshino province south of Nara (fig. 63). He is variously identified as a manifestation of the historical Buddha Śākyamuni, of the thousand-armed Bodhisattva of compassion Kannon, and of the future Buddha Miroku. In appearance, however, he bears the characteristics of a ferocious esoteric Buddhist figure—frightening face, bulging eyes, fanged mouth, flaming hair, and vajra thunderbolt brandished in one upheld hand. Zaō Gongen's sacred site on Mt. Kinpu became a pilgrimage destination for aristocrats and retired emperors in medieval times and ultimately inspired a tradition of ascetic practices known as Shugendō

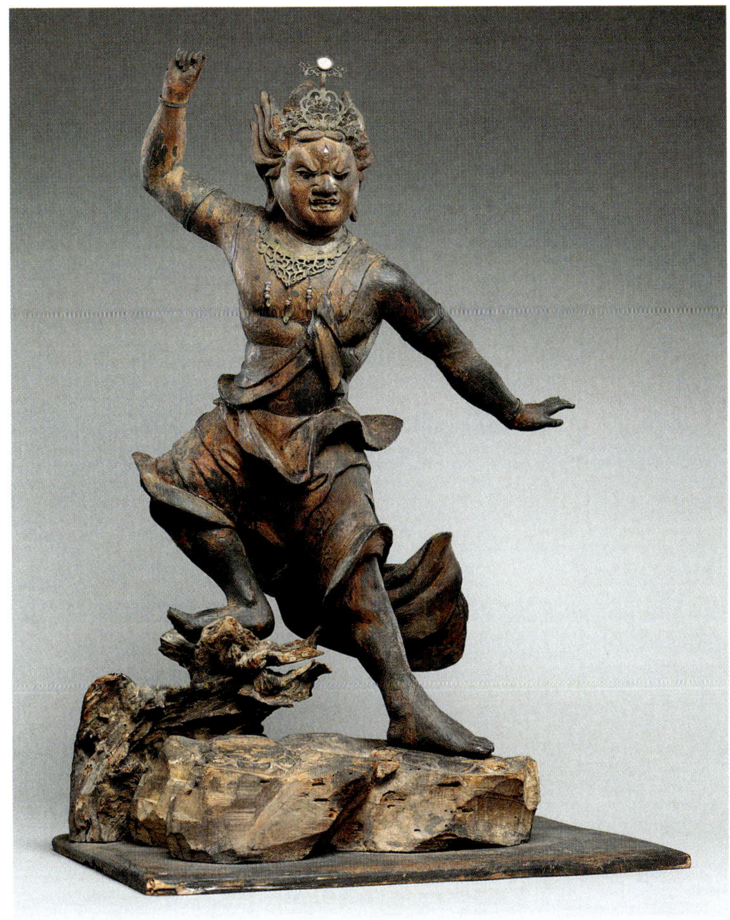

Fig. 63. Zaō Gongen, 14th cent. Zaō is a kami, or Shinto deity, residing on Mt. Kinpu, who is treated variously as a manifestation in Japan of past, present, and future Buddhist figures—Śākyamuni, Kannon, and Miroku. His frightening appearance—grimacing face, upswept hair, and a vajra thunderbolt in his raised right hand (missing from this image)—conveys his intention to strike down obstacles to enlightenment and defeat opponents of Buddhism. Zaō is a classic example of the merging of Buddhist beliefs with localized veneration of kami in Japan.

that seamlessly merged Buddhist religious aspirations with the veneration of mountain deities.[18]

This panoply of spiritual beings—Myōō, guardian figures, and deities in addition to the many Buddhas and Bodhisattvas—makes up a mindboggling array, but in fact the ones mentioned here are just a tiny fraction of the myriad Buddhist figures populating Japan's religious landscape. In certain ways they come across as a hodgepodge of divinities, some propitiated to allay misfortunes and others beseeched for concrete benefits. Many seem to have an accidental or peripheral connection to Buddhism, and their competing cults tend to produce a spiritual cacophony that is hard to comprehend. Suffice it to say that all of them operate within a Buddhist framework. In essence, the Buddhist threefold paradigm of quest, enlightenment, and compassion intersects or underlies all these spiritual beings and the practices associated with them. These three Buddhist ideals are thus understood broadly and loosely in the Japanese context so that a far-flung array of spiritual figures and religious activities can be interpreted as embodying them, even if their connection seems tenuous or faint. In short, an image of the Buddha with compassionate hand gestures is seen as Buddhist, but so is a local divinity to whom propitiatory offerings and prayers are made. People might stand in the presence of either one and feel that the goals and principles of Buddhism are fully expressed. Ultimately, it is the expansive, porous, and multidimensional character of Mahayana Buddhism that makes this teeming world of Buddhist spirituality possible in Japan.

PART III

BUDDHIST IMAGES IN THE WORLD

CHAPTER 7

BUDDHIST ICONS AS LIVING ENTITIES

The magnificent Tōdaiji Temple, enshrining the Great Buddha of Nara, was first dedicated in a grand ceremony held in 752. This was the culmination of a long and ambitious project to produce the mammoth bronze image and to build the cavernous hall around it. Emperor Shōmu (701–756) launched the project in 743 and committed a large portion of Japan's resources to it. The casting of the image was done in place using an earthen mold in a series of eight pourings of molten metal between 747 and 749. Finishing work, including the production of the image's head, continued for several years beyond that. Simultaneously, the massive hall was constructed around it while the image itself was being completed. The Great Buddha and its hall were actually larger then than they are today, having been destroyed and rebuilt on a slightly smaller scale twice in Japanese history. The work was largely finished in 752 when the dedication ceremony was held (fig. 64).

Befitting a project of this magnitude, the dedication of the image and temple was also conducted in a grand fashion. Supposedly over ten thousand priests attended as well as aristocrats, military officials, bureaucrats, regional authorities, musicians, and dancers—with the recently retired Emperor Shōmu at the head, along with Empress Kōmyō and their daughter Kōken, the new emperor. The exact content of the dedication is known only in rough outline—vegetarian banquet, sutra lectures, incantations, banners and flowers, and so forth—but the highpoint of it was a ritual known as the eye-opening ceremony, conducted by a priest from India named Bodhisena. In it he took a large ink brush and painted in the pupils of the Great

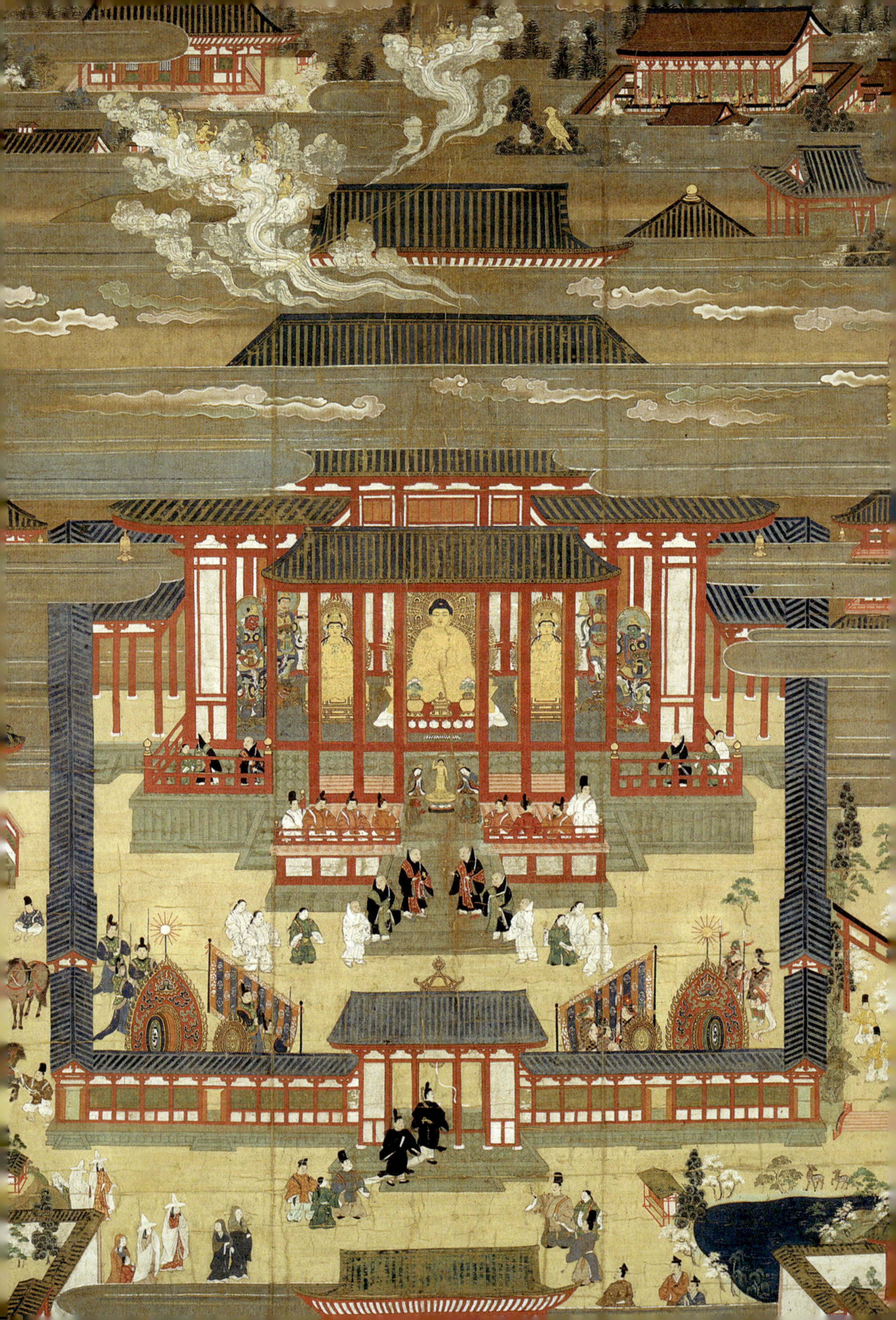

Buddha's eyes (fig. 65). The brush itself had a long cord attached stretching to the hands of Shōmu, his wife, their daughter, and others so that they too would be indirect participants—thereby accruing karmic merit—in enlivening the Great Buddha. Even today the brush, ink stick, and cord from the ceremony survive in the Shōsōin, the imperial storehouse of treasures from Shōmu's reign. This ritual act, also known as "dotting the eyes" (*tengen*), was a standard Buddhist practice to awaken or bring to life a Buddhist image. From that point, the Tōdaiji's great icon was thought to be a living Buddha in the world.[1]

The eye-opening ceremony was not invented in Japan. It was inherited from the Asian continent where it was widely performed in the installation of Buddhist icons. There are many variations to the ceremony, depending on the location in Asia and the type of Buddhism in which it is conducted. In the Theravada Buddhism of Southeast Asia and Sri Lanka, for instance, it is typically accompanied by offerings of food, flowers, and incense, lighting of lamps, chanting of mantras, petitions to deities, meditation of monks, and recitation of religious texts and episodes from the Buddha's life—with the image finally awakened by uncovering or painting in its eyes. In Tibetan Buddhism, the consecration centers more on engaging, inviting, and infusing the spirit of the Buddha into the image through ritual, invocatory, and meditative means, with an eye-opening rite appended to it. Similarly, in the esoteric Buddhism of the Japanese Tendai and Shingon traditions, the inspiriting process occurs through mudras, mantras, and meditative acts, in which not only the physical eye of the image is opened, but also the so-called heavenly eye, wisdom eye, Dharma eye, and Buddha eye. And in Japanese Sōtō Zen, the ceremony of "dotting the eyes" with brush and ink is conducted in conjunction with flower and incense offerings, recitation of the ten great appellations of the Buddha and a eulogy of praise, a consecration statement of the image, and a dedication of karmic merit. In sum, despite the variations that occur in different forms of Buddhism, the eye-opening ceremony is universally thought to bring the

Fig. 64. Great Buddha Hall. Illustration from *Tōdaiji Engi*, 16th cent. This illustration, from a collection of stories about extraordinary events at the Tōdaiji Temple, is considered by some to be a depiction of the original consecration ceremony of the Great Buddha. On both sides he is flanked by a Bodhisattva and beyond them by the Four Heavenly Kings, creating a protected sacred space in the central hall. Below the Great Buddha, a small icon of Śākyamuni Buddha at birth is installed (fig. 11). Priests dressed in black are the main celebrants of the ceremony, with a variety of other people in attendance outside—aristocrats, warriors, court ladies, nuns, and children. Historians point out that the various buildings in the illustration reflect the layout of the temple after it was rebuilt in the late twelfth and early thirteenth centuries rather than its original configuration.

Buddhist image to life, and from that point people can interact with it as if in the presence of a living Buddha.[2] In the icon, therefore, a person can "behold" the Buddha, and the Buddha can in turn fix the person in his gaze.

ARE BUDDHIST IMAGES ALIVE?

The impression that Buddhist images are alive is rare among most people today, especially those conditioned by a reductionist and materialist understanding of the world. There is a prevailing sense that a distinct line divides the animate from the inanimate. Premodern Buddhists too recognized such a line, for they regarded Buddhist images

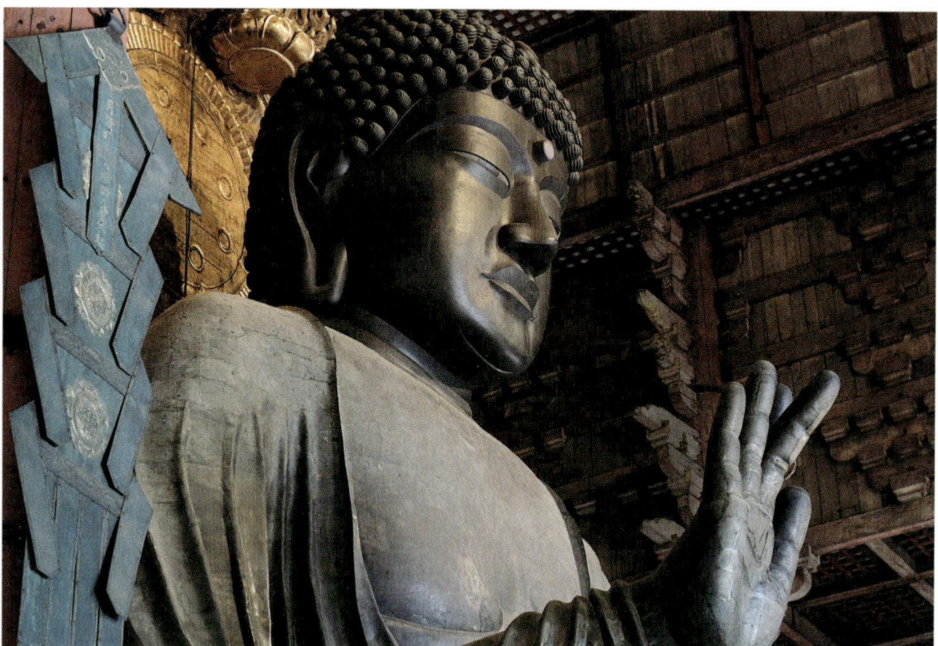

Fig. 65. Painted eyes of the Great Buddha. Tōdaiji Temple, Nara. At the original consecration of the Great Buddha in 752, the so-called eye-opening ceremony, the act of painting in the pupils of the Buddha's eyes was used as a ritual procedure to "enliven" the figure. The painted pupils can be seen today, though these are the result of later reconsecrations. The icon was destroyed by fire in 1567 and recast in the late 1600s.

prior to consecration as simple objects, but as living entities once their eyes were "opened." Science and secularism, for their part, tend to treat this eye-opening ceremony as a quaint custom at best and an outdated superstition at worst. Yet, there is ample evidence that through much of Japanese history Buddhist images were recognized as living, pulsating, dynamic beings with whom people could interact.

To problematize the modern differentiation of living beings from inanimate objects, it might be helpful to reflect briefly on people's behavior after the loss of a beloved or revered person in their life—a grandmother, for instance. While fully aware that she is no longer alive in the same sense that she was, people nonetheless continue to relate to her in ways somewhat analogous to how they did before. They seek her company by visiting her gravesite or enshrined ashes. They feel her presence in the personal objects she has left behind—a comb or a letter. Her physical appearance remains vivid in their mind because of a favorite photo kept in a special place in their home. Certainly, in their most rational moments people would never claim that their grandmother's ashes or comb or photo is any more alive than a rock. And yet behaviorally they interact with them more as they would with a person than with a physical object. Nowadays there are ways to explain away such behavior, describing it as nostalgic or personal or subjective. But the point is that many objects in life cannot be reduced simply to the categories of the living and the non-living. Some are experientially different even if they are judged to be inert scientifically. In certain respects the relics of the Buddha, the written sutras preserving his Dharma, and the icon perpetuating his physical appearance function analogously to one's grandmother's ashes, letters, and photo. Or, at least, thinking of them in that way may be the closest that people today can come to a premodern Buddhist understanding of images.[3] The major difference, of course, is that the Buddha embodies all the complexities and profundities of Buddhism's many meanings—Dharma, Nirvana, wisdom, compassion, emptiness—that one's grandmother may not. These meanings are considered inherent in and radiating out from his iconic image.

Fig. 66. Seiryōji Śākyamuni Buddha, 10th cent. Seiryōji Temple, Kyoto. This famous icon has long been regarded as a "living body" of Śākyamuni Buddha. Hidden in a compartment inside and also in other parts of the statue were a number of objects that were thought to enliven the icon: relics of the Buddha, religious texts, mirrors, precious stones, patches of clerical robes, coins, and even sewn fabric replicas of bodily organs.

The simultaneously elusive and captivating identity of the Buddha has been expressed in various ways throughout Buddhist history. The Buddha, for instance, is famously quoted as saying, "Whoever sees the Dharma sees me; whoever sees me sees the Dharma." A philosophical interpretation of this might emphasize the primacy of the Dharma over the person of the Buddha. But in traditional Japanese Buddhism the statement would suggest the inseparability of Buddhism's truths from the identity of the Buddha. That is, to behold the Buddha is to perceive his Dharma, and vice versa. To the extent, though, that the Dharma encompasses not just ethical and ritual dimensions but also the deconstruction of seeming realities and people's reliance on them—that is, the realization of emptiness and nonattachment—seeing the Buddha is also a matter of encountering his religious quest, his enlightenment, and his compassion. All those associations with the person of the Buddha are attributed to the image of the Buddha as well.

Another way to approach the living character of Buddhist images is via the significance of the eye in the eye-opening ceremony. Vision is a widely cited trope in Buddhism, referring not only to seeing the physical world clearly but to religious insight into the nature of things. In a sense, the eye-opening ritual is a re-enactment of the Buddha's original enlightenment wherein the Buddhist icon is awakened to the truths of the universe in the same way that the Buddha was.[4] And just as the Buddha was imbued with the aura of this liberating and compassionate vision, so too do Buddhist images exert a mysterious and liberating power over those who confront them. The icon captivates people, and they cannot help but behold the Buddha.

Besides these conceptual approaches to the life of icons, there is also material evidence of belief in their living character based on the ancient custom of placing objects inside the hollow cavity of statues. Perhaps the most famous example is the revered standing image of Śākyamuni Buddha at the Seiryōji Temple in Kyoto (fig. 66). This icon is a replica (or, according to some legends, the original itself) of a portrait statue of Śākyamuni said to have been made in India while

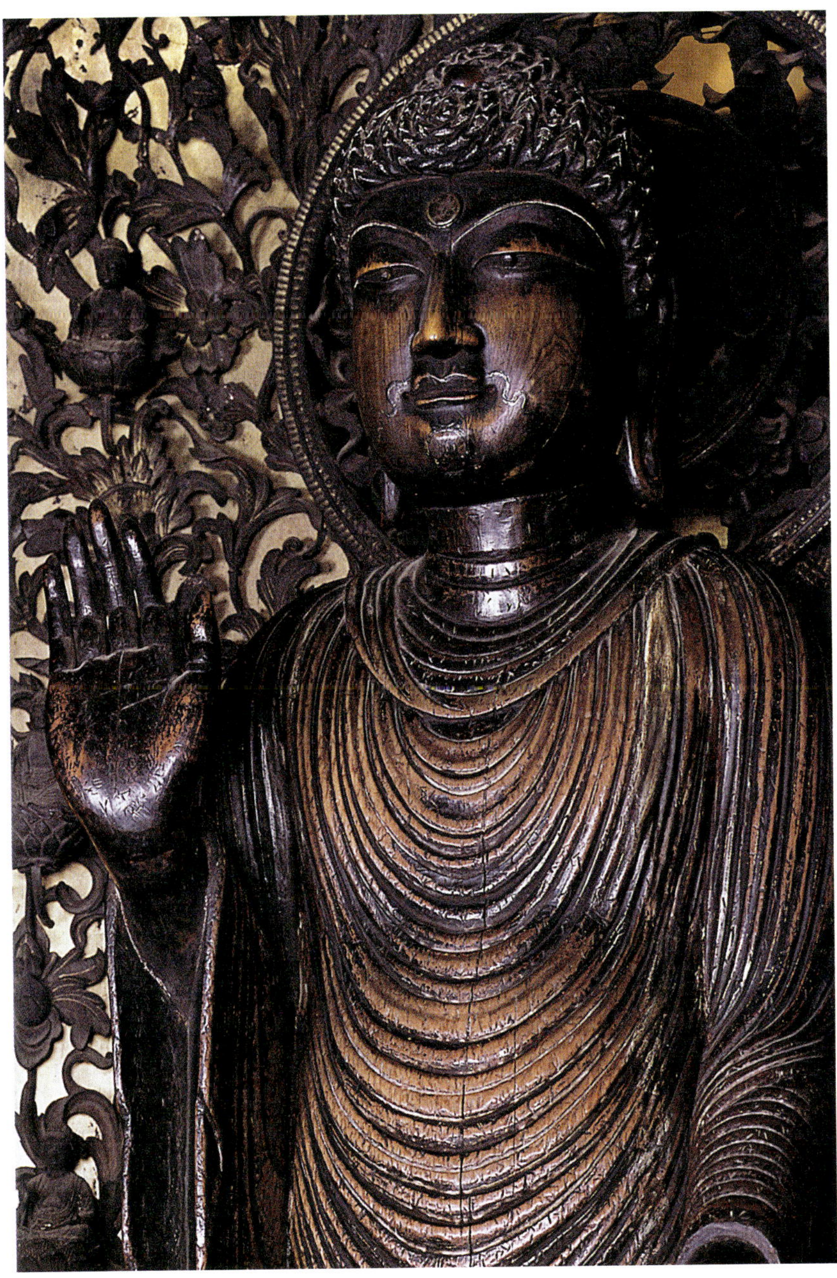

he was still alive, which supposedly was later transported to China. Because it is considered an exact likeness of the historical Buddha, its power and efficacy as an icon are especially intense. The priest Chōnen brought the image to Japan in 986 after sojourning in China for three years.

In 1954 a long-sealed compartment at the back of the Seiryōji icon was opened and examined by the head priest of the temple and other scholars. It contained several hundred objects and fragments, as well as a list of some of the items placed inside the Buddha. Among them were a variety of pious offerings from clerical and lay Buddhists who no doubt sought to participate in the awakening of this image: gems, precious stones, patches of priests' robes, coins, and so forth. Several objects, though, seem particularly noteworthy. First, there were copies of three sutras and other religious documents. The teachings of the Buddha, which were thought to have enlivening properties, were frequently inserted into icons—authenticating, in a sense, the inseparability of the Buddha and the Dharma. Second, the list refers to a tooth of the Buddha, supposedly a relic from the historical Śākyamuni, that was imbedded in the face of the image. From earliest times in Buddhist history, relics of the Buddha—teeth, bone fragments, and bead-shaped crystals from his cremation—were treasured as extensions of the Buddha that retain his numinous qualities. Placement of relics inside icons has occurred throughout the Buddhist world as another potent method of enlivening images. Third, the list mentions four mirrors, though only one was found inside the compartment itself. (Others may have been placed in different parts of the statue, including the head.) Mirrors were a common instrument in consecration ceremonies and were used to look obliquely into the Buddha's eyes as his pupils were painted or to project the Dharma into the Buddha. They are thus associated with both the Buddha's teachings and his enlightened vision. Finally, a complete set of inner organs—heart, lungs, liver, kidneys, stomach, and so forth—made out of silk and each containing a precious core (a gem, incense, or Sanskrit writing), was discovered inside the compartment. These organs were sewn by nuns and laywomen, according to the list—a rare but not unknown insertion in icons. Nonetheless, they are another indication of this image's status as a "living body" of the Buddha.[5]

The objects hidden in the Seiryōji icon possess great symbolic value, each providing a different array of meanings for bringing the icon to life. From a modern perspective, the inner compartment may be considered a kind of time capsule, offering a glimpse into the material culture of tenth-century Buddhism. But to the people placing those items in it, the objects were more than mere expressions of faith—they were objects of empowerment. The symbolic messages they expressed were kept secret, since they were supposed to be hidden away forever from the gaze of people on the outside. But if the items served their real purpose—to enliven the image—then people would sense their power in their experience of a living Buddha. And that is precisely how the Seiryōji image was perceived, as reflected by the Japanese term *shōjin,* meaning "living body," which was used to refer to the Seiryōji Buddha and other images around which icon cults developed. The implication of this term is that the historical Śākyamuni has been incarnated yet again as the icon of the Seiryōji Temple, and people who long to be in his presence should seek him there.

The Seiryōji Buddha is a prime example of a renowned icon that was experienced as vibrant and responsive in premodern Japan. At the same time, people were aware that the enlivened quality of images is also fragile, contingent, and mysterious, just as the life of a human body is. Actually, there have been occasional expressions of suspicion toward icons in Buddhist history, and even anti-iconic behavior. The most famous instance is a story well known in Japan and popularized in the West by D. T. Suzuki about the Chinese Zen monk Danxia Tianran (739–824). Once when Danxia was staying at a temple on a very cold night, he took a wooden image of the Buddha and burned it to keep himself warm (fig. 67). A person at the temple reprimanded him, asking why Danxia would do such a sacrilegious act. Coyly, he answered that he burned the Buddha in order to discover his relics, just as occurred in the cremation of Śākyamuni. The person responded by asking how a wooden image could possibly have such things. Danxia replied that he should then not be reprimanded, since the image is only a block of wood, not the Buddha.

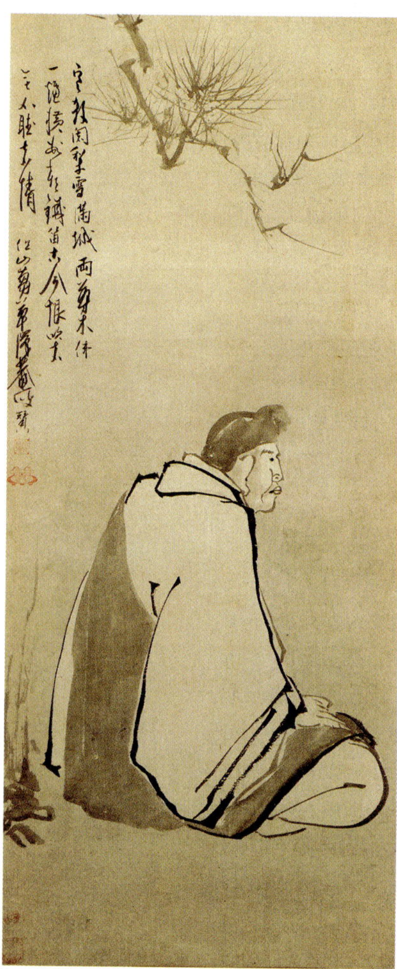

Fig. 67. Zen monk Danxia burning the Buddhist image, 16th–17th cent. This ink painting illustrates Danxia Tianran's boldness in setting a wooden Buddha afire to keep himself warm. The artist, Unkoku Tōgan (1547–1618), reinforces the anti-iconic message of the story by emphasizing the resolute posture of the Zen monk and relegating the tiny fire to the left edge of the painting. Tōgan became a Buddhist priest late in life.

The story of Danxia's burning the image is typically cited to remind people never to allow anything to become an object of attachment, not even something sacred. Certainly, this is how the story has been interpreted in Zen Buddhism. But its shock value derives from the fact that in Danxia's time the norm was to regard such images as the living embodiment of the Buddha, especially if they had a relic of the Buddha hidden inside. This is as true of the Zen tradition in both China and Japan as it is of other Buddhist traditions. Even D. T. Suzuki, while affirming the standard Zen interpretation of the story, did not endorse such iconoclastic behavior but instead upheld the conventional monastic practices characteristic of Zen religious life.[6]

A good counterexample to Danxia is the Shakakō, or Śākyamuni Fellowship, that was based at Vulture Peak Hall (Ryōzen'in) in the Tendai monastic complex on Mt. Hiei outside Kyoto in the eleventh century (a hall that no longer exists). It enshrined an image of Śākyamuni Buddha who was recognized—in keeping with his characterization in the *Lotus Sutra*—as an eternal Buddha perpetually proclaiming the *Lotus* teachings in a transcendent and miraculous Pure Land on Vulture Peak. In fact, the hall was seen as a microcosmic double of that miraculous realm, and the icon as an earthly instantiation of Śākyamuni. Around this hall developed a fervent community of over five hundred devotees—men and women, clerics and laypeople—who took turns looking after the Buddha in twenty-four-hour shifts. Their activities included chanting the Buddha's name, performing music and song, reciting parts of the *Lotus Sutra,* and being constantly mindful of appropriate thoughts, words, and actions while inside the hall—all typical religious behavior for the period. But in addition, they tended to every need of the Buddha as if he were a living person. The fellowship's procedures state:

> 1. Every day we should pay respect and make offerings [to the Buddha].
>
> After the signal at the time of the rabbit [5:00 to 7:00 a.m.], [offer] rice gruel, one or two types of vegetables with sauce, and chopsticks. At the time after the signal at the hour of the serpent [9:00 to 11:00 a.m.], [offer] four or five measures of fragrant rice, and one or two types of soup made with salt, vinegar, etc. Fruit, when available[, should be offered]. At daybreak, [offer] water; at twilight [offer] votive lights (with a measure of new oil).
>
> In addition, as appropriate to cold or heat, such things as a brazier or a folding fan should be offered. (The brazier and fan should be ready in the hall; the charcoal, however, should be brought by the person whose turn it is.)
>
> 2. In the afternoon and evening, we should keep watch and guard [the Buddha].
>
> From the early morning of that day to the early morning of the following day, [we should] keep watch, and perform the various tasks as they have been designated, such as rolling up the blinds and lowering the awnings, opening the door, cleaning, etc.
>
> We should not approach the Buddha at undesignated times. Walking or sitting, we must maintain firm resolve, and we must not behave roughly. We absolutely must wait for the entrance of the next person, and then leave.[7]

As far as the members of the fellowship were concerned, within the confines of the hall they were in the presence of Śākyamuni, and their mundane service to him was considered a demonstration of their reverence and an inspiration for their own spiritual awakening.

THE SACRED SPACE OF BUDDHIST IMAGES

In Japan, the most likely place for people to encounter a Buddhist image is a temple. Japan has countless temples, and virtually all of them contain images in one guise or another. It is difficult to generalize about Japanese temples because there are many types with different functions: public temples, private temples, sectarian temples, monasteries, memorial halls, pilgrimage sites, cultic centers, personal hermitages, wayside chapels, mausoleums, and so forth. Whatever the type, it is common for a Buddhist image or multiple images—a sculpted or painted representation of a Buddha, Bodhisattva, or Buddhist divinity—to be the centerpiece of the temple (though in certain cases other sacred objects may take their place). The description of Buddhist temples offered below is far from exhaustive, and considerable variation exists. But it applies in some degree to most medium-size and large temples in Japan.

Generally speaking, a temple is considered a sacred space inhabited by the Buddhist icon that is enshrined there. In addition, temples serve as a site for communal religious activity, where members congregate to perform the rites and practices of their particular tradition. These two temple functions, enshrinement and practice, go back to Buddhism's earliest institutions in India. Nowadays there is a tendency to emphasize the dimension of religious practice in temples over the role of enshrinement, especially in monasteries where monks follow strict routines. But when analyzed structurally, it is apparent that temples are largely icon-centered in layout. That is, icons provide the pivot around which the activity of the temple takes place. Even in Zen monasteries, halls enshrining Buddhist images occupy the heart of the monastic compound, whereas meditation halls are located to the side.

The layout of Japanese temples was influenced by Chinese models, which in turn emulated imperial palace design in China. The palace was a walled compound oriented on a north-south axis. At the south end was a main gate or series of gates through which one approached the emperor's reception hall or a set of halls toward the north. On each side of this axis, to the east and west, were buildings housing various support functions for the emperor. Under ideal conditions, temples are laid out in a similar pattern with a north-south axis and a southern gate leading into a closed compound. The hall enshrining a primary Buddhist image, the functional equivalent of the emperor, is centrally located or placed slightly to the north. Temples follow this configuration even when the particular landscape does not allow a southerly approach; in such cases, they are built around a notional north-south axis.

When people enter a Buddhist compound via the south gate, they make their way through successive layers of sacred space that ultimately lead to the icon at the heart of the temple. The gate itself may feature the Twin Benevolent Kings, guardians defending the area from threats to Buddhism (fig. 59). Inside the compound a bell tower might be seen in one corner and a drum tower in the other, or there might be a pagoda on one side of the central axis, containing its own installation of Buddhist images (fig. 78). Ancillary structures arrayed along the east and west sides of the compound support the activities of the temple, including quarters for the priests and related facilities (a study hall, sutra repository, refectory, bath, and toilet), an ancestor hall, and the abbot's quarters at the northeast corner. Each of these might also contain its own collection of Buddhist images enshrined in places of honor. Proceeding straight ahead along the central axis, one arrives at a large building (possibly two or even three buildings in a row in some temples) placed at the center or north end of the compound. This building is usually called the main hall (*hondō*), the golden hall (*kondō*), the Buddha hall (*butsuden*), or something similar, and it is here that the central icon (*honzon*) of the temple is found. Admittedly, Buddhist temples can vary greatly in layout and function, but this general configuration characterizes temples in Japan to some degree (fig. 68).[8]

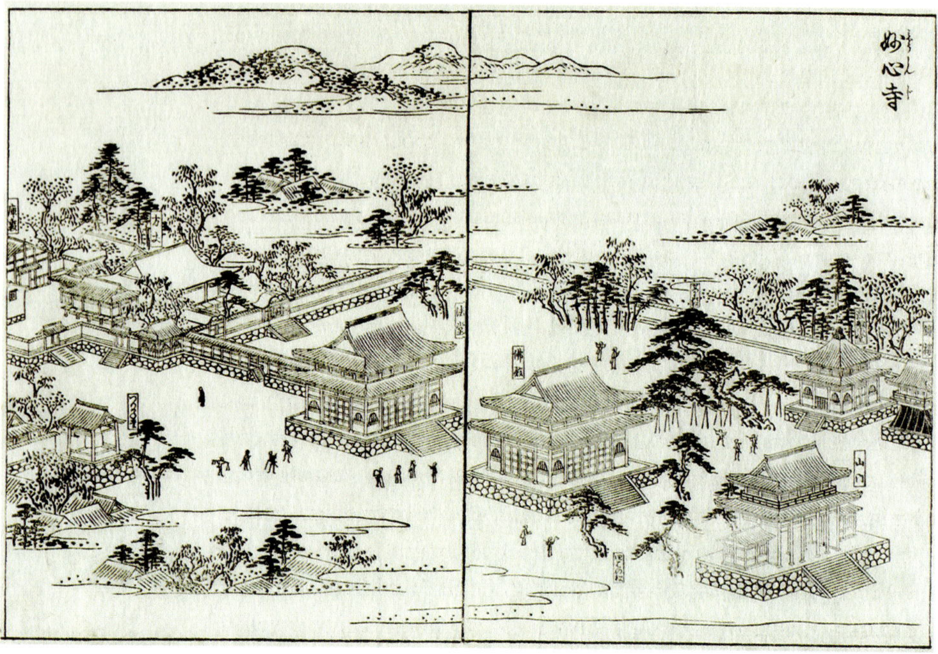

Fig. 68. **Illustration of Myōshinji Zen monastery, Kyoto, 18th cent.** In this rendering of the Myōshinji monastery, from a guidebook to famous places in Kyoto, the north-south axis of the temple compound is visible along a diagonal stretching from the lower right corner to the left center of the frame. The wall enclosing the south end of the compound is not visible in the illustration and would be off to the lower right. From there, the first building is the main gate of the monastery, which has a chapel with icons on the second floor. The next building is the central one in the complex, the Buddha hall, where rituals are performed each morning and on special occasions. It contains an enshrined image of Śākyamuni flanked by his disciples Kāśyapa and Ānanda. Behind it is the Dharma hall, used for monastic assemblies, lectures, and special rituals. From there a covered walkway leads to the abbot's quarters and reception hall, and at the end of the axis is the monastery kitchen. Landmarks on the sides of the compound include a covered tower to the upper right of the main gate, labeled a belfry. Next to it is a building called the Nirvana hall, which originally enshrined a deathbed image of Śākyamuni and memorial tablets of Zen patriarchs. Near the lower left corner of the illustration is another pavilion containing a large temple bell.

Upon entering the main hall, one is again confronted with a delineation of sacred space. First, there is a separation between an outer area (*gejin*) on the south side of the chamber, where ordinary people may congregate, and an inner area (*naijin*) on the north side, which only priests and functionaries may enter. The inner area itself may also be partitioned into sections—usually left, center, and right—that enshrine various images, the most important of them usually occupying the central section. In some temples this inner area dominates the entire chamber, with only a small area apportioned to the congregants outside it. Often there is a raised platform on which an array of Buddhist images is installed. Around the periphery there may be guardian figures—for instance, the Four Heavenly Kings at the corners (fig. 57) or the Twelve Divine Generals encircling it (fig. 60). Within this protected space are images of Buddhas, Bodhisattvas, and sometimes Myōō, typically arranged in quasi-independent units across the three sections, left, center, and right. Each unit itself may also contain multiple images—say, a Buddha, two flanking Bodhisattvas, and others. Based on the identity of these figures, the entire assembly creates an intricate interplay of religious meanings, with the central icon usually carrying the greatest significance (fig. 69). When the Buddhist images inhabiting this inner sanctum dominate the chamber in this way, the edifice functions more as their sacred palace than as a congregational hall.[9]

Some temples may allot a larger proportion of space to the outer congregant area, but the chamber itself is always configured to acknowledge the preeminence and centrality of the enshrined icon. Adorned with hanging banners, decorative lamps, and celebrative pendants, and painted with celestial flowers and other bright images, the hall has the air of a regal palace or even a paradise of the Buddha. In front of the central icon is an altar table equipped with an assortment of ritual paraphernalia: incense burners, flower vases, candleholders or lamps, water vessels, containers for food and drink, bells or gongs or clackers, and so forth (fig. 2). In esoteric Buddhism the altar is set up on a broad low table where the Buddhist divinity is invited, hosted, and communed

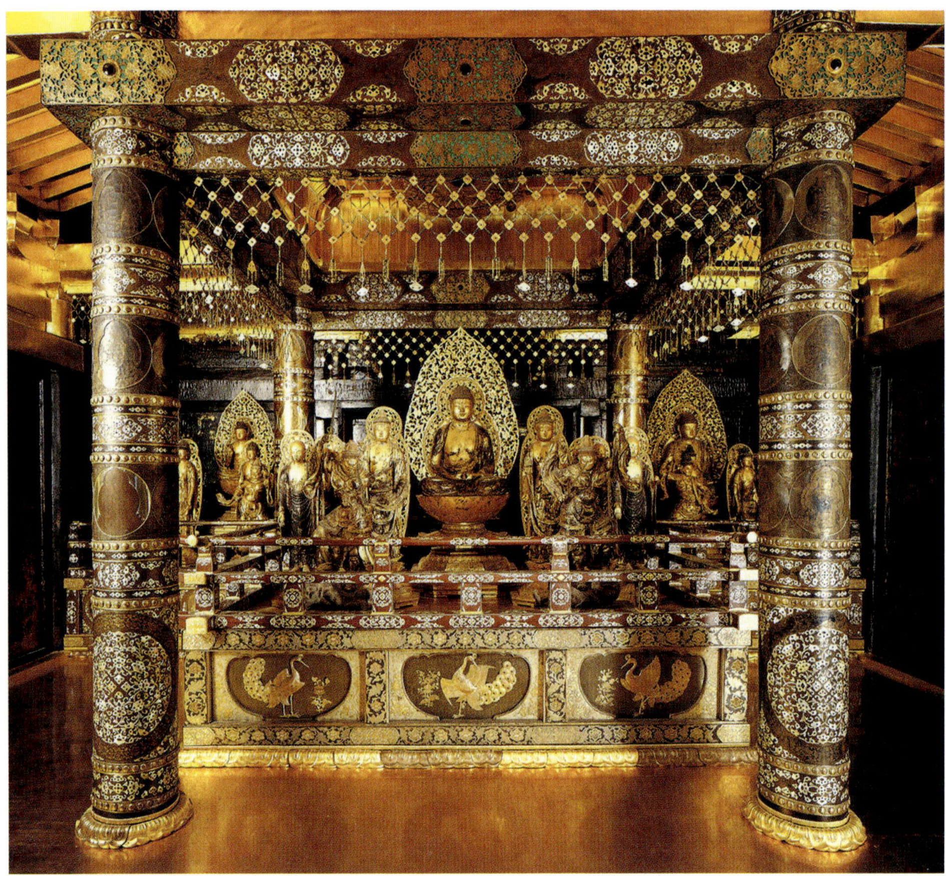

Fig. 69. **Altar area of Konjikidō Hall, 12th cent. Chūsonji Temple, Hiraizumi.** This is the interior of a small but well-known chapel in northern Japan. The space is dominated by three raised altar areas, each surrounded by railings. The two ancillary ones are barely visible to the left and right behind the central one. On each altar Amida Buddha is flanked by his attendant Bodhisattvas Kannon and Seishi, and by six images of the Bodhisattva Jizō at the outer edges. Two of the Four Heavenly Kings, Jikokuten and Zōchōten, guard the space at the front of the altar. This particular ensemble of figures is rare in Japanese iconography. The opulence of the interior—adorned with gold leaf, mother-of-pearl, and an ornate canopy—evokes the richness of Amida's Pure Land and the promise of salvation. This message is made even more poignant by the fact that the bodies of three generations of regional rulers are interred under the three altars. The chapel cum mausoleum is now preserved and displayed behind plexiglass within a large ferro-concrete building.

with using cleansing water, incense, unguents, flowers, food, drink, and other offerings. In addition, a majestic canopy is suspended from the ceiling over some icons, just as a royal parasol would be held over a king. The icon itself is installed on an ornate Sumeru platform, suggesting that the Buddha resides atop the highest mountain in the world (fig. 10). Or it can be placed inside an elaborate shrine (*zushi*) with doors on the front that open and close. The enclosure might look like a cabinet in which the icon is stored, but it is more appropriate to regard it as the icon's miniature palace.[10]

In tracing the route from the entrance gate of the compound to the enshrinement spot in the main hall, it is apparent that the temple is laid out in layers or zones of increasingly sacred space. To the extent that icons were treated as living entities in premodern Japan, the temples enshrining them were regarded as numinous and specially charged places. When people entered their precincts, they would move in stages to the sacred center, and their awareness of the vibrant pulsating icon would quicken as they approached. In short, temples were structured as spaces where people could step outside their daily routine and encounter the Buddha—that is, behold the Buddha—in the form of a living icon.

THE RITUAL LIFE OF BUDDHIST IMAGES

The Buddhist sutras frequently describe how people interacted with the Buddha Śākyamuni during his lifetime. There was nothing casual or informal about it. They considered themselves to be in the presence of the World-Honored One (*seson*) and the Conqueror (*shōsha*) of suffering and death, whose wisdom and compassion emanated in all directions. Hence, set patterns of etiquette and signs of reverence, similar to the respect shown to other highborn persons in ancient India, became standard in their responses to the Buddha. There are many descriptions of these gestures, and the offerings that accompanied them, in sutras that circulated in Japan:

Lotus Sutra, chapter 4: "At that time . . . Subhūti, Mahākātyāyana, Mahākāśyapa, and Mahāmaudgalyāyana . . . rose from their seats, arranged their robes, bared their right shoulders, and bowed their right knees to the ground. Pressing their palms together with a single mind, they bent their bodies in a gesture of respect and, gazing up in reverence at the face of the Honored One, said to the Buddha. . . ."[11]

Sutra of the Great Nirvana Without Remainder, chapter 17: "Then Cunda . . . hung up silken banners and parasols, and carried in, along with these, incense, flowers, and garlands."[12]

These passages describe the formalities that accompanied interaction with Śākyamuni Buddha. Their stylized gestures of respect and veneration, as well as the variety of gifts and offerings, have been recast and perpetuated as a repertoire of ritual activities and offerings performed at Buddhist temples.

In most temples, the day begins with some type of morning routine. If the icon is cordoned off or hidden away overnight, its enclosure is ceremonially opened. The altar table in front is furnished with fresh supplies if needed—principally, incense, flowers, and candles. The first ritual event of the day is a morning ceremony. If the site is a small community temple, the resident priest might perform it alone. If it is a major temple such as a large Zen monastery, dozens or even scores of Buddhist priests might participate. They would file into the hall in a solemn and orderly fashion and bow to the Buddha, often with their palms held together reverentially. The senior priest leading the service would approach the altar and bow, perhaps offering incense or some other type of offering. The participants would form lines or rows, either in front or at the two sides of the hall, and prostrate themselves on the floor before assuming a formal sitting position. The ceremony itself consists of a series of recitations or chants, some performed by the senior priest and others by everyone in chorus. They typically include an opening invocation, ritualized confession and repentance, taking the Three Buddhist Refuges (in the Buddha, the Dharma, and the Sangha), singing praises to the

Buddha, reciting Buddhist scripture (the famous *Heart Sutra* is quite common), chanting the Buddha's name, reaffirming Bodhisattva vows, and offering up karmic merit for the benefit of all living beings. The length of the ceremony may be short (perhaps fifteen minutes) or long (over an hour), and the actual content varies tremendously depending on the type of temple and the particular Buddhist figure enshrined.[13] In many temples a parallel ceremony is held at the end of the day, though it is usually not as long as the morning one. Thus, in Japanese temples there is a ritualized occasion every day in which one stands in the presence of the Buddhist icon and interacts with it.

Temples also have regular routines to supply the icon's "material" needs. Food is the most common item and is usually provided on a daily basis. It can be a simple presentation of fresh fruit on the altar or, on special days, a fully prepared vegetarian meal (*shōjin ryōri*), including rice, pickled vegetables, tofu, steamed vegetables, and soup (fig. 70).[14] The food is placed before the icon and removed later before it has a chance to spoil. The presentation of food to the image in this way emulates the merit-making practice of almsgiving to the Buddha and his disciples in Śākyamuni's day. In rare cases the image is provided with clothing too. A few icons are sculpted naked (fig. 24) and then regularly clothed in actual Buddhist robes. A well-known example is the Bodhisattva Jizō at the Denkōji Temple in Nara, who is dressed in new robes each summer in a community ceremony at the temple (fig. 71).[15] This again emulates the ancient custom of offering new robes to the Buddha and his disciples each year after the rainy season.

Interaction with an enshrined figure follows a somewhat different format in esoteric Buddhism—primarily in Shingon and Tendai temples—where the ritual takes place at a low square altar table bearing ritual implements and vessels with food, flowers, candles, incense, and liquids, all set up to symbolically serve the Buddhist divinity a meal. The ceremony is complex, with many meticulous steps conducted in five stages: preparation of the practitioner; preparation of the ritual space; inviting, greeting, and feting the

Buddhist divinity; merging with the divinity; and finally departure of the divinity, dissolution of the ritual site, and withdrawal of the practitioner. Perhaps the most famous example of this type of ritual is the *goma* or fire ceremony, often performed with Fudō Myōō as the principal icon. The wooden sticks burned in the fire, typically with a vow or prayer written on each, "feed" the deity (fig. 72). To the extent that the ritual is said to include a merging of the priest with the divinity, the ceremony seems to go beyond a mere material offering to a god.[16]

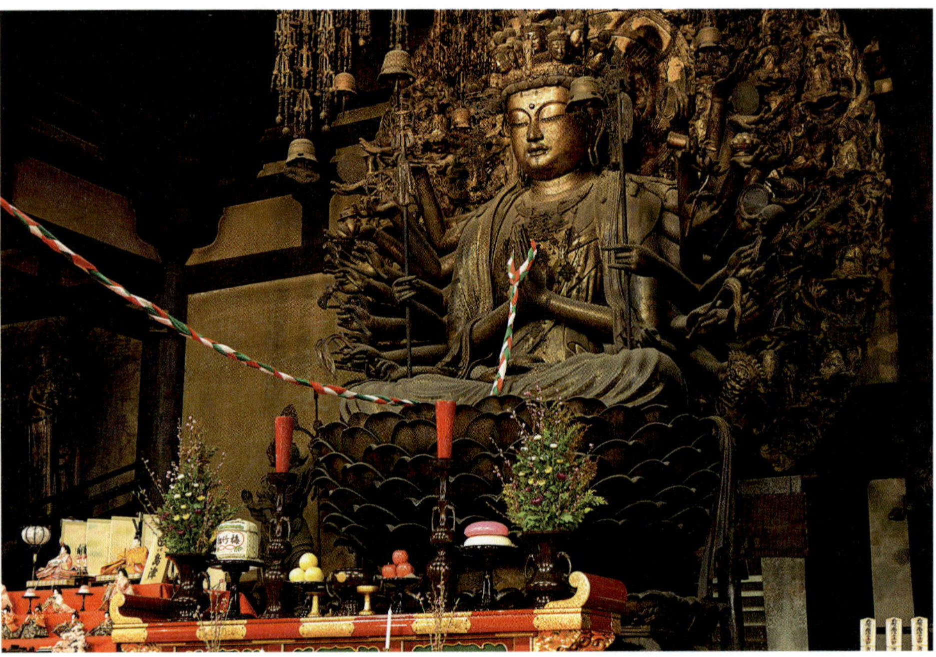

Fig. 70. Food offerings to Kannon Bodhisattva, 12th cent. Sanjūsangendō Temple, Kyoto. Offerings of fresh fruit and rice cakes, along with flowers, votive candles, incense, and even a small cask of Japanese sake, have been placed before the eleven-headed thousand-armed Kannon Bodhisattva of the Sanjūsangendō Temple. The occasion is a celebration of spring replete with a seasonal display of Japanese dolls to the left of the altar table. The multicolored cord draped from Kannon's hands extends outside the restricted inner area so that celebrants may touch or hold it as they offer prayers, thereby experiencing a tangible link to the Bodhisattva.

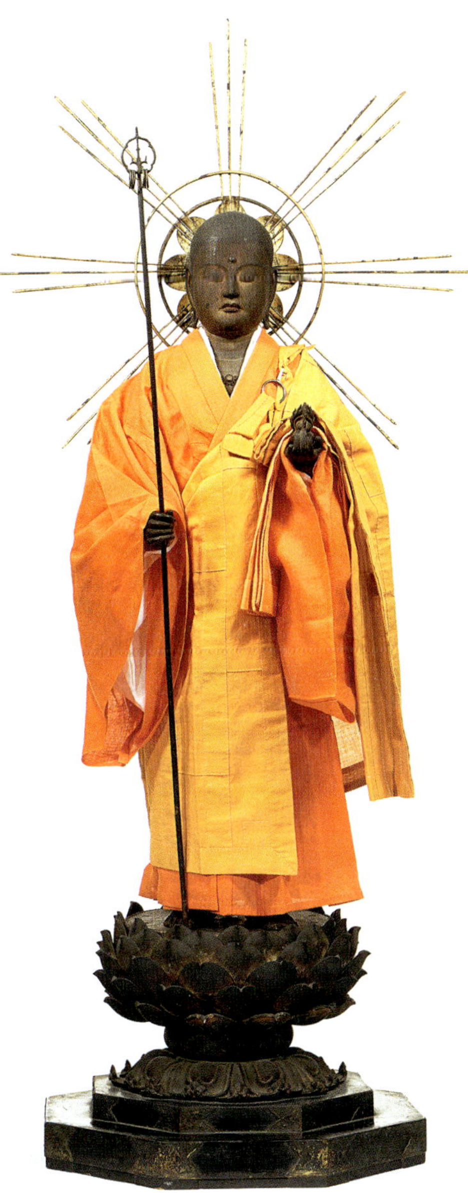

Fig. 71. **Jizō Bodhisattva clothed in robes, 13th cent. Denkōji Temple, Nara.** This three-foot image, known as the Naked Jizō, is ritually dressed in miniature Buddhist robes during a mid-summer ceremony each year conducted by the temple's priests. The new robes are sewn by temple parishioners as an offering and an act of piety.

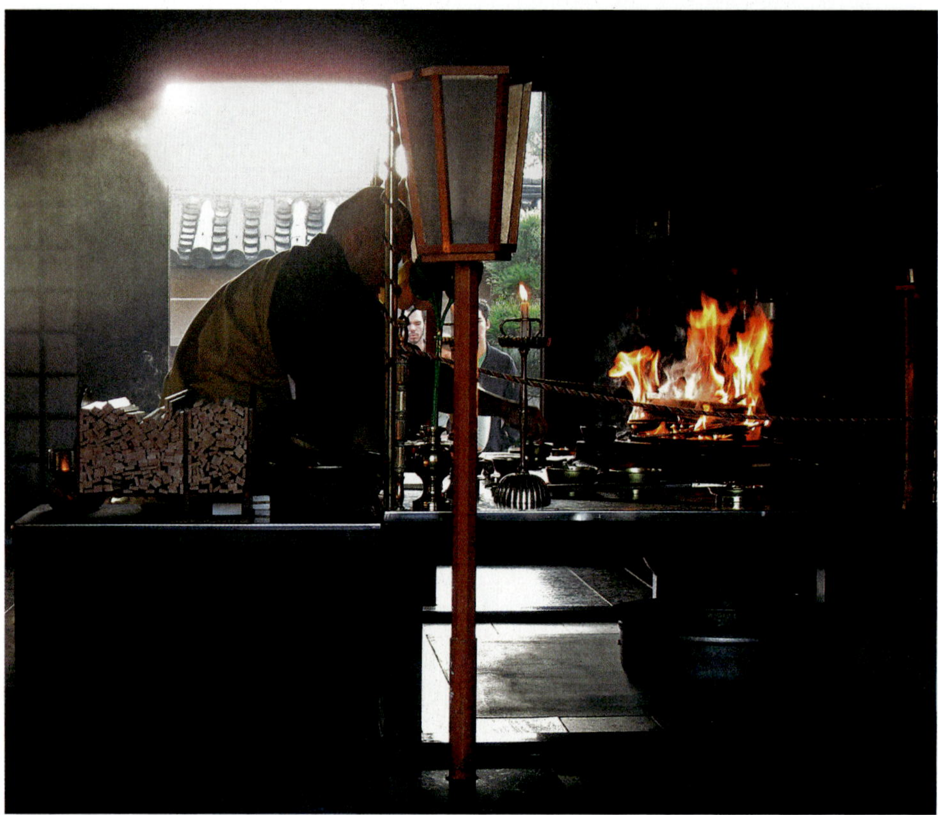

Fig. 72. Shingon *goma* fire ceremony. Tōji Temple, Kyoto. The *goma* ritual, performed before an esoteric Buddhist image, treats the figure as an honored guest to be invited, hosted, feted, given offerings, and sent off. This esoteric altar is a special type where small sticks of wood with written supplications (from the stack next to the priest) can be fed to the fire as offerings. The priest engages the Buddhist divinity through hand-signs, invocations, and mental reflections, while other participants chant or sound gongs in the background.

Virtually every temple has a calendar of holy days and ritual occasions that it follows each year. These events address a host of religious and communal concerns, some structured around direct engagement with Buddhist icons, and others marking seasonal transitions or commemorative activities. Frequently, though not universally, the calendar includes the following events: services of celebration, thanksgiving, and prayer at New Year's; commemoration of Śākyamuni's death in the second month (fig. 18); ceremonies at the time of the spring and autumn equinox in the third and ninth months; festivities surrounding Śākyamuni's birthday in the fourth month (fig. 11); the Obon remembrance of the ancestors in the seventh or eighth month; celebration of the Buddha's enlightenment in the twelfth month; a ritual meal offered to "starving ghosts" (*gaki*) and sentient beings reborn in the hells; and commemoration of the founder of the school of Buddhism to which the temple is affiliated (fig. 73).[17]

In addition, many temples have ritual days dedicated specifically to their primary icon. For instance, the Kiyomizu Temple in Kyoto recognizes the eighteenth day of each month as the *ennichi,* or "karmic bond day," on which one can establish a spiritual tie to

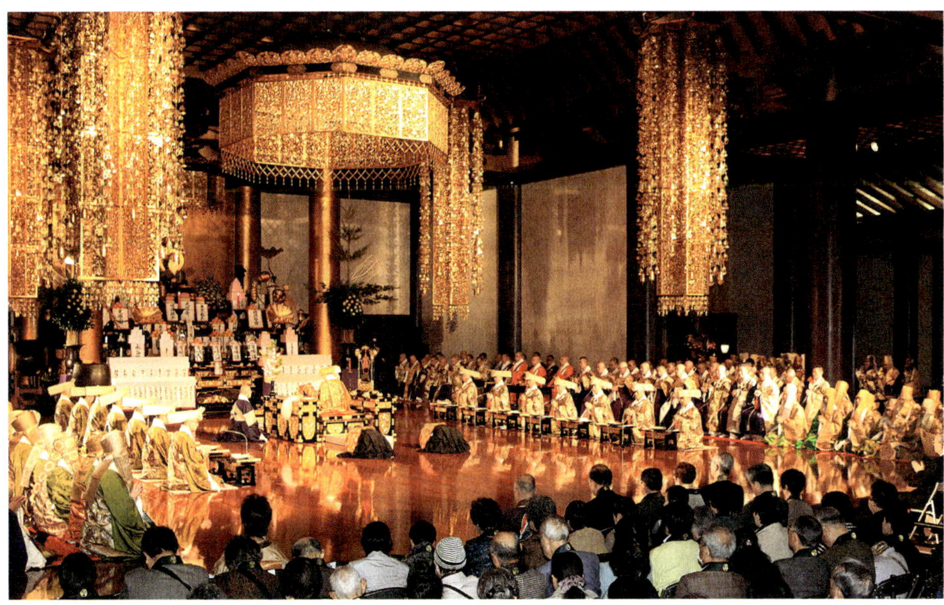

Fig. 73. Founder Memorial Service. Zōjōji Temple, Tokyo. Each year, in early April, a grand memorial service known as the Gyoki Daie is held at the Zōjōji Temple for the founder of the Jōdo school of Buddhism, Hōnen (1133–1212). It is conducted in the main hall of the temple, where an image of Hōnen is installed on a provisional altar placed in front of the central icon of Amida Buddha (fig. 10). Priests from throughout the country come to Zōjōji to participate in this commemoration and to express gratitude for Hōnen's teachings propounding the saving message of Amida Buddha.

its miraculous eleven-headed thousand-armed image of Kannon Bodhisattva, which is known for its efficacy and responsiveness to supplications. Kiyomizu is one of thirty-three temples on the Kannon pilgrimage route of western Japan. Pilgrimage in order to reverence an icon directly has been a perennial practice in Japanese Buddhism, which has helped spread and amplify the fame of many images. It is in this context that the Kiyomizu icon has been celebrated, as crowds would historically flock to the temple on a monthly basis to make offerings and pay homage to the Bodhisattva.[18]

One curious tradition at some temples in Japan is to hide their principal icon from public view. Such images are known as *hibutsu,* "hidden or secret Buddhas," and they typically reside behind the closed doors of a shrine cabinet. This custom can create a spiritual tension in that people may come to the temple to "behold" the Buddha and stand in his presence but are not allowed to view him. The eleven-headed thousand-armed Kannon Bodhisattva at the Kiyomizu Temple, for example, is only put on display once every thirty-three years. But to accommodate visitors who yearn to see his physical form at other times, a replica of the icon is exhibited in front of the closed shrine cabinet.[19] This replica is known as *maedachi,* or figure "standing in front," an object that is found in many temples that have hidden images. In a few extreme cases secret icons are never displayed. The most famous example is the Amida Buddha triad at the Zenkōji Temple in Nagano. This Buddha, flanked by two Bodhisattvas, has been hidden away for so many centuries that a few art historians have questioned whether the original image even exists anymore. As with other celebrated icons such as the Śākyamuni image of the Seiryōji Temple, reputed replicas of the Zenkōji triad have been produced in abundance since medieval times, thereby offering people a visual surrogate of the icon (fig. 74). These replicas circulated throughout Japan over the centuries, generating a nationwide network of satellite chapels that have spread the rituals and renown of the Zenkōji icon far and wide.[20]

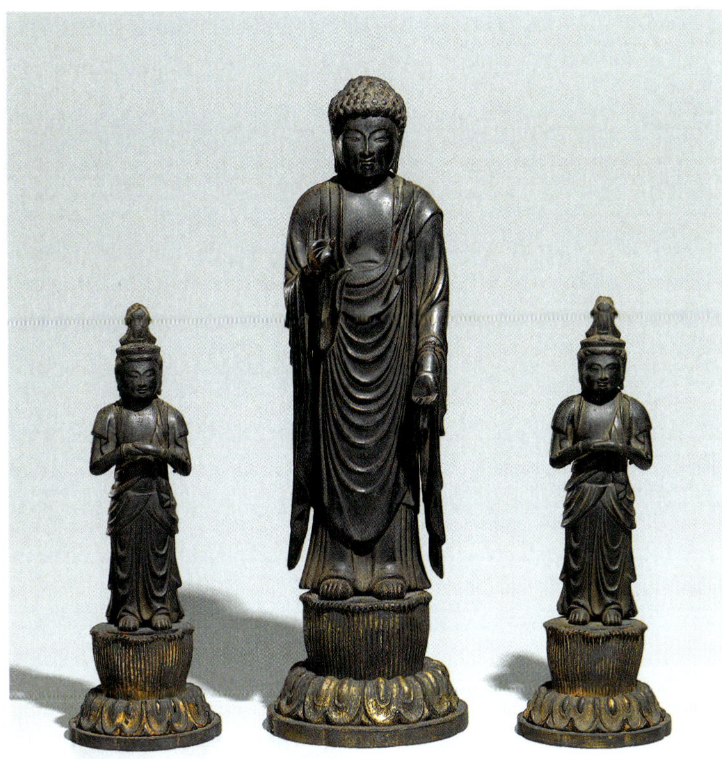

Fig. 74. Zenkōji Amida Triad, 13th–14th cent. These figures depict Amida and his companion Bodhisattvas Kannon and Seishi in a unique iconographic style made famous by the Zenkōji Temple. They are reputed to be a replica of its famous "secret Buddha," which was believed to have miraculous powers even though it was never displayed. Replicas, which were disseminated widely and open to view, were considered extensions of the hidden original and conduits of its spiritual potency. Miracle stories about the Zenkōji triad and its replicas contributed to a popular cult of devotion to the image.

The interaction between devotees and secret Buddhas provides additional insights into the traditional Japanese understanding of Buddhist images. The first is that, even though beholding the Buddha in a literal sense is a characteristic of temple culture, hidden images can evoke just as much veneration as displayed ones. This suggests that the act of standing in the presence of the Buddha does not depend on the Buddha's visibility and can occur when the image is hidden. The second is that, just as the historical Buddha can be replicated in an icon, likewise an icon can impart the Buddha's presence to yet another physical representation. The upshot is that the Buddha makes his presence known in palpable objects, even hidden ones, but those objects are theoretically infinite in number.

As described here, rituals pervade temple life in Japan, many of them involving interaction with "living" Buddhist images. Though it may not be obvious on the surface, these rituals are considered perfectly consistent with and expressive of the threefold paradigm of quest, enlightenment, and compassion that defines the Buddha. There has been a tendency in the modern period to showcase enlightenment among the three—interpreted mostly as a sudden, personal, and transformative awakening. Certainly in the history of Buddhism this event has been crucial to the religion. But Buddhist life has always encompassed a wider, more diverse, and more routinized array of experiences. Ritual experience is one of them. In ritual engagement with an icon people feel that they have entered the world of the Buddha. The temple is a physical setting that can provide this sacred space to encounter and commune with the Buddha, and thereby to experience the compassionate, enlightened, and questing dimensions of his identity. The ritual act, whether aimed widely at the complete enlightenment of all living beings throughout time, or narrowly at the simple healing of a sick child, is always played out against the backdrop of this threefold Buddhist paradigm.

THE GREAT BUDDHA AND THE NUN

Seeing Buddhist images as living entities runs contrary to the reductionist impulse of modern culture. Nonetheless, such a view of icons was pervasive in premodern Japan. This worldview is well illustrated in a painted narrative scroll from the twelfth century entitled the *Miraculous Accounts of Mt. Shigi*. The work is a collection of three stories, with illustrations, about a ninth-century priest named Myōren, who lived an exemplary religious life secluded on Mt. Shigi southwest of Nara. Originally, Myōren was from the remote province of Shinano (present-day Nagano), but as a young man he underwent Buddhist ordination at the Tōdaiji Temple and then withdrew to Mt. Shigi, where he dedicated himself to intensive religious practice for many years. As a result, his spiritual powers increased enormously, and he was reputedly capable of curing illness and other miraculous acts, as recounted in the first two stories in the *Miraculous Accounts of Mt. Shigi.*

The third story, however, is actually about Myōren's older sister, referred to simply as "the nun" (*amagimi*). When her brother left home to become a priest, she lost contact with him, but some twenty years later, after she herself took up the life of a Buddhist nun, she decided to search for him. The text recounts her story as follows:

> Alas, there was one older sister in Shinano [province]. Since she had not seen [Myōren] for years, she thought: "So, this young cleric said he would undergo ordination at the Tōdaiji Temple, and he seems to have gone up to the capital [of Nara] and stayed. Ah! I wonder how he is." She [too] left for the capital thinking, "I will seek him out." As she searched in the vicinity of the Yamashinadera [i.e., Kōfukuji] and Tōdaiji temples, every person just said, "No, I do not know him," whenever she asked, "Is there a young cleric named Myōren?" As might be expected, since more than twenty years had passed, there was no one who knew about these earlier matters. She [began to] despair as she asked people, and she thought, "What shall I do? If only I could hear of his condition, I would then return home."
>
> With that, she spent one night before the Great Buddha of the Tōdaiji Temple doing [religious] practices. Throughout the night she [implored the Buddha] saying, "Please tell me even in a dream the place where Myōren might be." Amid this, she dozed off and in a dream saw this Buddha saying, "The place that you seek, where this priest is, is to the west, and then south. There is a mountain in the "sheep-monkey" [astrological] direction [i.e., southwest]. Go seeking the place where purple clouds hover around that mountain." She then awoke and wondered intently when it would become daylight. As she detected a faint light, she looked out in the sheep-monkey direction and there the mountain appeared faintly with purple clouds hovering. She was overjoyed as she departed (fig. 75).[21]

According to the text, the nun proceeded to Mt. Shigi and was soon reunited with her brother. There she presented him with a heavy

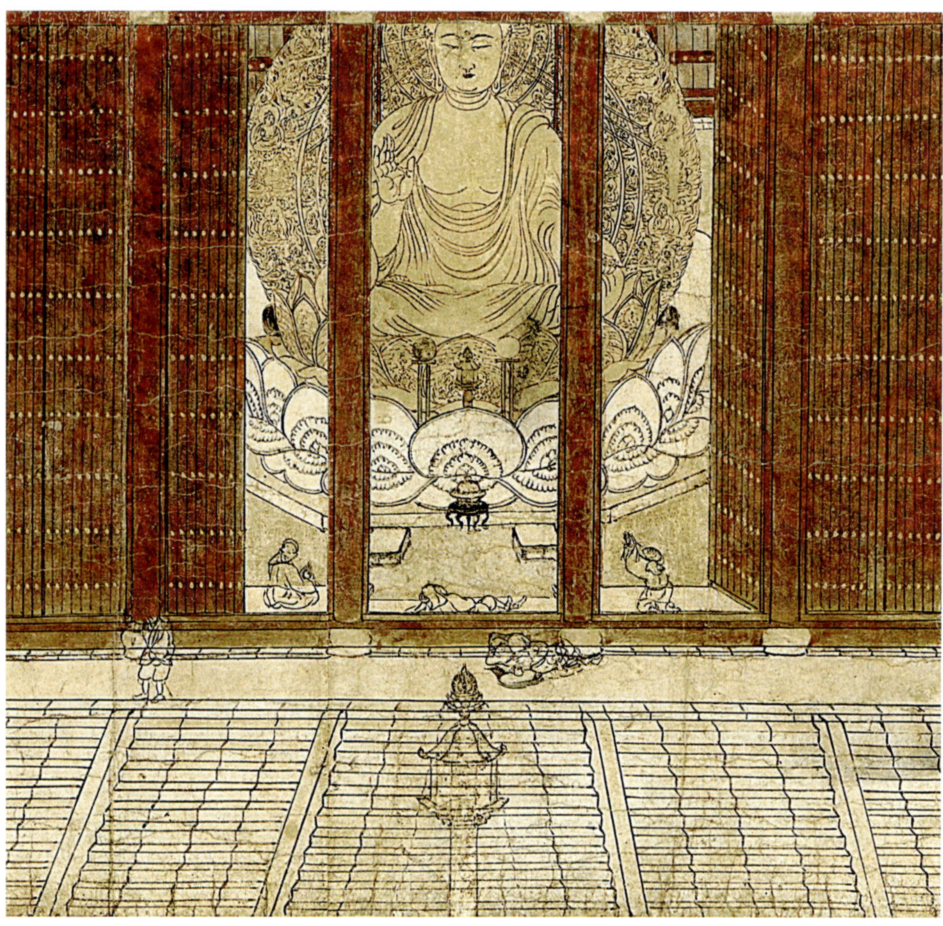

Fig. 75. Illustration from *Miraculous Accounts of Mt. Shigi*, 12th cent. This scene from a narrative scroll illustrates the night spent by the nun before the Great Buddha of Tōdaiji. The line drawings of figures on the threshold of the main hall and just outside it represent her actions over the course of the night—praying to the Buddha (*right*); reclining inside the door gazing up at the Buddha and then sleeping outside where the Buddha speaks to her in a dream (*middle*); sitting reverently, perhaps chanting and expressing gratitude (*left*); and finally departing from the temple for Mt. Shigi (*far left*), where she will be reunited with her brother. It is noteworthy that the nun remains at the threshold, never venturing far into the temple. Women were supposedly barred from entering Tōdaiji during this period—a type of gender discrimination found in many forms of Buddhism at the time. But they would still pray to the Great Buddha from outside.

robe to keep him warm during his ascetic austerities. He, in turn, ultimately invited her to join him in a life of Buddhist practice on Mt. Shigi, thus culminating her own religious quest.

This story of the nun's visit to the Great Buddha of Tōdaiji exemplifies the premodern Japanese urge to come into the presence of the Buddha and to interact with him in matters of great concern. What this meant in practice was to be in the presence of his iconic image. There, bathed in his wisdom and compassion, miraculous things could occur. This type of activity, expressed in ritual gestures, is what Buddhist life in traditional Japan was all about. Ritual interaction, far from being a hollow or mechanical process, became the form and substance of communication with the Buddha. And the Buddhist icon, far from being a lifeless object, became the identifiable locus of the Buddha's presence in the world.

CHAPTER 8
BEYOND THE BUDDHA IMAGE

One of the largest and most pervasive forms of Buddhism in Japan is the Nichiren school. It is named after the charismatic Buddhist master Nichiren (1222–1282), who preached complete devotion to the *Lotus Sutra* as the hallmark of Buddhist life. He also championed the recitation of the title of the sutra, called the Daimoku, as the primary religious practice for people, urging them specifically to chant the words *Namu Myōhō Rengekyō,* "I take refuge in the *Lotus Sutra of the Marvelous Dharma.*" And he envisioned the various powers of the universe—Buddhas, Bodhisattvas, and other figures—working together to advance the truth and preeminence of the *Lotus.* Nichiren depicted the convergence of these forces in a calligraphic mandala known as the Gohonzon, or "Principal Object of Reverence," in which he inscribed the letters of the Daimoku down the middle as a central axis, and then arrayed on each side the names of specific Buddhas, Bodhisattvas, and other figures who upheld the *Lotus,* ending with his own name just under the Daimoku. This design expresses in a nutshell Nichiren's *Lotus*-centered worldview (fig. 83).

The vision found in Nichiren's calligraphic mandala is detectable in the configuration of the images installed on the central altar of Nichiren temples such as the Kuonji on Mt. Minobu (fig. 76). At first sight its altar area looks much like the inside of other Buddhist temples: gold leaf ornamentation, overhead canopy, large votive lamps, and elaborate floral decorations; a grand altar table for offering incense, flowers, and food; and a raised platform for enshrined images and objects. What is noteworthy is that the central and highest image on the platform is not the Buddha per se but rather a combination of the written letters of the Daimoku and a statue of Nichiren at its base.

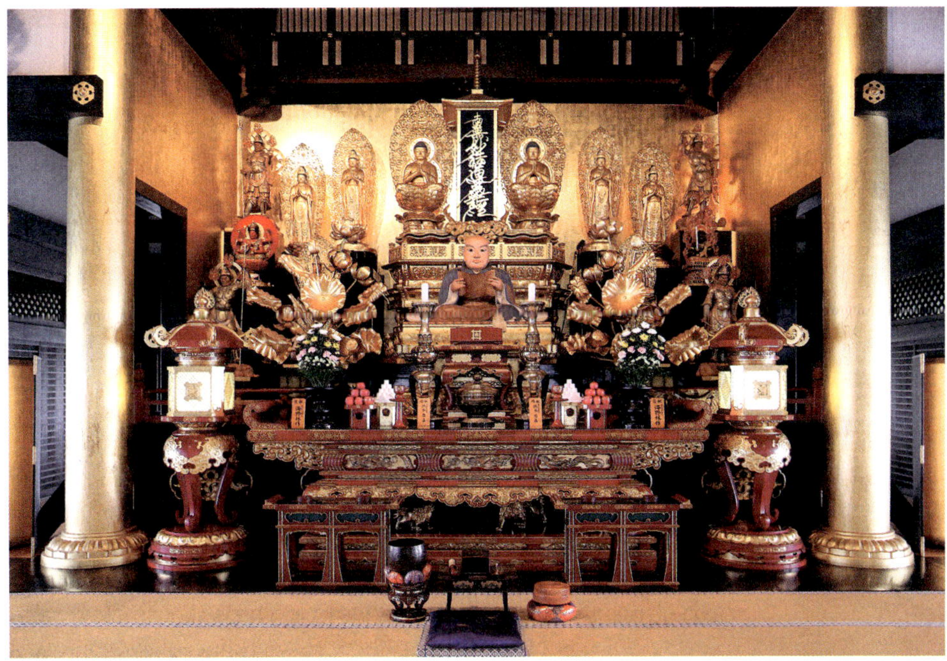

Fig. 76. **Central altar of the Great Hall. Kuonji Temple, Minobu.** Upon the central altar the primary object of reverence is the vertical inscription of the Daimoku at the top center, written in cursive Chinese characters on a black background. The inscription is adorned with a pagoda roof on top, and just below it is an icon of Nichiren himself holding the *Lotus Sutra*. On each side of the inscription are the two principal Buddhas of the sutra, Śākyamuni and Tahō, and beyond them are four Bodhisattvas revered in the sutra. At the four corners of the altar are the Four Heavenly Kings, and between each pair on the left and right are the Myōō Aizen and Fudō, all guarding the periphery of the sacred space. Below the altar is a table for incense, flowers, and food offerings, with a cushioned platform in front where a priest can sit to offer incense and chant the Daimoku or the sutra. Located on Mt. Minobu, the Kuonji Temple was founded by Nichiren in 1281, the year before his death.

In addition, the two main Buddhas of the *Lotus Sutra* are shown alongside the Daimoku, as are *Lotus*-related Bodhisattvas and guardian figures at the edges—all roughly following the layout of the mandala. Different Nichiren temples have variations of this arrangement—adding or subtracting iconographic figures—but even in its most elaborate format the centerpiece is always the Daimoku inscription (or the entire Gohonzon mandala), paired with an image of Nichiren.

What the example shows is that in some Buddhist temples—actually, in many—the central object of reverence is not an image of the Buddha. In fact, a number of things besides classical icons have served to inspire Buddhists over the centuries: images of revered masters, religious inscriptions, sutra scrolls, physical relics of the Buddha, and other objects. In seeking to understand their function, one should approach them much as one does icons. Just as an icon has a complex association with the Buddha—sometimes as a representation or a symbol, but more often as an instantiation—likewise these objects are more than commemorative tokens or models for behavior. As in the case of icons, they can be a palpable manifestation of the Buddha in the world. That is, people may behold the Buddha and encounter his Dharma in such objects as much as in an icon. In essence, there is an easy transposition or substitution among Buddhism's many sacred objects, so that the meaning of one may be effortlessly discovered in another. Hence, if one encounters a sacred inscription such as the Daimoku in a temple instead of an image of the Buddha, the experience is considered commensurate with encountering the Buddha himself. And just as the Buddha embodies compassion and enlightenment and the Buddhist quest, so these objects exude and inspire them as well.

BUDDHIST RELICS

One type of object revered in Buddhism throughout its history is a relic of the Buddha. Known in Sanskrit as *śarīra* and in Japanese as *shari* or *Busshari,* the term Buddhist relics refers in most cases to the bodily remains of Śākyamuni after his cremation—things such as his bones and teeth, and the crystalline beads that formed in the funeral pyre. Besides bodily relics, Buddhism also recognizes contact relics of the Buddha—objects that he came into contact with, such as his begging bowl or robe or walking staff—and also commemoration relics—indicators of the Buddha's activities, such as the images installed at important sites in his life, or his footprint with its multi-spoke Dharma-wheel mark (fig. 19). But among Buddhist relics, bodily ones seem to have attracted the most veneration. For instance, the Temple of the Tooth, or Daḷadā Māligāwa, in Kandy, Sri Lanka, is renowned for enshrining a tooth relic of the Buddha (fig. 77). Likewise, the Famensi Temple outside the traditional Chinese capital of Chang'an (present-day Xi'an) is celebrated for its finger-bone relic. In Japan, however, it was the bead-like crystal remains of the Buddha that became the most widely recognized type of relic.[1]

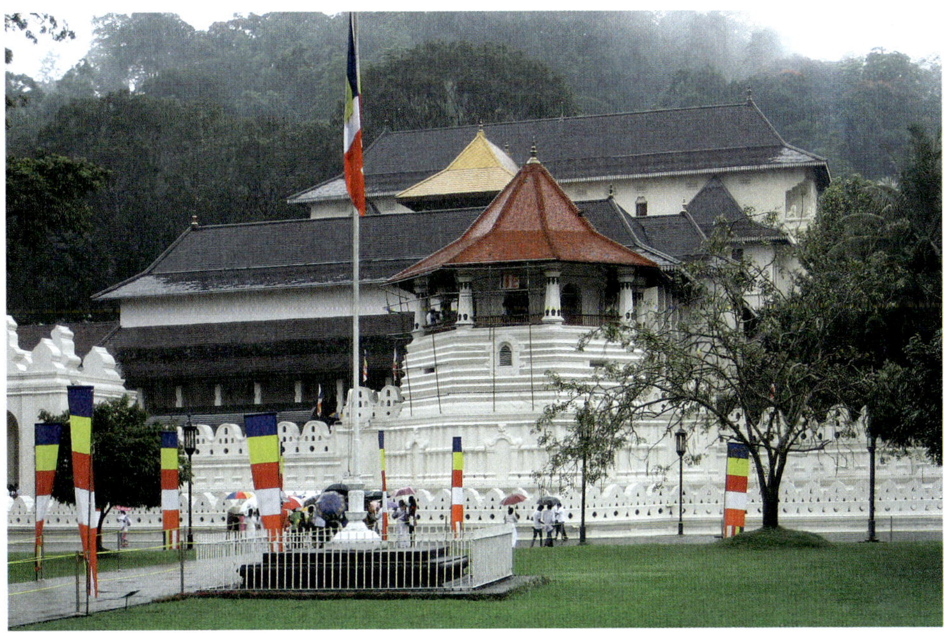

Fig. 77. **Temple of the Tooth (Daḷadā Māligāwa), Kandy.** The tooth relic of Śākyamuni Buddha enshrined here is one of the most revered objects in Sri Lankan Buddhism. Supposedly retrieved from the Buddha's funeral pyre, the relic was preserved for hundreds of years in India before being carried to Sri Lanka in the early fourth century, where it was entrusted to the ruler for safekeeping. Successive kings and dynasties became the custodian of the relic until it was carried to Kandy, the mountain fortress of the last Sri Lankan kings, during the colonial period. In Kandy this moat-encircled temple was built for its enshrinement, where the relic is preserved in seven nested, stupa-shaped reliquaries made of gold. Ceremonies are performed before the relic three times a day, with a ritual bath weekly. During the annual Esala Perahera festival, it is paraded through the streets of Kandy on the back of a magnificently caparisoned elephant.

The veneration of the Buddha's relics began, it seems, almost immediately after his demise. According to accounts of Śākyamuni's final days, he gave instructions on his deathbed that his remains should be treated the same way that a "chariot-wheel-turning" king's would be. After his death the Mallas, a powerful tribe from the nearby town of Kuśinagara, took charge of making these arrangements. Once they had allowed people to show their final reverence to the Buddha's body, they wrapped it in many layers of new cloth, immersed it in oil, and cremated it on a pyre of aromatic woods and fragrances. At that point the remains were to be interred in a stupa, or large hemispherical burial mound, at a crossroads or public place where people could pay homage, just as they would to a wheel-turning king. But another tribe arrived wanting to take possession of the relics from the Mallas, and then six more appeared, all vying for control. In the end the relics were divided into equal portions for the various contending parties and enshrined in stupas at different locations. According to tradition, the great Indian king Aśoka (ca. 3rd cent. BCE) subsequently took possession of all the relics, subdivided them into 84,000 parts, and placed them in stupas throughout his empire.[2]

In ancient India, Buddhist stupas became a focal point for the efflorescence of the religion. They were considered sites where one could come into the presence of the Buddha, since his relics were enshrined there. At first, stupas and monasteries were located separately, supposedly to distinguish between the religious activities of the Buddhist laity and the clergy. But gradually the two types of institutions tended to merge. Stupas were the place where the life of the Buddha was rehearsed and celebrated, and where worship, praises, and offerings were made to him. As icons of the Buddha came into common use, especially at pilgrimage spots associated with his life, they too were installed in stupas, endowing these sites with a dual presence: the Buddha as enshrined image and as interred relics. This convergence of images and relics prefigured the practice of putting relics inside an icon as a way of bringing it to life. Both lay Buddhists and clerics who frequented stupas wished that after death their own cremated remains would be placed in the precincts of stupas so that they would benefit spiritually from proximity to the Buddha's relics. As Buddhism spread to East Asia, the Indian stupa underwent an architectural metamorphosis into the multi-tiered pagoda.[3] But its association with relics of the Buddha and the enshrinement of his image persisted, and was subsequently transmitted to Japan (fig. 78).

References to Buddhism in the ancient *Nihon shoki,* or *Chronicles of Japan,* indicate that relics—in addition to icons, ritual objects, and religious texts—were treasured during Buddhism's earliest period in Japan. The chronicle records that in 584 a relic spontaneously appeared atop a serving of sanctified vegetarian food. It was tested for authenticity—pounded to no effect with a hammer and anvil, and thrown into water to see if it could be made to float or sink telepathically. Passing these tests, the relic was subsequently enshrined at the top of the central pillar of a newly built pagoda, thereby paralleling the link between relics and stupas in India.[4] Serendipitously, excavations in 1956 of the site where the pagoda originally stood yielded a gilded box containing a relic, presumably the one mentioned in the text, which apparently had been placed in a new reliquary in the late twelfth century after a fire destroyed the pagoda.[5] This episode reflects not only the reception and veneration of Buddhist relics in Japan but also a belief that they could materialize miraculously, in addition to being transported physically from one country to another. Needless to say, such a conviction led to a proliferation of relics throughout the Buddhist world.

Though not as prevalent as icons of the Buddha, relics nonetheless have had a visible and enduring place in Japanese Buddhism. The enshrinement of relics and the performance of a relic ceremony (*sharie*) occurred at major temples in early Japanese history such as the Tōshōdaiji in Nara and Shingon Buddhism's Tōji in Kyoto. A similar relic ceremony was instituted at the Tendai monastic complex on Mt. Hiei outside Kyoto in the ninth century after the Tendai priest Ennin (794–864) traveled to China and brought back relics to

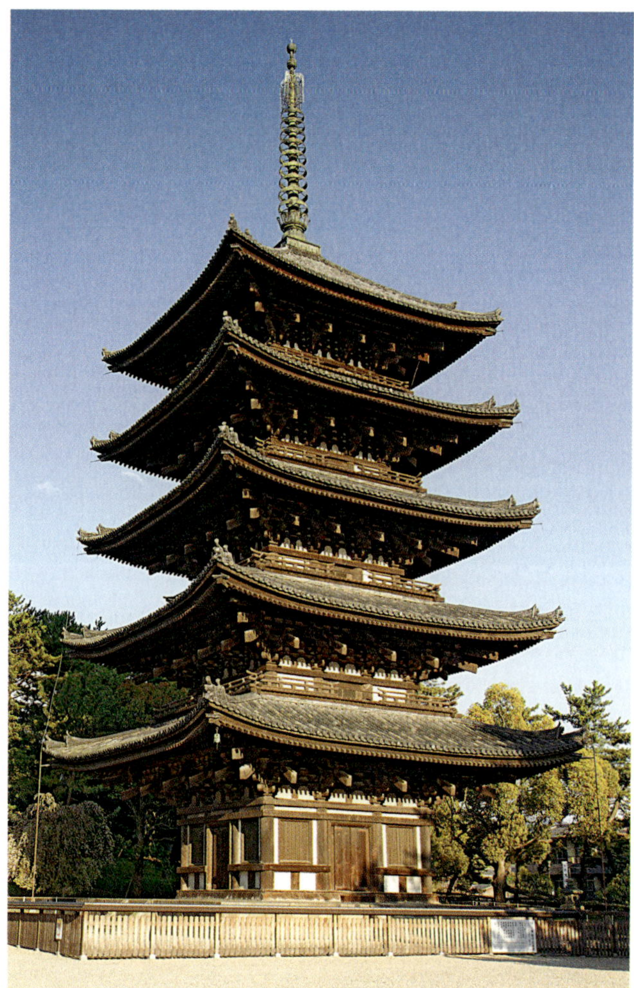

Fig. 78. **Five-tiered pagoda, 15th cent. Kōfukuji Temple, Nara.** The evolution of the hemispherical stupa of India into the multi-tiered pagoda of East Asia was one of the notable architectural developments of Buddhism. Shown here is the five-tiered pagoda of the Kōfukuji Temple in Nara, the second tallest in Japan, built in 1426. Like stupas, pagodas were associated with the Buddha's relics from the first, and a receptacle for them was often embedded in the foundation stone on which the central pillar of a pagoda rested. Eventually images of the Buddha came to embody his presence as much as relics did, and many pagodas gained renown as repositories of revered icons. The Kōfukuji pagoda contains four triads of images, each consisting of a Buddha and two flanking Bodhisattvas, on the four sides of the central pillar on the pagoda's first floor. The Buddhas of the past and future, Śākyamuni and Miroku, are positioned on the north-south axis, while the Buddhas of the present, Yakushi and Amida, who preside over Pure Lands in the eastern and western direction, respectively, are on the east-west axis.

enshrine. An account of the ceremony in the tenth-century work *The Three Jewels* quotes the Buddha as saying:

> Whether you make offerings to the Buddha's relics or to the living Buddha, the merit is exactly the same, and there is no difference in the benefits yielded. One instance of relic worship will erase sins and lead to rebirth in heaven. Prepare jeweled caskets and place the relics inside them. Build jeweled stupas and place the caskets inside them.[6]

The text goes on to proclaim that the Buddha is eternal, and that any one venerating relics will have a purified heart because the Buddha himself is pure and empty. This culture of relic veneration developed further in the thirteenth and fourteenth centuries when a new format of Buddhist liturgy known as the *kōshiki,* containing popular styles of chanting and singing, was used for relic services. Sometimes this relic *kōshiki* was performed in conjunction with *kōshiki* dedicated to the commemoration of Śākyamuni's death, the remembrance of momentous places in his life, and the praise of his sixteen eminent arhat disciples. But other times the celebration occurred separately, depending on a temple's yearly ritual calendar and the pedigree of its relics.[7] Even today the relic ceremony is conducted annually in many temples in Japan. For instance, the Engakuji Zen monastery in Kamakura performs it each year in mid-October.

The most common relics in Japan are tiny gem-like beads of various colors and shades, reflecting the widespread belief that Śākyamuni, when cremated, left behind precious adamantine stones that are quite different from ordinary human remains. Opulent reliquaries were crafted in Japan to hold these numinous treasures, often constructed so that the relics inside could be seen. In some cases reliquaries might be placed in a small casket, or in nested caskets, especially if they were interred under the central pillar of a pagoda at a temple. In other cases, they might take the form of an elaborate miniature pagoda or stupa, placed inside a shrine cabinet or on an altar just as a Buddhist icon would be (fig. 79). Such installations invite the same type of reverence for relics that is shown to enshrined images of the Buddha.[8]

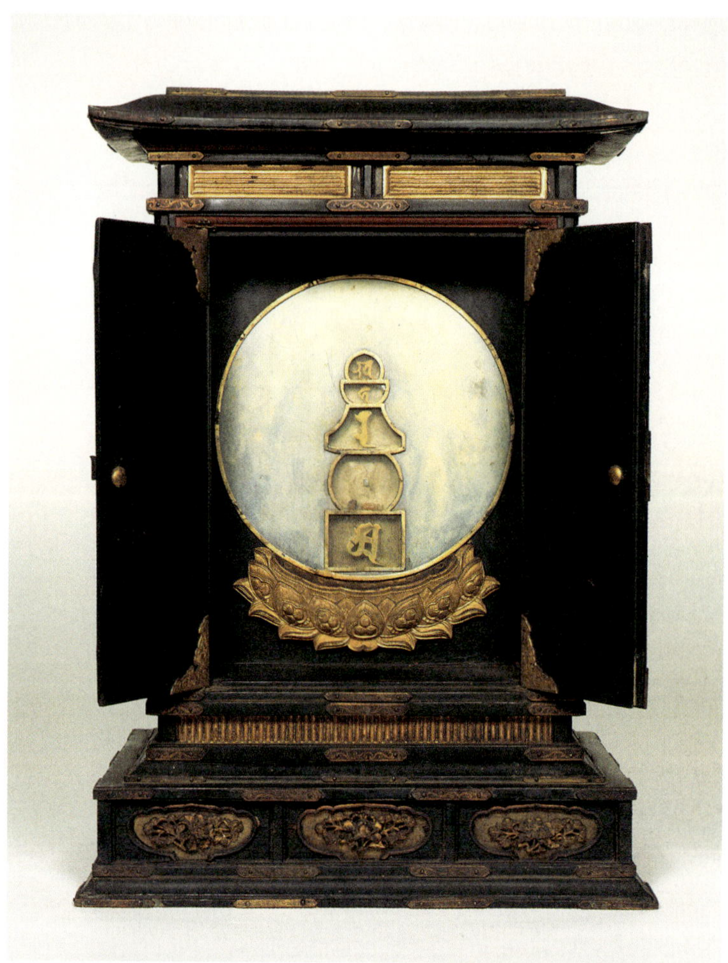

Fig. 79. Buddhist reliquary in the form of a five-element stupa, 15th cent. Five-element stupas display symbols of the five elements of the universe: the square block at the bottom symbolizes earth; the round orb, water; the triangular roof-like pyramid, fire; the bowl-shaped hemisphere, wind; and the teardrop jewel on top, emptiness. On four of the five elements shown here the Sanskrit letter representing that element is inscribed in gold. Inside the fifth, the round orb of this reliquary, four small stone-like relics have been placed and are faintly visible. The reliquary is installed in a *zushi,* or shrine cabinet, suitable for placement on an altar table in a temple or private chapel. The doors of the cabinet could be opened during the day and closed at night, or whenever needed, just as they would be if an image of the Buddha were enshrined.

Relics, though parallel to icons in certain ways, have sometimes performed other functions. Historically, they were thought to imbue the possessor with special powers and authority, and hence were coveted by rulers and contending parties. The story of the eight tribes vying for Śākyamuni's relics after his cremation and of King Aśoka later taking control of them indicates how old the tie is between Buddhist relics and rulership. Possessing and protecting them was part and parcel of the ancient paradigm of the virtuous Buddhist king. In Japan too relics became treasured by the imperial household, aristocratic regents, and samurai warlords, all of whom thought they bestowed legitimacy on their rule. Relics were also believed to have magical properties: to insure good fortune, thwart enemies, cure disease, and make rain. In fact relics were commonly conflated with Buddhism's mythical wish-granting jewel, a miracle-producing orb associated with various Bodhisattvas and supposedly possessed by the wheel-turning king. As a result, ornate reliquaries frequently took the appearance of tear-shaped jewels, in contrast to the traditional pagoda or stupa motif (fig. 80).[9]

Although the perception of relics as magic talismans may seem at odds with their spiritual identity as instantiations of the Buddha, using them for worldly benefits was never considered problematic in traditional Japan. The prevailing view was that the Buddha makes his presence known in both the spiritual and the material realm, so his relics were recognized simultaneously as sources of authority and power and as objects of veneration, embodying the Buddha's compassion and enlightenment.

RELIGIOUS TEXTS

Sacred texts of Buddhism are another type of object revered alongside icons, or occasionally in place of them. These texts have a more complex and multivalent meaning, for while they are physical objects, like icons and relics, that can be enshrined and ritually

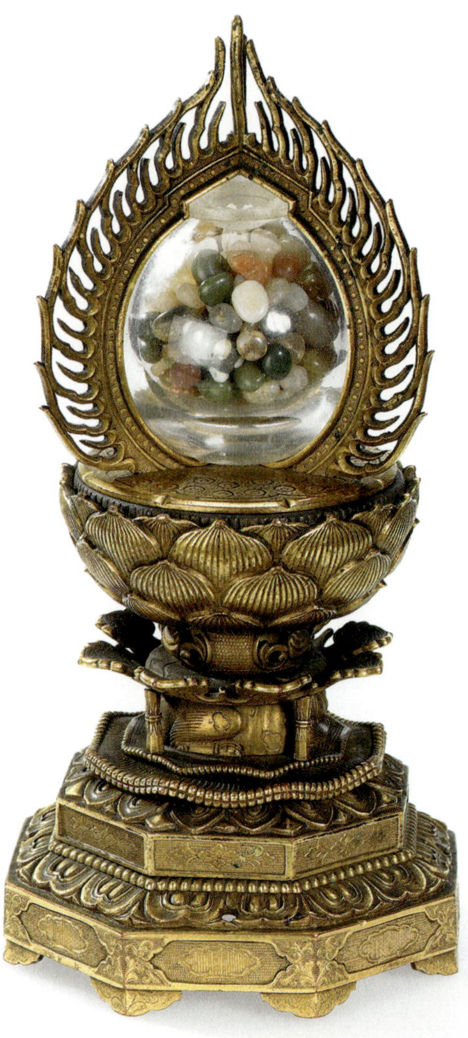

Fig. 80. Buddhist reliquary in the shape of a wish-granting jewel, 16th–17th cent. This reliquary combines the veneration of relics with the aura of a wish-granting jewel, a sacred object with miraculous powers associated with certain Bodhisattvas and other figures. The jewel rests on a lotus pedestal and is enclosed by a flaming nimbus, just as an image of the Buddha might be. The crystal container reveals an abundance of relics—polished stones, bead-like objects, and possibly glass—all of which were treated as the numinous remains of the Buddha or other revered figures, no matter where the relics were acquired. Reliquaries were commonly enshrined in a case or cabinet or enclosure of some type and displayed for ritual purposes and on special occasions.

engaged, they are also conceptual objects, discourses that can be grasped mentally and proclaimed verbally. Traditionally in Buddhism all karmic actions, and by extension all things produced by them, can be divided into three categories: physical, verbal, and mental. Hence, the Buddha Śākyamuni was considered to have not only a physical body but also a verbal and a mental one too. His verbal identity is commonly equated to his teachings, or the Dharma, as preserved in Buddhism's scriptures. In fact, some classifications of the Buddha's relics list the so-called Dharma relics as the third category instead of commemoration relics—encompassing anything proclaimed to be the teachings of the Buddha. It is not surprising, then, that religious texts, in addition to bodily relics, are sometimes placed inside Buddhist icons to bring them to life—as in the case of the Śākyamuni image at the Seiryōji Temple in Kyoto. This close association of images, relics, and texts can be found throughout the Buddhist world.[10] Nonetheless, religious texts sometimes take on a separate significance and stand apart from icons and relics as the centerpiece of Buddhist reverence.

According to tradition, the Buddhist canon began when five hundred disciples of Śākyamuni assembled after his death to recount the teachings they had heard. This gathering has become known as the First Buddhist Council. While living, the Buddha presented his teachings orally, leaving behind no writings. Hence, Ānanda, who was Śākyamuni's constant companion and personal attendant, was selected to recite the discourses of the Buddha that he recalled, which became the basis of the sutra section of the canon. The reason these texts begin with the words "Thus have I heard" is because Ānanda supposedly heard them firsthand. The actual evolution of Buddhist sutras as a canonical body of literature is complex, but suffice it to say that the teachings attributed to the Buddha were memorized and transmitted orally for generations and only later committed to writing. Once in written form, the sutras circulated as another type of embodiment of the Buddha around which the religion could coalesce.

Although the sutras of Mahayana Buddhism appeared in India several centuries after Śākyamuni's death, they too were widely accepted as authentic teachings of the Buddha. Many of these sutras contain self-referential statements urging Buddhists to focus their devotion on the text itself. A prime example is in the *Lotus Sutra:*

> If there are persons who embrace, read, recite, expound, and copy the *Lotus Sutra . . . ,* even only one verse, and look upon the sutra with the same reverence as they would the Buddha, presenting various offerings of flowers, incense, necklaces, powder incense, paste incense, incense for burning, silken canopies, streamers and banners, clothing, and music, and pressing their palms together in reverence, then . . . you should understand that such persons have already offered alms to a hundred thousand million Buddhas and in the place of the Buddhas have fulfilled their great vow. . . .[11]

This statement reflects the extent to which the sutra was conceived as a surrogate of the Buddha, functioning as the object of praises, devotions, and offerings that previously were directed to the Buddha in person or to his icon. Some Mahayana sutras even portray devotion to sutras as superior to devotion to stupas where the Buddha's relics are enshrined. This trend has been described as a "cult of the book" in Mahayana Buddhism, resulting in a glorification of sutras as much as images and relics.

East Asia was heir to these Indian tendencies and ultimately developed a strong sutra culture of its own. This is seen particularly in the practice of sutra copying. Written texts quickly became foundational in Buddhism, and transmission of them occurred everywhere that the religion spread. But their production was not merely a mechanical activity. Rather, there was great religious virtue associated with the act of copying and spreading the sutras. Just as one could accrue karmic merit by producing a Buddhist icon, merit also flowed from transcribing sutras. And just as an icon took on a life of its own once produced, sutras likewise came to function as an autonomous voice of the Buddha. Thus, the creators of images and texts, after their work was done, entered into a deferential relationship with the very objects they produced. China in particular offered a hospitable environment for revering sutras, since the veneration of the Confucian classics and other ancient texts was already widespread. Sanskrit and other Indian sutras were, of course, translated into the Chinese language, but that did not lessen their special status as the word of the Buddha. In fact, it integrated them into the Chinese aesthetics of calligraphy, the art of transcribing celebrated texts and inscriptions in masterful handwriting, which was widely practiced in East Asia.[12]

Japan inherited all these conventions surrounding Buddhist sutras and built on them. The practice of sutra copying became common and widespread. In addition to pious individuals, professional scribes and scribal bureaus emerged that performed this activity for devout aristocrats, wealthy patrons, and government-sponsored sutra-copying initiatives. One product of these endeavors was the creation of lavishly produced calligraphic sutra scrolls—for instance, on indigo paper with silver or gold ink, or framed by gorgeous illuminations and decorations. The *Lotus Sutra,* which styled itself as the repository of the Buddha's highest teaching, lent itself to such adornments. Certain calligraphic productions of it place every Chinese character of the text on a tiny lotus-flower pedestal or beside an image of the Buddha or inside a small stupa, as if each letter were a fully embodied Buddha in its own right (fig. 81). Here the differentiation of the text from the icon becomes hazy, since every character of the sutra is revered as an ever-present Buddha.[13]

The sacred status of sutras led to a number of practices in Japan whereby texts and scrolls became the central objects of Buddhist ritual. In the tenth through the twelfth centuries, for instance, powerful Buddhists from aristocratic and imperial families initiated projects to have sets of the entire Buddhist canon copied, typically comprising over five thousand scrolls. Some of these sets were produced in beautiful calligraphic editions and stored in the sutra

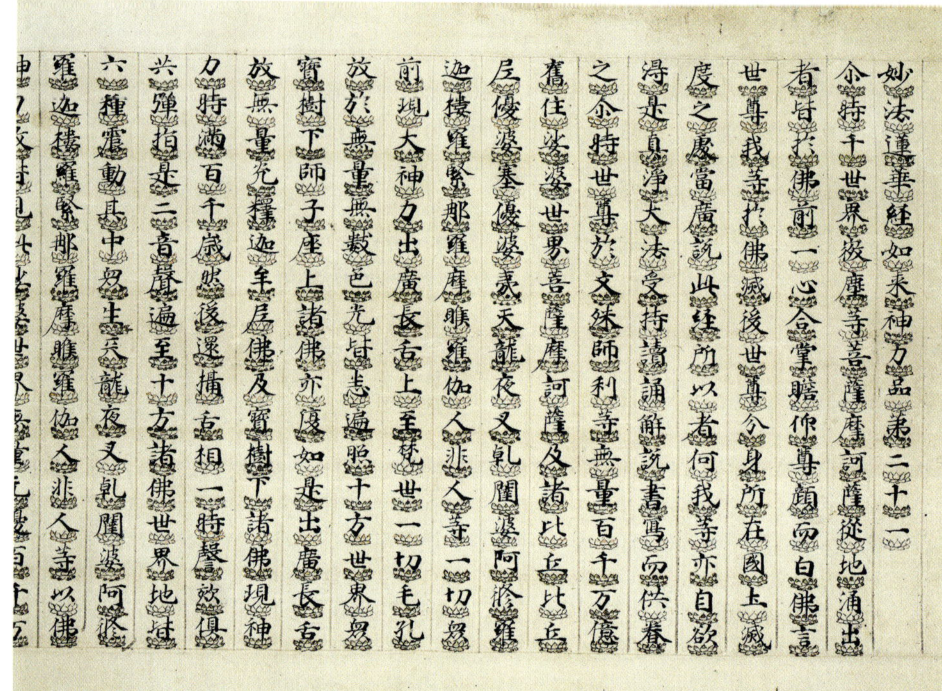

妙法蓮華經如來神力品第二十一
尓時千世界微塵等菩薩摩訶薩從地涌出
者皆於佛前一心合掌瞻仰尊顏而白佛言
世尊我等於佛滅後世尊分身所在國土滅
度之處當廣說此經所以者何我等亦自欲
得是真淨大法受持讀誦解說書寫而供養
之尓時世尊於文殊師利等無量百千万億
舊住娑婆世界菩薩摩訶薩及諸比丘比丘
尼優婆塞優婆夷天龍夜叉乾闥婆阿修羅
迦樓羅緊那羅摩睺羅伽人非人等一切衆
前現大神力出廣長舌上至梵世一切毛孔
放於無量無數色光皆悉遍照十方世界衆
寶樹下師子座上諸佛亦復如是出廣長舌
放無量光釋迦牟尼佛及寶樹下諸佛現神
力時滿百千歲然後還攝舌相一時謦欬俱
共彈指是二音聲遍至十方諸佛世界地皆
六種震動其中衆生天龍夜叉乾闥婆阿修
羅迦樓羅緊那羅摩睺羅伽人非人等以佛

Fig. 81. Ornamented manuscript of the *Lotus Sutra*, 12th cent. This elegant handwritten copy of "The Supernatural Powers of the Tathagata," chapter 21 of the *Lotus Sutra,* was created with silver rules between vertical lines of text—read from right to left—and multicolored lotus flowers painted exquisitely under each character. The *Lotus Sutra* presents itself as the highest Dharma of the Buddha, and thus as an embodiment of his identity. This confluence or interchangeability of the sutra with the Buddha is conveyed symbolically by the lotus pedestal beneath every character, suggesting that each one is a manifestation of the Buddha.

repositories (*kyōzō*) of grand temples built by these elites. While one might think that these repositories operated as libraries, they in fact functioned as a sacred space for the sutras. At some temples there were annual ceremonies during which the sutra scrolls were ritually celebrated and offered flowers and incense just as a Buddhist image would be. Icons were installed in other halls of the temples and regular rituals were performed in their presence as well, so the sutra repositories operated in parallel with them rather than in

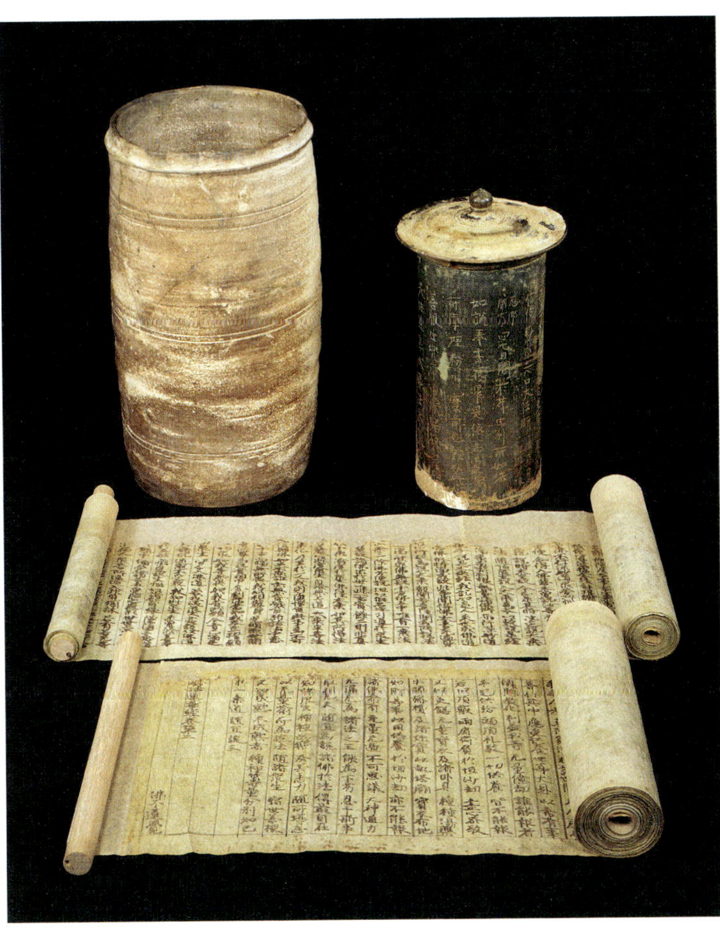

Fig. 82. Sutra canister, 12th cent. These objects, excavated at Kokawa in Wakayama prefecture, were retrieved from a mound in which sutras were buried, a practice in medieval times for preserving the Dharma when people thought Buddhism was in decline. The scrolls contain several sections of the *Lotus Sutra.* The inner canister in which they were placed is made of bronze with an inscription identifying the person who sponsored the sutra copying and the circumstances in which the burial occurred. The lid of the canister has a knob in the shape of a wish-granting jewel. Once sealed, the bronze canister was placed in the ceramic container, which was covered with a plate-like stone and buried in the ground.

competition—simply making the Buddha present at the temple in his Dharma guise too. This veneration of written scriptures led to another interesting practice in which sutra scrolls were encased in decorated canisters and buried in sutra mounds at religious sites (fig. 82). Some of these canisters took the form of pagodas and stupas, creating a strong association between sutras and relics.[14] Admittedly, Buddhist texts have had many different functions in the history of the religion: as records of the Buddha's teachings, as a medium for transmitting them, as products of karmic merit making, as status symbols for religious and political elites, and so forth. But one of the crucial functions has been as a physical manifestation of the Buddha—that is, as another place to behold the Buddha. And as such, sutra scrolls stand alongside icons and relics as objects of reverence.

CALLIGRAPHIC INSCRIPTIONS

Another multivalent object in Japanese Buddhism is the calligraphic inscription. Like a sutra, it is written in Chinese characters, but instead of taking the form of a long text, it is usually produced as a simple one-sheet inscription that can be exhibited and viewed. Typically these inscriptions consist of the sacred name of a Buddhist text or figure rather than a famous saying or words of wisdom. In a religious context they are often enshrined where one might expect an icon to appear, and thus they function as a devotional object in their own right. Like drawn or painted images of the Buddha, they can be mounted on a scroll that is unrolled and hung up for display, and rerolled for storage or transport. Though such inscriptions are commonly written in fine calligraphy, historians point out that their popularization in Japan was not based on their aesthetic qualities. Aristocrats and highborn believers could commission artists to produce exquisite statues or paintings of the Buddha to meet their needs, thereby fusing aesthetics with religion. But such objects were beyond the means of ordinary people. Religious inscriptions by contrast required little more than ink, a brush, and a piece of paper on which to write the sacred name. They could be produced in abundance and distributed widely. As a result, calligraphic inscriptions helped to spread Buddhism outside the aesthetic culture of elite society, becoming the devotional object of choice for many believers in Japan.[15]

A prime example of this kind of inscription is Nichiren's calligraphic mandala, the Gohonzon, or Principal Object of Reverence, mentioned earlier (fig. 83). It is called a mandala because it offers a graphic representation of figures in the universe that Nichiren Buddhists consider foundational. Instead of presenting actual depictions of these figures, the mandala just gives their names in Chinese characters. The names are arranged in a symmetrical layout on the page suggesting the relationship of these figures with each other. At its center are the words *Namu Myōhō rengekyō* written vertically in seven characters, the title of the *Lotus Sutra* as chanted by Nichiren believers. Its placement indicates that the sutra is the central pillar holding up the universe and that its power and truth are concentrated in the title itself. On each side at the top are the names of the two main Buddhas of the sutra, Śākyamuni and Tahō, and beyond them the four leading Bodhisattvas highlighted in the sutra. In addition, flanking the central axis are the names of other Bodhisattvas, arhats, divinities, legendary personages, and Buddhist masters, some appearing in the *Lotus* and others revered by Nichiren as defenders and proponents of the *Lotus*. At the corners of the mandala are the names of the Four Heavenly Kings, and along the left and right edges are Aizen Myōō and Fudō Myōō, represented esoterically by their Sanskrit "seed letter" (*shuji*) rather than their Chinese name. These guardian figures at the periphery provide a protected space for the other figures inside the mandala. Symbolically, the mandala recreates the idealized world of Vulture Peak where the *Lotus Sutra* was originally preached, which according to Nichiren transcends and encompasses all other possible worlds. It thus represents a miniature cosmology in which the figures listed play a cosmic role. Historically, it is not clear when this mandala became a widespread object of worship in the Nichiren tradition, for some early temples enshrined images of Śākyamuni, or the two main Buddhas, with the four Bodhisattvas alongside. But Nichiren himself distributed hundreds of copies of the mandala to his followers, and today it is found ubiquitously in Nichiren Buddhism.[16] Whether in a large temple or a private chapel or a home shrine, the mandala provides a complete assembly of iconographic figures on a single sheet of paper. What is distinctive about it is that all the names recorded on it

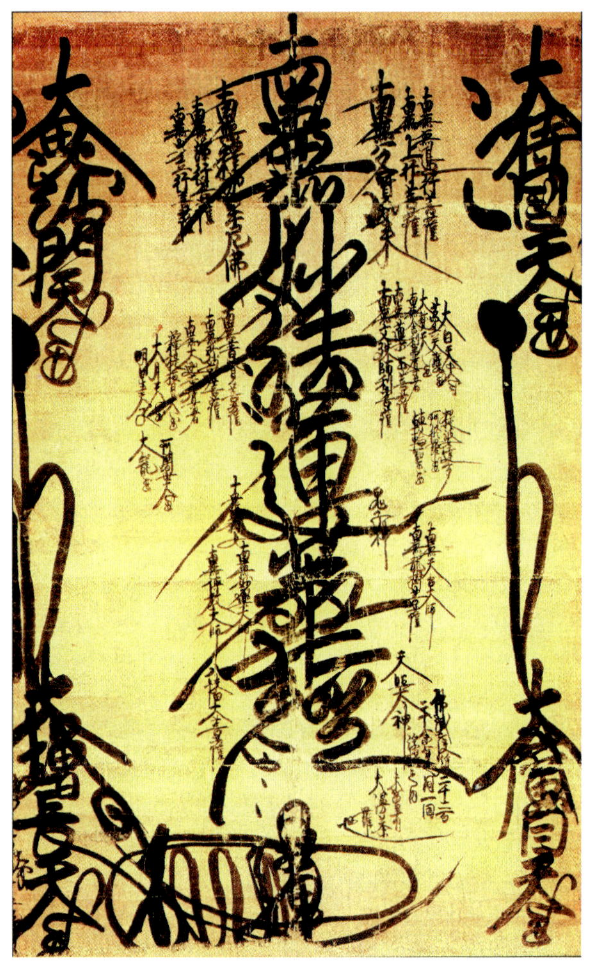

Fig. 83. Nichiren's Gohonzon or Principal Object of Reverence, 13th cent. Hikigayatsu Myōhonji Temple, Kamakura. This special copy of the calligraphic mandala, handwritten by Nichiren in 1280 and widely known as the Great Mandala and Principal Object of Reverence at the Time of Passing, was supposedly enshrined next to his bed when he died. The seven large characters down the center form the Daimoku, the title of the *Lotus Sutra* as chanted by adherents. On either side at the top are the names of the two revered Buddhas, Śākyamuni and Tahō, and of the four faithful Bodhisattvas. Below them are the names of various Bodhisattvas, arhats, divinities, Tendai Buddhist masters, and Shinto deities that venerate and proclaim the *Lotus.* At the bottom center is Nichiren's own name. The large characters at the four corners are the names of the Four Heavenly Kings, with the stylized Sanskrit "seed letters" of Aizen and Fudō between them down the sides, creating a protective border along the edges. This mandala is both a graphic representation of the *Lotus* universe and an iconic object of reverence for Nichiren believers.

are personages except for the most important one down the middle. That is the name of the *Lotus Sutra* itself.

Another type of calligraphic inscription widespread in Japanese Buddhism is the Amida Buddha inscription, frequently referred to in Japanese simply as the Myōgō Honzon, or "venerated name" (fig. 84). It became common in Pure Land Buddhism, especially the Shin branch whose founder, Shinran (1173–1262), is sometimes credited with its popularization. The wording on Amida inscriptions can take several different forms, but the most prevalent one reads *Namu Amida Butsu,* "I take refuge in Amida Buddha," written in Chinese characters. These are the same words found in the Nenbutsu invocation, the simple and rhythmic chant of Amida's name that pervaded Pure Land Buddhism. In its basic structure the Amida inscription consists of the six characters written vertically on a piece of paper. Though not as complex as Nichiren's mandala, these inscriptions are sometimes adorned or elaborated in various ways. For instance, it is not unusual for a small lotus flower to appear below the last character of the inscription indicating that, like a Buddhist icon situated on a lotus pedestal, the inscription is an object of reverence. In other instances, the inscription may have salient passages from the Pure Land sutras written in panels above and below it when mounted on a scroll hanging. And in its most ornamented and intricate form, known as a Kōmyō Honzon, or "sacred light inscription," rays of light are shown streaming from the letters at the center onto small portraits of illustrious religious figures, suggesting that the inscription is none other than Amida Buddha shedding his light. As in the case of Nichiren's mandala, Amida inscriptions were produced in abundance and became the centerpiece of worship for countless ordinary believers whether they could actually read the words or not.[17]

Though representative of two very different types of Buddhism, the Nichiren Gohonzon and the Amida Buddha inscription have some common characteristics. The first is that they are constructed around a written name—the name of a sutra in one case and the name of a Buddha in the other. For both, there is the presupposition that the name is not simply a pointer to another entity but rather

Fig. 84. Six-character inscription of Amida's name, 13th cent. The six characters written down the center, *Namu Amida Butsu,* "I take refuge in Amida Buddha," is the Nenbutsu chant found ubiquitously in Pure Land Buddhism. In this particular inscription, produced by Shinran in 1256, the lotus flower beneath the characters implies that the name of Amida, whether written or spoken, is as much an icon as an image of the Buddha is, placed on a lotus pedestal. At the top and bottom of this inscription are quotations from the *Larger Pure Land Sutra*, including Amida's widely cited eighteenth vow. This six-character version of the Amida inscription is the most common format, though eight- and ten-character versions also survive in Shinran's handwriting.

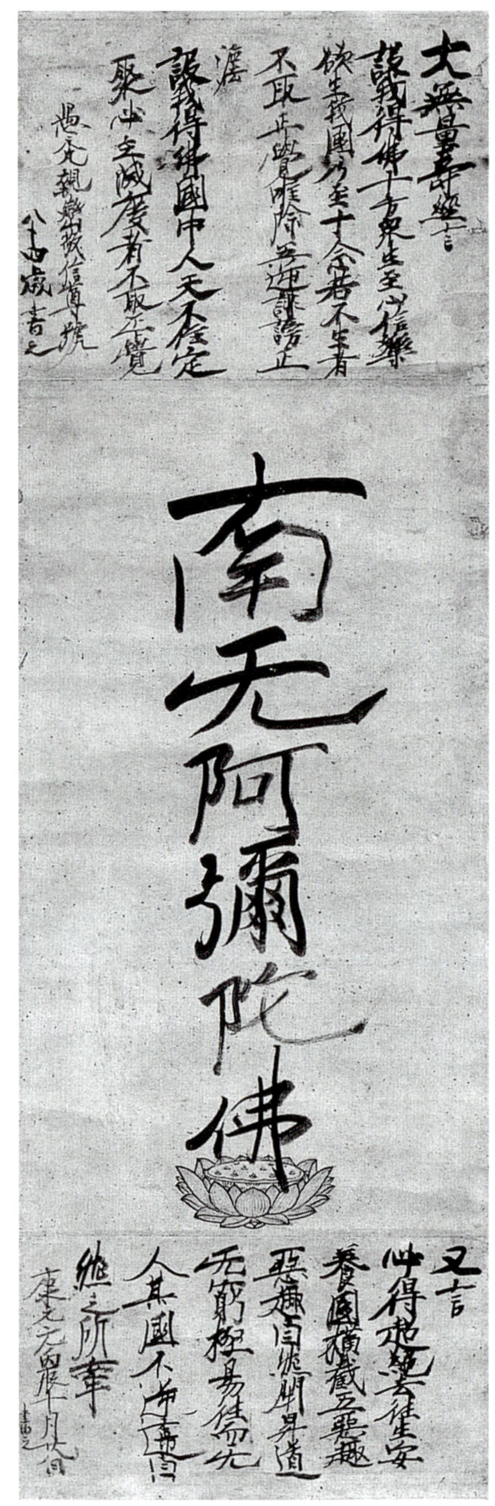

a concentrated manifestation of it. And just as the *Lotus Sutra* and Amida Buddha are infused with power, so too are their names. Calligraphic inscriptions are thus another way for the Buddha to be present in the world. The second characteristic is that both inscriptions are not just objects of reverence but also invocations that people perform. Chanting the title of the *Lotus Sutra* in the form of the Daimoku or the name of Amida in the form of the Nenbutsu is the core religious practice in these two Buddhist traditions. The words themselves—which originate with the Buddha and embody the Buddha—exist both inside and outside the believer, as a verbal invocation on the one hand and as a written inscription on the other. Hence, the calligraphic inscription is another place where the enlightened and compassionate identity of the Buddha and the religious quest of the believer intersect.

Another type of inscription that merits a brief discussion is *bokuseki,* or "ink traces," in Zen Buddhism. They bear some similarities to the *Lotus* and Amida inscriptions described above, but also important differences. Today ink traces are typically characterized as enlightened calligraphic inscriptions—either written in an enlightened moment or by an enlightened person or in an enlightened manner—or as objects that provoke enlightenment in the observer. The content of these inscriptions is not fixed as in the case of Nichiren and Pure Land inscriptions. They typically draw from an extensive repertoire of famous Zen expressions and symbols, such as the phrase "A separate transmission outside the teachings, not relying on words or letters" (*kyōge betsuden furyū monji*), or a unique saying by a particular Zen figure, or the single word "nothingness" (*mu*), or an empty circle, or an inscription with a monochrome sketch of Bodhidharma, the semi-legendary transmitter of Zen from India to China. The modern portrayal of ink traces as enlightened calligraphy does not adequately convey their historical evolution and use in Zen. It is clear that monasteries valued calligraphic writings of great masters, but it is not clear that they functioned as icons. They may have been regarded more as aesthetic treasures or keepsakes from the past than as living religious objects. What complicates their meaning is the extensive use of ink traces in tea ceremony culture beginning in the sixteenth century, just as the concept of *bokuseki* was becoming widespread in Japan. Tea ceremony was an aesthetic pursuit of the rich and powerful, an activity that Zen monasteries themselves helped cultivate and advance. Calligraphic scrolls were frequently displayed as spiritual adornments in tea rooms as much as in monasteries. Although they occupied a place of honor in tea culture, and perhaps lent it a religious air, they did not evoke the same type of ritual response—bowing, chanting, making offerings, as one would to the Buddha—that *Lotus* and Amida inscriptions did. In sum, the iconic quality of the ink traces popularized in Zen—though not totally absent—rarely approached that of Nichiren and Pure Land inscriptions, and so in Zen settings they were not ordinarily enshrined as icons per se.[18]

PORTRAITS OF BUDDHIST MASTERS

There are a host of images in Japanese temples that look like standard Buddhist icons but are in fact sculpted or painted portraits of historical figures in Japan and China. In most cases these are revered Buddhist masters who have been memorialized. In some instances their images are set up in a small personal shrine; in others they are installed in a large alcove or room; and in still others they occupy an entire temple building. These images often have an altar table in front replete with standard ritual furnishings. And on a regular basis rituals are conducted before them. In short, these portraits of Buddhist masters are recognized as living images and serve a similar function as icons of the Buddha.

Perhaps the richest trove of such portraits can be found in the Zen tradition. Curiously, though the "ink traces" of Zen masters rarely rose to the level of full-fledged icons, their portraits did. The role of the master in Zen monastic life is enormous, since he serves as the spiritual arbiter, model, and guide of the monks in training.

From early in Zen history, painted portraits of masters, known as *chinzō* or "true likenesses," were produced in great numbers. For many years scholars assumed that these portraits functioned as certificates of authentication bestowed by masters on disciples testifying to their spiritual attainments. But subsequent scholarship has demonstrated that *chinzō* were more closely tied to death rituals for masters and the perpetuation of their "presence" among the so-called patriarchs of the monastery. Moreover, the connection of Zen portraits to the postmortem remains of masters has also been well documented. In China, for instance, the mummified bodies of masters were sometimes transformed into icons themselves by lacquering over them. In other cases, cremation ashes were used in the production of images or preserved in an inner cavity of portrait statues. There has thus been a strong connection between images of Zen masters and their relics, just as there has been with the Buddha. Since in the Zen setting the living master functions as a surrogate of the Buddha, the postmortem image of the master can similarly act as a stand-in or extension of the icon of the Buddha—evoking similar religious meanings and ritual responses.[19] In their most common format, *chinzō* images appear as painted portrait scrolls. But in their most powerful and elaborate expression, they take the form of lifelike statues of the master in a formal sitting pose (fig. 85).

Reverence for Buddhist masters and depiction of them in iconic form is not limited to the Zen school. Virtually every form of Buddhism has its own founding figure or saintly exemplars, who have inspired physical representation and ritual apotheosis of various types. This is certainly true of Nichiren, whose image is typically enshrined on the altar of Nichiren temples along with the Daimoku inscription of the *Lotus Sutra* title (fig. 76). Nichiren's life story as an indefatigable proponent and defender of its teachings—revered as a reincarnation of the Bodhisattva Jōgyō, named in the sutra, and even as an earthly manifestation of the Buddha—undergirds the grand memorial service, called Oeshiki, that is performed each year before his image. Likewise, Kūkai (774–835), or Kōbō Daishi, the founder

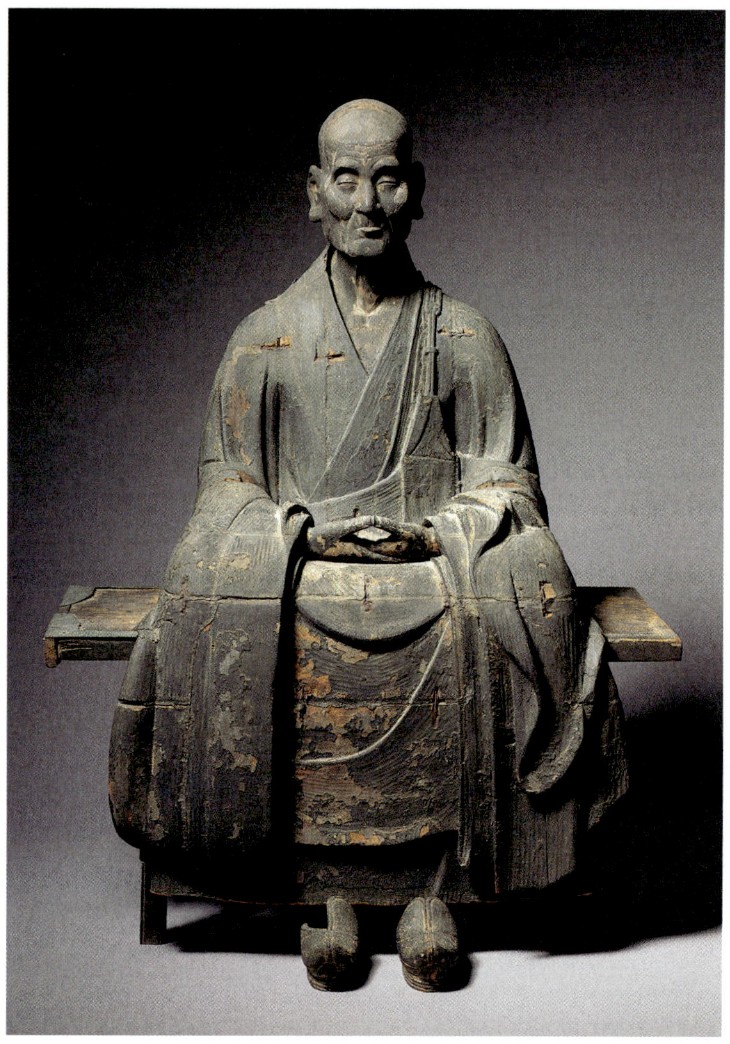

Fig. 85. Portrait statue of Zen master Hottō Enmyō Kokushi, 13th–14th cent. This figure epitomizes the power and realism of images of eminent Zen masters produced after their death. Such statues and painted portraits are enshrined in side altars of main halls or in patriarch halls or in other specially designated spots in the monastery, and rituals are conducted before them on a regular basis. Their lifelike appearance enhances the sense of the master's abiding presence in the monastery. This master, known also as Shinchi Kakushin (1207–1298), transmitted the Mumon lineage of Zen from China to Japan in the thirteenth century, together with its collection of Zen koans known as the *Mumonkan* (Gateless Gate).

of Shingon Buddhism in Japan and semi-legendary miracle worker, has inspired a saintly cult replete with sacred sites, pilgrimage routes, ritual invocations, annual ceremonies, and of course iconic portraits. The standard depiction of Kūkai, whether in painted, sculpted, or printed form, shows him seated formally on a Chinese-style high seat holding a vajra ritual implement in one hand and a Buddhist rosary in the other (fig. 86). Such images are pervasive in Japan, ranging from large temple settings to small personal shrines. In these contexts Kūkai is venerated just as a Bodhisattva might be.

An interesting architectural development resulting from reverence for Buddhist masters is the establishment of memorial halls, or literally "portrait halls" (*mieidō* or *goeidō*), dedicated to masters. In them an iconic image, or "portrait," of the master is installed on the central altar. Such halls might be located at the gravesite of the master or within a large temple complex as a side building or ancillary hall. In a few instances memorial halls have emerged as large temples in their own right. The most prominent of these is the Honganji (both the East and West branches) of the Shin school of Pure Land Buddhism. Historically, the temple started as a small gravesite chapel dedicated to Shinran, the founder of Shin Buddhism. From its beginning in the thirteenth century, it had a sculpted image of him installed on the altar, possibly with his ashes enshrined inside. Over the centuries the Honganji evolved into a massive temple and a widely influential religious organization. Throughout its development the hall dedicated to Shinran has remained the centerpiece of the temple. It stands alongside a hall to Amida Buddha but in fact dwarfs it. Inside, both halls have a central altar, and around this focal point are all the adornments and ritual accouterments that characterize Japanese temples, including ancillary installations of portraits of other Buddhist masters and inscriptions of Amida's name. The two halls thus have a similar interior layout, but one has Shinran enshrined on the central altar and the other has Amida. From this similarity it is possible to identify Shinran as a stand-in for Amida within the larger hall. This is consistent with his sectarian portrayal as a worldly manifestation of

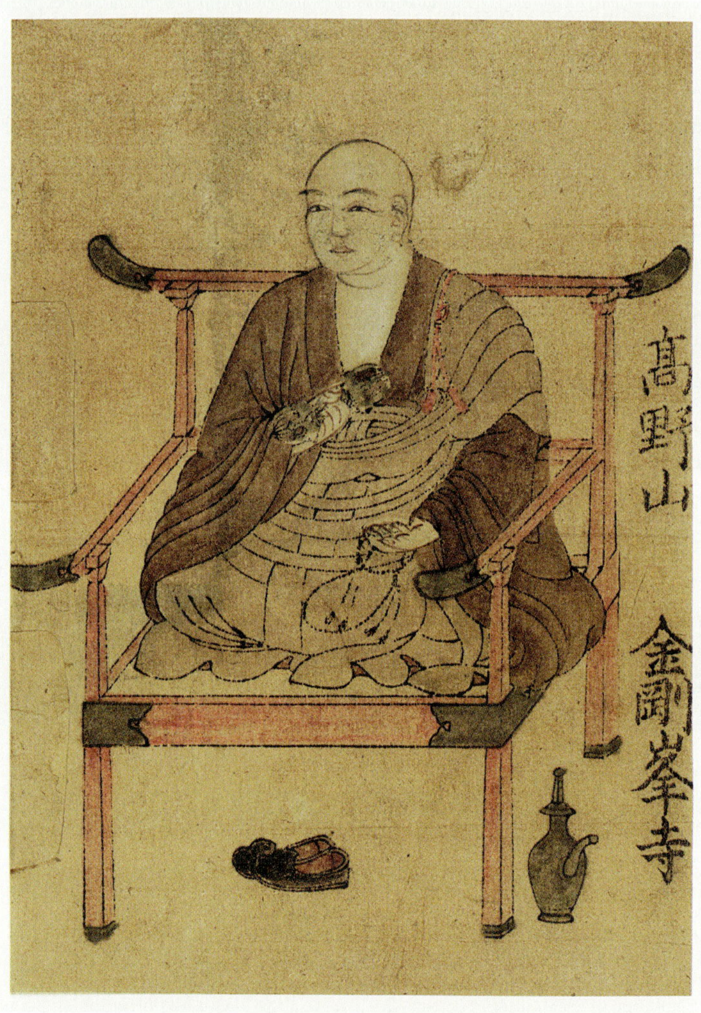

Fig. 86. **Portrait of Master Kūkai (Kōbō Daishi), 18th–19th cent.** This woodblock print of Kūkai (774–835), the founder of Shingon Buddhism in Japan, bears the imprint of Kongōbuji, the head temple of the monastic center established by Kūkai on Mt. Kōya, where his mausoleum—revered as his place of "eternal meditation"—is located. Mt. Kōya, as well as an eighty-eight temple circuit on the island of Shikoku, became pilgrimage destinations for his devotees. Small images like this print, which were produced in great numbers, circulated widely among them and could be installed in simple personal shrines. Photo © 2020 Museum of Fine Arts, Boston.

Amida throughout Shin Buddhist history. What this means is that to "behold" Shinran in the portrait hall of the Honganji is tantamount to beholding Amida. To the extent that the temple is dedicated to Shinran, ritually engaging him becomes an avenue for experiencing the wisdom and compassion of the Buddha himself.[20]

As these examples show, ritual interaction with images of masters is as much a part of Japanese Buddhism as interaction with icons of Buddhas and Bodhisattvas. This pattern in the treatment of masters and the enshrinement of their images follows the same paradigm as that of the historical Buddha, who was himself a revered master in his own day. As a result, Buddhist masters have become yet another category in the panoply of sacred figures found in Mahayana Buddhism. As with other figures, encountering a master, whether as a living individual or as an enshrined iconic personage, offers one more portal into the threefold ideal of Buddhism—spiritual quest, enlightenment, and compassion. Masters both embody this ideal and evoke it in others.

JAPAN AS A SACRED LANDSCAPE

Japan is a landscape dotted with expressions of the sacred. The most visible examples are temples themselves. It is hard to travel through any city or village in Japan without happening upon a temple. Some are grand and famous, occupying prominent spots or claiming illustrious histories. Others are small and obscure, conducting religious services and celebrations for the local parishioners. Virtually all are laid out with a main hall at the center in which an image of the Buddha or some other Buddhist figure is installed as the ritual centerpiece. This image acts as a pivot or *axis mundi* around which religious life and practice revolve. In addition to Buddhist temples, Japan is also the location of countless Shinto shrines, considered the dwelling places of spirits and deities known as kami. Although Shinto is classified as a separate religion today, through most of Japanese history it operated interdependently and harmoniously with Buddhism. Its many sacred sites have augmented and amplified the spiritual landscape of Japan.

Besides these institutions, there are ubiquitous wayside shrines along roads and paths throughout the country. Typically these are miniature structures that contain small images of Buddhas, Bodhisattvas, or other divinities carved out of stone. Perhaps the most popular figure installed in these shrines is the Bodhisattva Jizō. He is considered a compassionate protector and rescuer of the vulnerable and the helpless, especially travelers and children. Members of the community maintain these shrines—cleaning and repairing them; making offerings of food, water, incense, candles, and flowers; and periodically dressing the Jizō in a child's bib and cap, thereby conflating its identity with that of the children it protects. Kyoto, the ancient capital of Japan, which remains a very traditional city, is filled with small, well-kept roadside shrines (fig. 87). A beloved neighborhood event each summer is a children's festival called Jizō Bon, held at certain street-corner shrines. It consists of a brief sutra-chanting service before the image and then games, snacks, and gifts for the children. This event occurs around the time of the Obon ceremonies at temples and homes when the ancestors are "invited back and hosted" for three days. Though Jizō is a common image in these wayside shrines, some are dedicated to other Buddhist figures such as the Bodhisattva Kannon as well as unidentified or indeterminate Buddhas or Bodhisattvas.

Another locus of religious activity is cemeteries and gravesites. Death rituals have generally fallen within the purview of Buddhism in Japan, and cemeteries are commonly (though not universally) located within temple compounds. Parishioners who have graves there entomb the ashes of family members either individually or collectively in a family grave. A typical gravesite consists of a stone construction with a central monument on a multi-tiered pedestal and a small offering space in front. The monument may be a simple vertical stone or it may be an elaborate *gorintō* or "five-element stupa" (fig. 88). Inscribed on it may be the name of the individual or the family, or a religious invocation to Amida Buddha or the *Lotus Sutra* or the five elements. In layout, gravesites bear a faint resemblance to the central altar area of a Buddhist temple—with the monument serving in place of the central icon.[21] People might visit a grave on the anniversary of a person's death or on commemorative dates in the temple's ritual calendar such as the equinoxes and Obon. They might clean the site, pray to (or for) the deceased, and make offerings of food, drink, incense, flowers, or other items. It is noteworthy that one of the standard euphemisms for death in Japanese is *hotoke ni naru,* "to become

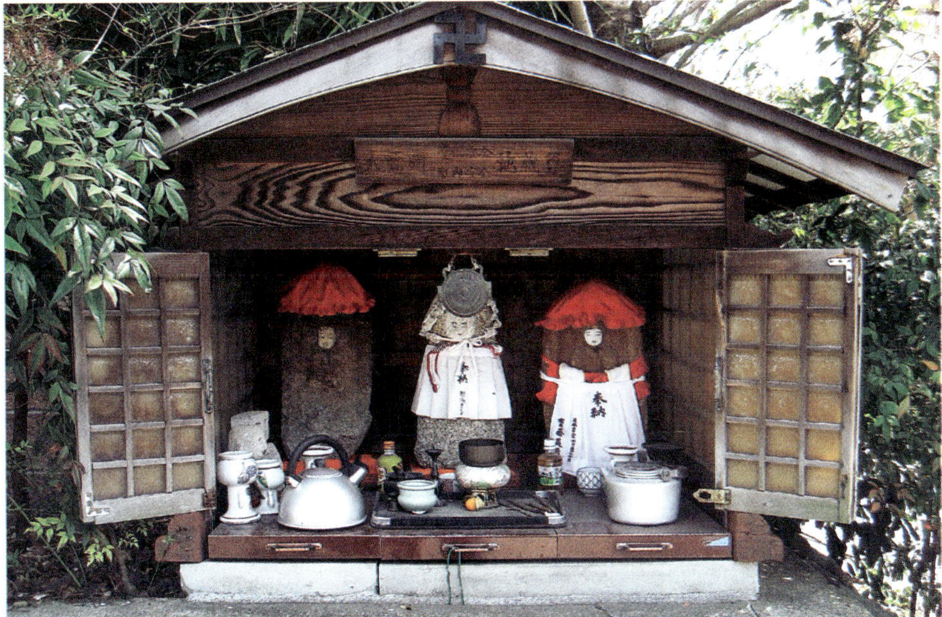

Fig. 87. Roadside Buddhist shrine. This small shrine is located in Iwakura on the northern edge of Kyoto. The three stone figures were originally roadside images and are identified by the plaque overhead as Jizō Bodhisattvas. The shrine consists of a cabinet with doors that open and close. Each Jizō has had his face painted in and is dressed in a child's bib and cap. A small gong above and a small inverted bell below may be rung whenever prayers are made or offerings given, including such things as incense, candles, tea, flowers, fruit, or a soft drink from a vending machine. The inverted swastika at the top is a sacred symbol marking this as a Buddhist site. It is not unusual for people in the neighborhood to pause briefly in front of the shrine and pay their respects.

a Buddha." That is, death is homologized to the moment of enlightenment and the attainment of Buddhahood. People thus interact with the deceased as if they are Buddhas, and their ritual responses at the gravesite resemble those before a Buddhist image at a temple.

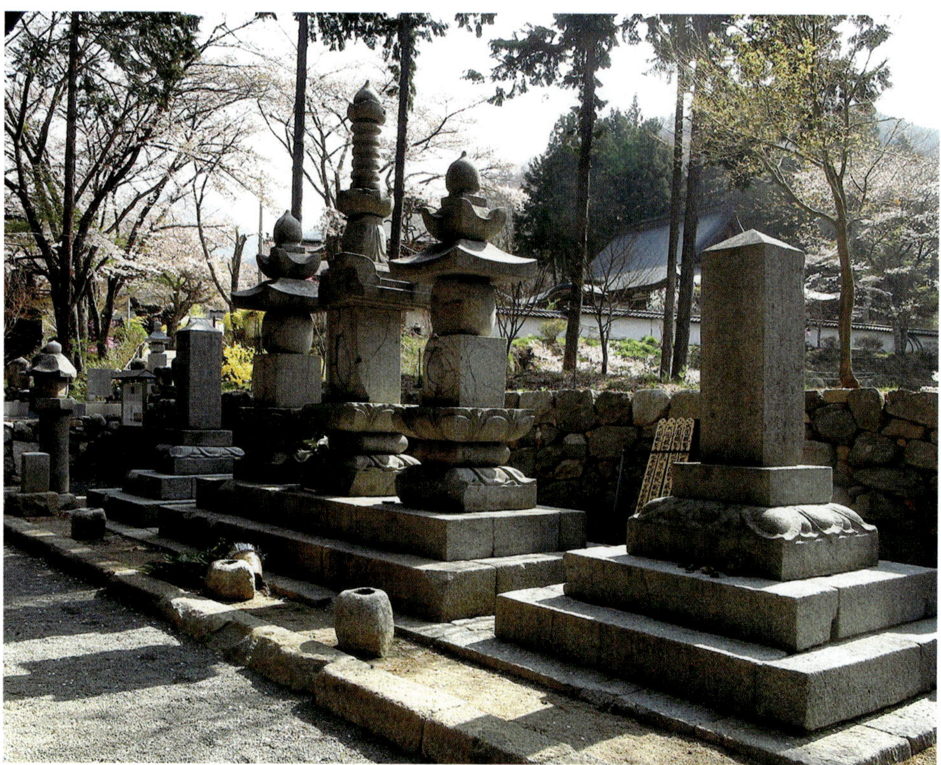

Fig. 88. Buddhist grave monuments, 18th cent. Keitokuin Temple, Kōshū, Yamanashi prefecture. The three monuments in the middle are the gravestones of an important warlord, Takeda Katsuyori (1546–1582), and his wife and son, all of whom died by suicide after his defeat in battle. They were erected in 1775 to replace earlier ones. Takeda's monument in the center is a stylized pagoda, and the other two are five-element stupas. All three are topped with a wish-granting jewel and rest on a lotus pedestal. Stone containers have been placed in front for incense, and offerings include a flower bouquet that has toppled over in this photo. At the far end is a votive stone lantern, and leaning against the wall, behind the monuments, are slats of wood with religious inscriptions on them known as *sotoba*—a Japanese transliteration of the word stupa, since the tops of the slats are cut slightly to resemble a stupa. Not all grave monuments in Japan take the shape of a five-element stupa or a pagoda. Some are simple standing monoliths like the ones at each end of this gravesite.

This same interlinking of the Buddha with deceased family members occurs inside the home at another site of religious activity: the *butsudan* or family Buddhist altar (fig. 30). In traditional households this is where people interact ritually with the Buddha and also with deceased relatives and ancestors. The *butsudan* is usually installed in a cabinet or an alcove that can be opened and closed. In extravagant cases the altar is just as ornately decorated as a temple altar, though much smaller in scale. Ordinarily, the centerpiece is a small sculpted or painted icon of the Buddha, often flanked by Bodhisattvas, Buddhist masters, other Buddhist figures, or religious inscriptions. Adornments and ritual vessels are arrayed in front and below, including lamps, candles, censers, flower vases, food and drink containers, bells, clackers for chanting, and liturgical manuals. Also integrated into this array are memorial tablets (*ihai*) to deceased relatives and sometimes a "roll book of the past" (*kakochō*) listing deceased members.[22] Hence, just as the Buddha is made present in the home altar in the guise of a miniature icon, likewise the ancestors are manifested in the form of memorial tablets. Daily rituals at the altar might include offerings of rice, water, incense and flowers; religious recitations and chants; and prayers of thanks and petition to the Buddha, the ancestors, or both. A common repertoire of ritual gestures and religious assumptions are thus directed at the Buddha and the ancestors alike. In this intimate domestic space before the home altar, the meanings that inhere in the Buddha spill over to the ancestors so that they become both the beneficiaries of the Buddha and his agents in the eyes of their descendants.

Japan is thus a multifaceted spiritual landscape where the Buddha's identity is present in all manner of spatial and material form. It encompasses diverse physical objects such as icons, religious texts, relics, inscriptions, and saintly personages. It also suffuses a wide variety of physical settings including temples, pagodas, roadside shrines, gravesites, home altars, and even the little stone piles that pilgrims stack up as tiny stupas along their route. Considering the pervasiveness of religious imagery in Japan, it might be tempting to think that the Buddha is everywhere. But one must be careful not to homogenize Japan into one vast and undifferentiated sacred landscape, for people experience the Buddha in specific locations and concrete objects. It is these encounters in fact that constitute beholding the Buddha—and, in doing so, becoming party to his spiritual quest, enlightened awakening, and all-pervasive compassion.

AFTERWORD
Museums Revisited

In the last couple of decades there has been a boomlet in the popularity of Buddhist art among ordinary Japanese. It is difficult to know what has stimulated this interest. It may be that the aging population has felt at leisure to indulge in pastimes and curiosities that they could not pursue during their working careers. Or it could be that Japan's economic paralysis of the 1990s has caused people to shift away from single-minded economic expansion to simpler and more edifying pursuits. Whatever the reason, there has been a proliferation of magazines and popular books on Buddhism, Buddhist temples, and Buddhist art. One example is the cute paperback *Butsuzō no himitsu* (Secrets of Buddhist Images, 2006), published in conjunction with an exhibit at the Tokyo National Museum explaining Buddhist art to children and their parents.[1] Another is the special-issue magazine *Kimochi ii Bukkyō* (Feel Good Buddhism, 2004) with feature articles on meditation for newcomers, touring Buddhist temples, connoisseurship of incense, temple etiquette, gourmet vegetarian meals, and Buddhist statues.[2] A third is the large, lavishly illustrated paperback introduction to Buddhist iconography *Butsuzō no mikata miwakekata* (How to View and Distinguish Buddhist Images, 2002), produced by Shufu to Seikatsu Sha (Housewives and Lifestyle Company), a major publisher of women's magazines and trade books.[3] This burgeoning interest has brought people into art museums and Buddhist temples to explore Buddhism firsthand.

Japan's national museums first appeared in the late nineteenth and early twentieth centuries. They were influenced by the model of foreign museums—only a few decades after the very concept of a museum emerged in Europe and the United States—and also by domestic Japanese policies aimed at creating a modern cultural identity for the nation and elevating Japan in the eyes of the world. The country had undergone a traumatic social and political revolution in the mid-nineteenth century as it sought to compete with the Western colonial powers. Amid this trauma, Buddhism was widely depicted as a backward and superstitious religion, and only gradually regained its reputation by recasting itself as a rational worldview compatible with modern science and international values. One tradition that lost credence in this process was Buddhism's deeply rooted practice of venerating Buddhist images as living icons. Fortunately, just as these images seemed destined for eclipse—if not disappearance—a number of influential Japanese intellectuals, inspired in part by the Western idea of art, began to portray Buddhist iconography as a reservoir of Japan's aesthetic and cultural heritage. For all intents and purposes, the concept of Japanese Buddhist images *as art* was invented at this point. Buddhist temples generally accepted this new valorization of their sacred treasures, and emergent art museums (as well as private collections) became alternative repositories for these objects.[4] Though temples, out of sheer force of custom, continued to conduct their long-established rituals for enshrined images, museums became new sites for displaying them in new ways and for comprehending them in the new conceptual framework of the "fine arts."

The Kyoto National Museum, which opened in 1897, was one of these sites, and its original building, the Meiji Kotokan, remains a classic of Western-influenced design in Japan (fig. 89). From the beginning it drew heavily from European and American ideas about museums, deploying them for a nationalist agenda to glorify Japan's "high civilization" and cultural achievements.[5] While Buddhist art was included among those achievements, it was celebrated not for its religious meaning but for its cultural value. Even today in the museum's magnificent new Heisei Chishinkan building, objects that originated in Buddhist temples are exhibited to maximize their visual effect, just as they might be in Western museums. Unlike Western museums, however, the Kyoto National Museum is located in a city full of Buddhist temples, which continue to enshrine their icons in

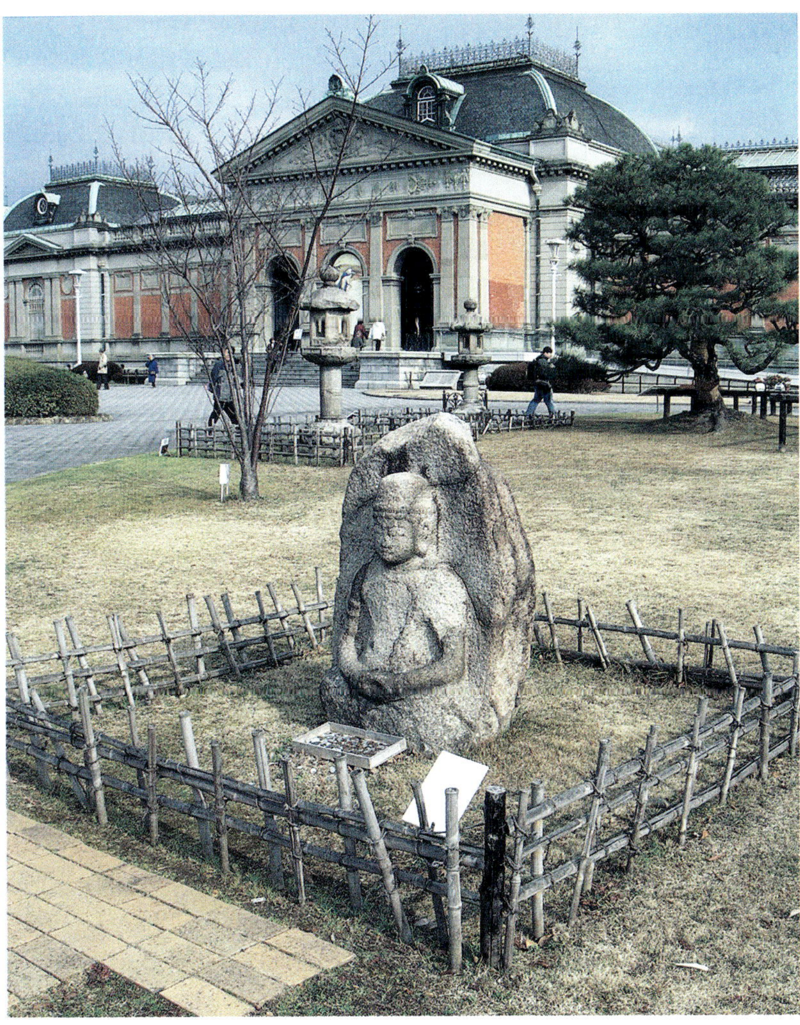

Fig. 89. Buddhist image on the grounds of the Kyoto National Museum. The Meiji Kotokan, seen in the background, is the original building of the museum, which opened in 1897. It largely follows the Neo-classical style of nineteenth-century European architecture, though a few elements in its decorative façade derive from Japanese imagery. From the beginning the museum had Japanese Buddhist statues on display. Today it also exhibits a variety of stone sculpture on its grounds, including the Buddhist image in this photo from 2007. Note the small box in front of the image containing coins that visitors have tossed. Offering coins to enshrined images, whether located in temples or by the side of the road, is a common act of devotion in Japanese Buddhism.

consecrated areas and to interact with them in ritualized ways. Hence, the average museumgoer in Kyoto is likely to have had exposure to Japan's dual characterization of Buddhist images: as works of art and as objects of reverence. This dual perception occasionally results in a slightly displaced response to images across the two settings. It is not unusual to see people in Japanese museums bow to a Buddha or join their hands together reverentially, just as they might in a temple, and then proceed to read the display's caption and to inspect the image closely, as they would in a museum. There is thus a blurring in the meaning of the Buddha in their minds—as a museum object on the one hand and as a temple icon on the other. Such instances suggest that it is difficult in Japan to sequester Buddhist images in a purely museum environment.[6]

The significance and function of museums has been debated in recent years as their place in society has come under scrutiny. One characterization has been that museums constitute a "contact zone" between dominant social interpretations and alternative claims. Here contact zone is a term used by scholars to indicate settings and occasions in which conflicting views—based on cultural, geographic, social, historical, or ideological differences, often with one side asserting dominance over the other—come into contact with each other. To the extent that museums have assumed the role of assigning meanings to the objects they curate—primarily through naming and captioning them—they have acted as arbiters of the object's identity and have potentially aligned their interpretations, whether consciously or not, with the views of mainstream society against dissenting voices.[7] The postcolonial analysis of museums mentioned at the beginning of this book exemplifies the recent critique of this role. That is, the display of Asian treasures in Western museums during the nineteenth and early twentieth centuries arose from colonial domination, and museums established the terms for interpreting them to the West. The question now is whether museums can act as a platform—or a different type of contact zone—for multiple interpretive experiences rather than privileging the predominant, authorized view.

In the light of such criticisms many museums today have become more sensitive to how they exhibit religious objects. They acknowledge their sacred origins and some create displays that replicate traditional religious settings (fig. 4). Also, religious groups are sometimes allowed and even encouraged to perform acts of piety to sacred objects—within the limits of the museum's protection of them. Not all museums have developed such open policies, but those that have seem to have created a space for multiple interpretations of its objects. Yet the delicate balance of providing an open forum for all voices can be elusive, for tensions may exist not only between the convictions of religious groups and the secular posture of public museums, but also between competing religious groups, all claiming to speak in behalf of the exhibited object. Hence, the conundrum for museum administrators is to find that sweet spot between openness and control where the museum, as a contact zone, can be a place of difference, exchange, and even discovery.

American and European museums may not have the temple-rich surroundings that the Kyoto National Museum has to counterbalance the curated, art-oriented atmosphere surrounding the Buddhist images in their collections. But they nonetheless operate in a more complex and diversified world than what the old-fashioned stereotype of East versus West might suggest. Museumgoers today come from a kaleidoscope of cultural backgrounds and include Buddhists by heritage, by conversion, and by simple self-declaration. These visitors bring a variety of responses to the images they see, no matter what the captions might say. Hence, the possibility of reacting to Buddhist objects with piety and even ritualized gestures is not out of the question today. This would suggest that museums, though not fully functioning as temples, have the capacity to accommodate temple-like experiences and to convey succinctly, for the benefit of museumgoers who may not know, the original temple-rooted identity of Buddhist images. In short, museums can function as hybrid spaces where the experience of their objects does not preclude the type of experiences that have historically been the norm for temples.

*

Let me conclude by recounting an experience I had at the Cleveland Museum of Art years ago. In 1998 the museum mounted a grand exhibition entitled "Buddhist Treasures from Nara" containing an array of objects from the Nara National Museum,[8] some of which are presented in this book. It was a cultural revelry for me. I had seen many of the works while living in Japan previously. But having them so close to home, I eagerly visited the museum a number of times and gave small, intimate explanatory tours to friends and colleagues. Among the objects was a famous portrait of the thirteenth-century Buddhist master Shinran sitting in a semi-formal pose on a bearskin rug (fig. 90). I had conducted extensive research on Shinran earlier in my career, so there was probably no one in the Cleveland area who understood the content and history of this portrait better than I did. It was thus a particular treat for me to view the portrait up close and at my own pace. As I meticulously inspected its every detail, it seemed to me that the figure of Shinran suddenly cut his eyes in my direction and met my gaze. It was uncanny, almost eerie. I was momentarily shaken, as if I had invaded someone's space and they had reacted by staring back. As I retreated a step, I immediately became aware of the intrusive way I had been scrutinizing the portrait. I would never have done such a thing if I were standing in the presence of Shinran himself.

This story is not meant to show that Buddhist images are alive. Personally, I do not have the capacity to experience them as living entities the way premodern Buddhists might have. Rather, it is meant to show that objects—especially religious ones, even in museums—have an awakening power if one is poised to perceive them in the right way. This delicate pose is a matter of suspending judgment, if only for a moment. It is a matter of approaching them without that deconstructive, reductionist gaze. In that instant the viewer becomes an empty vessel to be filled. That, I imagine, is what it means in this day and age to behold the Buddha.

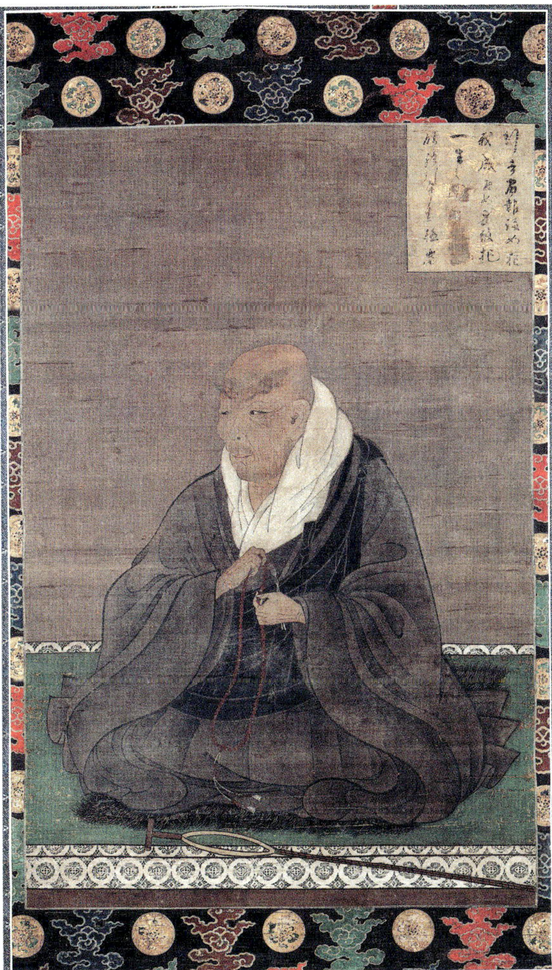

Fig. 90. Portrait of Master Shinran, 13th–14th cent. Shinran was a thirteenth-century proponent of Pure Land Buddhism, and the religious movement he founded became the largest in Japan two centuries after his death. He was revered by disciples and ordinary followers alike and came to be venerated as an earthly manifestation of Amida Buddha. Portraits such as this one depicting him in old age show informal touches that set them apart from standard portraits of great Buddhist masters—for instance, his walking cane laid out in front and the bearskin rug on which he sits. These details hint that Amida, if incarnated as a human, might assume a humble guise such as this. The inscription in the upper right is a four-line verse that came to Shinran in a dream when he was a young man, inspiring his exclusive devotion to Amida. Portraits of this type were often displayed on commemorative occasions such as the monthly and yearly remembrance of Shinran's death, and religious practices such as Nenbutsu and scriptural chanting were performed before them.

TEMPLES

The following list includes only those temples mentioned in the book.

Byōdōin. Uji Renge 116, Uji-shi, Kyōto-fu 611-0021, Japan
Chōgosonshiji. See Mt. Shigi
Chūsonji. Aza Koromonoseki 202, Hiraizumi-chō, Nishi Iwai-gun, Iwate-ken 029-4195, Japan
Daḷadā Maligāwa (Temple of the Tooth). Sri Dalada Veediya, Kandy 20000, Sri Lanka
Denkōji. Ogawa-chō 24, Nara-shi, Nara-ken 630-8233, Japan
Engakuji. Yamanouchi 409, Kamakura-shi, Kanagawa-ken 247-0247, Japan
Enryakuji. Hieizan, Sakamoto Honmachi 4220, Ōtsu-shi, Shiga-ken 520-0116, Japan
Famensi. Fufung 722200, Baoji, Shaanxi, China
Hikigayatsu. See Myōhonji
Hōkōji. Chayamachi 527-2, Shōmen-dōri Yamato-ōji Higashiiri, Higashiyama-ku, Kyōto-shi 605-0931, Japan
Honganji. Nishi Honganji, Horikawa-dōri Hanaya-chō-kudaru, Shimogyō-ku, Kyōto-shi 600-8501, Japan; and Higashi Honganji, Karasuma-dōri Shichijō-agaru, Shimogyō-ku, Kyōto-shi 600-8505, Japan
Hongwanji. See Honganji
Hōryūji. Hōryūji Sannai 1-1, Ikaruga-chō, Ikoma-gun, Nara-ken 636-0115, Japan
Jionji. Sōhonzan Jionji Chiseki 31, Sagae-shi, Yamagata-ken 990-0511, Japan
Keitokuin. Yamato-chō Tano 389, Kōshū-shi, Yamanashi-ken 409-1202, Japan
Kiyomizudera. Kiyomizu 1-294, Higashiyama-ku, Kyōto-shi 605-0862, Japan
Kōfukuji. Noboriōji-chō 48, Nara-shi, Nara-ken 630-8213, Japan
Kongōbuji. Kōyasan 132, Kōya-chō, Ito-gun, Wakayama-ken 648-0294, Japan

Konjikidō. See Chūsonji

Kumano Shrine. Nachisan 1, Nachikatsuura-chō, Higashimuro-gun, Wakayama-ken 649-5301, Japan

Kuonji. Minobusan, Minobu-chō 3567, Minamikoma-gun, Yamanashi-ken 409–2593, Japan

Mt. Hiei. See Enryakuji

Mt. Kinpu. Kinpusenji, Yoshinoyama 2598, Yoshino-chō, Yoshino-gun, Nara-ken 639-3115, Japan

Mt. Kōya. See Kongōbuji

Mt. Minobu. See Kuonji

Mt. Shigi. Chōgosonshiji, Shigisan 2280-1, Heguri-chō, Ikoma-gun, Nara-ken 639-0923, Japan

Myōhonji. Ōmachi 1-15-1, Kamakura-shi, Kanagawa-ken 248-0007, Japan

Myōshinji. Hanazono Myōshinji-chō 64, Ukyō-ku, Kyōto-shi 616-8035, Japan

Rengeōin. See Sanjūsangendō

Sanjūsangendō. Sanjūsangendō-mawari-chō 657, Higashiyama-ku, Kyōto-shi 605–0941, Japan

Seiryōji. Saga Shakadō, Fujinoki-chō 46, Ukyō-ku, Kyōto-shi 616-8447, Japan

Shin'yakushiji. Takabatake-chō 1352, Nara-shi, Nara-ken 630-8301, Japan

Temple of the Tooth. See Daḷadā Maligāwa

Tōdaiji. Zōshi-chō 406-1, Nara-shi, Nara-ken 630-8587, Japan

Tōji. Kujō-chō 1, Minami-ku, Kyōto-shi 601-8473, Japan

Tōshōdaiji. Gojō-chō 13-46, Nara-shi, Nara-ken 630-8032, Japan

Zenkōji. Motoyoshi-chō 491, Ōji Nagano, Nagano-shi, Nagano-ken 380-0851, Japan

Zōjōji. Shibakōen 4-7-35, Minato-ku, Tōkyō-to 105-0011, Japan

PRIMARY TEXTS

The following list includes only those primary sources mentioned in the book.

Brahma's Net Sutra (*Bonmōkyō*)
Chronicles of Japan (*Nihon shoki* or *Nihongi*)
Flower Garland Sutra (*Daihōkō Butsu kegonkyō*)
Heart Sutra (*Hannya shingyō*)
Kannon Sutra (*Kannongyō*)
Larger Pure Land Sutra (*Muryōjukyō*)
Lotus Sutra (*Myōhō rengenkyō* or *Hokekyō*)
Miraculous Accounts of Mt. Shigi (*Shigisan engi*)
Miraculous Tales from the Japanese Buddhist Tradition (*Nihon ryōiki*)
Pure Land Meditation Sutra (*Kanmuryōjukyō*)
Record of Miracles of the Bodhisattva Jizō (*Jizō Bosatsu reigenki*)
Sand and Pebbles (*Shasekishū*)
Sutra of Teachings Bequeathed by the Buddha (*Butsuyuikyōgyō*)
Sutra on Past Causes and Present Effects (*Kako genzai ingakyō*)
Sutra on the [Buddha's] Great Nirvana Without Remainder (*Daihatsunehangyō*)
Sutra on the Merits of the Fundamental Vows of Yakushi, the Lapis Lazuli Radiance Buddha (*Yakushi Rurikō nyorai hongan kudokukyō*)
Sutra of the Past Vows of Earth Storehouse Bodhisattva (*Jizō Bosatsu hongangyō*)
Sutra That Expounds the Descent of Maitreya Buddha and His Enlightenment (*Miroku geshō jōbutsukyō*)
The Three Jewels (*Sanbōe*)
Vimalakīrti Sutra (*Yuimagyō*)

NOTES

INTRODUCTION

1 Bernard Faure, "The Buddhist Icon and the Modern Gaze," *Critical Inquiry* 24 (Spring 1998): 768–778; and Stanley K. Abe, "Inside the Wonder House: Buddhist Art and the West," in *Curators of the Buddha,* ed. Donald S. Lopez, Jr. (Chicago: University of Chicago Press, 1995), 64–69.

2 Langdon Warner, *The Long Old Road in China* (Garden City, NJ, and New York: Doubleday, Page, 1926), 123–145; Peter Hopkirk, *Foreign Devils on the Silk Road* (Amherst: University of Massachusetts Press, 1980), 209–225; and Dunhuang Wenwu Yanjiusuo, ed., *Zhongguo Shiku Dunhuang Mogao-ku,* vol. 3 (Beijing: Wenwu Chubanshe, 1987), plates 66 and 67. See also Patricia J. Graham, "Langdon Warner's Vision of the Japanese Collection at the Nelson-Atkins Museum of Art, 1930–35," *Journal of the History of Collections* 28, no. 3 (2016): 367–382.

3 Svetlana Alpers, "The Museum as a Way of Seeing," 25–32; and Susan Vogel, "Always True to the Object, in Our Fashion," 191–204, in *Exhibiting Cultures: The Poetics and Politics of Museum Display,* ed. Ivan Karp and Steven D. Lavine (Washington: Smithsonian Institution Press, 1991).

4 Asaeda Zenshō, Samuel C. Morse, and Anne Nishimura Morse, eds., *Buddhist Art and Ritual* (Kyoto: Tankyūsha, 1998), 5–65.

5 Richard H. Davis, *Lives of Indian Images* (Princeton, NJ: Princeton University Press, 1997), 8–10.

CHAPTER 1: ATTRACTION AND AVERSION TO BUDDHIST ICONS

1 Michael Cooper, comp., *They Came to Japan: An Anthology of European Reports on Japan, 1543–1640* (Berkeley: University of California Press, 1965), 337.

2 Exodus 20:4–5, Leviticus 26:1, and Deuteronomy 4:15–18. See also Isaiah 44:9–20 and Jeremiah 10:1–5.

3 St. John of Damascus, *On the Divine Images: Three Apologies Against Those Who Attack the Divine Images* (Crestwood, NY: St. Vladimir's Seminary Press, 1980), 58–59, 63–64.

4 Peter Eichstaedt, *Above the Din of War* (Chicago: Lawrence Hill Books, 2013), 203–219; Takagi Tōru, *Daibutsu hakai: Bāmian iseki wa naze*

hakai sareta no ka (Tokyo: Bungai Shunjū, 2004); and Finnbar Barry Flood, "Between Cult and Culture: Bamiyan, Islamic Iconoclasm, and the Museum," *Art Bulletin* 84, no. 4 (December 2002): 641–659.

5 Robert H. Sharf, "Prolegomenon to the Study of Japanese Buddhist Icons," in *Living Images: Japanese Buddhist Icons in Context*, ed. Robert H. Sharf and Elizabeth Horton Sharf (Stanford, CA: Stanford University Press, 2001), 9–12.

6 See, for example, the *Encyclopaedia of Religion and Ethics*, edited by James Hastings (New York: Charles Scribner's Sons, 1908–1926), in which W. Crooke wrote on "Images and Idols (Indian)," 7:142–146; Tasuku Harada wrote on "Images and Idols (Japanese and Korean)," 7:146–148; and L. A. Waddell wrote on "Images and Idols (Tibetan)," 7:159–160.

7 Donald S. Lopez, Jr., *Buddhism and Science: A Guide for the Perplexed* (Chicago: University of Chicago Press, 2008), 1–37.

8 Sharf, "Prolegomenon," 3, 6, 8.

9 Edward Conze, *Buddhism: Its Essence and Development* (New York: Harper Torchbooks, 1959), 80–81; and A. B. Griswold, *What Is a Buddha Image?* (Bangkok: Fine Arts Department, 1968), 3–28.

10 Donald F. McCallum, *Zenkōji and Its Icon: A Study in Medieval Japanese Religious Art* (Princeton, NJ: Princeton University Press, 1994), 5–6.

11 See, for example, the *Larger Pure Land Sutra*, in Hisao Inagaki, *The Three Pure Land Sutras* (Kyoto: Nagata Bunshodo, 1994), 234.

12 For example, *The Sūtra of Contemplation on the Buddha of Immeasurable Life*, trans. Ryūkoku University Translation Center (Kyoto: Ryūkoku University Press, 1984).

13 Cynthea J. Bogel, *With a Single Glance: Buddhist Icon and Early Mikkyō Vision* (Seattle: University of Washington Press, 2009), 3, 180–181.

14 Robert E. Morrell, *Sand and Pebbles (Shasekishū): The Tales of Mujū Ichien. A Voice for Pluralism in Kamakura Buddhism* (Albany: State University of New York Press, 1985), 116.

CHAPTER 2: THE BUDDHIST IMAGE AS SACRED STORY

1 Concerning narrative theory and the interpretative community of religious images, see Stephen Crites, "The Narrative Quality of Experience," *Journal of the American Academy of Religion* 39, no. 3 (September 1971): 291–311; William K. Wimsatt and Monroe C. Beardsley, "The Intentional Fallacy" and "The Affective Fallacy," in *The Verbal Icon: Studies in the Meaning of Poetry* (New York: Noonday Press, 1958), 3–18 and 21–39; Roland

Barthes, "The Death of the Author," in *Image, Music, Text* (New York: Hill and Wang, 1977), 142–148; Michel Foucault, "What Is an Author?" in *Language, Counter-Memory, Practice: Selected Essays and Interviews* (Ithaca, NY: Cornell University Press, 1977), 113–138; Stanley Fish, *Is There a Text in This Class? The Authority of Interpretive Communities* (Cambridge, MA: Harvard University Press, 1980), 1–17, 167–172; and Richard H. Davis, *Lives of Indian Images* (Princeton, NJ: Princeton University Press, 1997), 8–10, 261–263.

2 For representative studies of the Buddha's life, see Edward J. Thomas, *The Life of Buddha as Legend and History* (London: Routledge and Kegan Paul, 1949); Nakamura Hajime, *Gotama Buddha—A Biography Based on the Most Reliable Texts,* 2 vols. (Tokyo: Kosei, 2000 and 2005); and Nagao Gadjin, "The Life of the Buddha: An Interpretation," *Eastern Buddhist,* n.s., 20, no. 2 (1987): 1–31.

3 The Japanese rendering of the sutra is *Kako genzai ingakyō,* collected in *Kokuyaku issaikyō,* ed. Iwano Shin'yu (Tokyo: Daitō Shuppansha, 1929), 32:1–120. The version found in the Buddhist canon is in vol. 3 of *Taishō shinshū daizōkyō,* ed. Takakusu Junjirō and Watanabe Kaigyoku (Tokyo: Issaikyō Kankōkai, 1924–1932), 620c–653b. Hereafter *Taishō shinshū daizōkyō* is cited as TD.

4 *Kokuyaku issaikyō,* 32:26.

5 Ibid., 32:91.

6 *Daihatsunehangyō,* TD, 1:191b–207c; and *Daihatsunehangyō,* TD, 12:365a–604a. For popular liturgical texts commemorating the death of the Buddha, see the *Nehan kōshiki* attributed to Genshin (942–1017), in *Dai Nihon Bukkyō zensho* (Tokyo: Meicho Fukyūkai, 1978), 33:183–185; and the *Shiza kōshiki* composed by Myōe (1173–1232), in TD, 84:898–906.

7 Marian Ury, *Tales of Times Now Past: Sixty-Two Stories from a Medieval Japanese Collection* (Berkeley: University of California Press, 1979), 44.

8 *Butsuyuikyōgyō,* TD, 12:1110c–1112b.

9 Jacob N. Kinnard, *Imaging Wisdom: Seeing and Knowing in the Art of Indian Buddhism* (Surrey, UK: Curzon Press, 1999), 25–44.

10 Susan L. Huntington, "Early Buddhist Art and the Theory of Aniconism," *Art Journal* 49, no. 4 (Winter 1990): 401–408; Vidya Dehejia, "Aniconism and the Multivalence of Emblems," *Ars Orientalis* 21 (1991): 45–66; and Susan L. Huntington, "Aniconism and the Multivalence of Emblems: Another Look," *Ars Orientalis* 22 (1992): 111–156.

11 Alfred Foucher, *The Beginnings of Buddhist Art and Other Essays in Indian and Central Asian Archaeology* (London: Milford, 1918); Ananda

Coomaraswamy, *The Origin of the Buddha Image* (Delhi: Munshiram Manoharlal, 1972); and A. K. Narain, "First Images of the Buddha and Bodhisattvas: Ideology and Chronology," in *Studies in Buddhist Art of South Asia*, ed. A. K. Narain (New Delhi: Kanak Publications, 1985), 1–21.

12 Robert H. Sharf, "The Scripture in Forty-Two Sections," in *Religions of China in Practice*, ed. Donald S. Lopez, Jr. (Princeton, NJ: Princeton University Press, 1996), 360–361.

13 W. G. Aston, trans., *Nihongi: Chronicles of Japan from the Earliest Times to A.D. 697* (Tokyo: Charles E. Tuttle, 1972), 2:65; and Masaharu Anesaki, *History of Japanese Religion: With Special Reference to the Social and Moral Life of the Nation* (London: K. Paul, Trench, Trubner and Co., 1930), 51–56.

14 Robert H. Sharf, "The Scripture on the Production of Buddhist Images," in *Religions of China in Practice*, 261–264; Benjamin Rowland, Jr., "A Note on the Invention of the Buddha Image," *Harvard Journal of Asiatic Studies* 11, no. 1–2 (June 1948): 181–183; and Martha L. Carter, *The Mystery of the Udayana Buddha*, supplement no. 64 agli Annali—vol. 50, fasc. 3 (Napoli: Instituto Universitario Orientale, 1990).

15 Sasaki Kōzō, *Seiryōji* (Tokyo: Chūō Kōron Bijutsu Shuppan, 2001), 21–40; and Gregory Henderson and Leon Hurvitz, "The Buddha of Seiryōji: New Finds and New Theory," *Artibus Asiae* 19, no. 1 (1956): 5–21.

CHAPTER 3: THE EXPRESSIVE DETAIL

1 Explanations of Buddhist iconography and symbolism in this chapter are derived from a wide variety of sources: Nakamura Hajime, ed., *Zusetsu Bukkyōgo daijiten* (Tokyo: Tokyo Shoseki, 1988); Louis Frédéric, *Buddhism: Flammarion Iconographic Guides* (Paris: Flammarion, 1995); E. Dale Saunders, *Mudrā: A Study of Symbolic Gestures in Japanese Buddhist Sculpture* (New York: Pantheon Books, 1960); Sawa Ryūken, *Bukkyō bijutsu nyūmon* (Tokyo: Shakai Shisōsha, 1968) and *Butsuzō zuten, Zōhoban* (Tokyo: Yoshikawa Kōbunkan, 1990); Sōgō Bukkyō Daijiten Henshū Iinkai, ed., *Sōgō Bukkyō daijiten*, 3 vols. (Kyoto: Hōzōkan, 1988); Nakamura Hajime, *Kōsetsu Bukkyōgo daijiten*, 4 vols. (Tokyo: Tokyo Shoseki, 2001); Furuta Shōkin et al., eds., *Buddhica—Bukkyō daijiten* (Tokyo: Shōgakkan, 1988); Nara Kokuritsu Hakubutsukan, ed., *Butsuzō no katachi to gihō* (Nara: Nara Kokuritsu Hakubutsukan, 1988); Meher McArthur, *Reading Buddhist Art: An Illustrated Guide to Buddhist Signs and Symbols* (London: Thames and Hudson, 2002); Mochizuki Shinkō, *Bukkyō daijiten*, 10 vols. (Tokyo: Sekai

Seiten Kankō Kyōkai, 1960); and Ariga Yoshitaka, *Butsuga no kanshō kiso chishiki* (Tokyo: Shibundō, 1996).

2 The exact items listed among the thirty-two marks vary somewhat from text to text. A representative list is found in Nakamura, *Kōsetsu Bukkyōgo daijiten,* 1:580a–581a, s.v. "Sanjūnisō." A scriptural example of such a list is found in *Kako genzai ingakyō,* in *Kokuyaku issaikyō,* ed. Iwano Shin'yu (Tokyo: Daitō Shuppansha, 1929), 32:22–24. Other works explaining the thirty-two marks include: Sōgō Bukkyō Daijiten, *Sōgō Bukkyō daijiten,* 1:483–484, s.v. "Sanjūnisō"; Furuta et al., *Buddhica—Bukkyō daijiten,* 350–351, s.v. "Sanjūnisō"; Sawa, *Bukkyō bijutsu nyumon,* 33–40; and McArthur, *Reading Buddhist Art,* 94–97.

3 Concerning the eighty minor characteristics, see Mochizuki, *Bukkyō daijiten,* 5:4212–4213, s.v. "Hachijūshukō"; Nakamura, *Kōsetsu Bukkyōgo daijiten,* 3:1355a, s.v. "Hachijūshukō"; Sōgō Bukkyō Daijiten, *Sōgō Bukkyō daijiten,* 1:1156, s.v. "Hachijūshukō"; and Furuta et al., *Buddhica—Bukkyō daijiten,* 793, s.v. "Hachijūshukō."

4 The three rings, though found ubiquitously in Buddhist icons, are not specifically listed among the Buddha's eighty minor characteristics. One of the eighty, however, indicates that the Buddha's upper body is perfect and full (*enman*), displaying the unparalleled dignity of a lion king. See Mochizuki, *Bukkyō daijiten,* 5:4212, s.v. "Hachijūshukō." This may have been the basis for depicting his neck as full and fleshy. Alternatively, the three rings may have been based on one of the thirty-two marks—the idea that the Buddha has seven places on his body that are abundant and full (*shichisho ryūmansō*), one of which according to some interpretations is the neck. See Sōgō Bukkyō Daijiten, *Sōgō Bukkyō daijiten,* 1:483, s.v. "Sanjūnisō."

5 James C. Dobbins, "Genshin's Deathbed Nembutsu Ritual in Pure Land Buddhism," in *Religions of Japan in Practice,* ed. George J. Tanabe, Jr. (Princeton, NJ: Princeton University Press, 1999), 173.

6 For iconographic lists of the most common hand gestures, see Saunders, *Mudrā,* 51–120; Nakamura, *Zusetsu Bukkyōgo daijiten,* 76–77, s.v. "Ingei"; Bijutsu Shuppansha, ed., *Butsuzō gaido* (Tokyo: Bijutsu Shuppansha, 1966), 180–181; McArthur, *Reading Buddhist Art,* 111–117; and Charles F. Chicarelli, *Buddhist Art: An Illustrated Introduction* (Chiang Mai, Thailand: Silkworm Books, 2004), 257–259.

7 Masaharu Anesaki, *Buddhist Art in Its Relation to Buddhist Ideals—With Special Reference to Buddhism in Japan* (1923; New York: Hacker Art Books, 1978), 15–16. The origins and significance of the lotus symbol are far more complex than this simple metaphor, though it is often cited as a popular

explanation. For an in-depth discussion of the issue, see Heinrich Zimmer, *The Art of Indian Asia: Its Mythology and Transformations* (Princeton, NJ: Princeton University Press, 1983), 1:158–230; and Ananda K. Coomaraswamy, *Elements of Buddhist Iconography* (Cambridge: Harvard University Press, 1935), 39–59.

8 This threefold explanation of icons is an adaptation based on Donald F. McCallum, *Zenkōji and Its Icon: A Study of Medieval Japanese Religious Art* (Princeton, NJ: Princeton University Press, 1994), 181–182.

CHAPTER 4: FULLY ENLIGHTENED BUDDHAS

1 Concerning the early iconographic layout of the Hōryūji Temple, see Bunsaku Kurata, *Hōryū-ji: Temple of the Exalted Law. Early Buddhist Art from Japan* (New York: Japan Society, 1981), 23–24; and Akiko Walley, *Constructing the Dharma King: The Hōryūji Shaka Triad and the Birth of the Prince Shōtoku Cult* (Leiden: Brill, 2015), 159–160.

2 Sarah J. Horton, *Living Buddhist Statues in Early Medieval and Modern Japan* (New York: Palgrave Macmillan, 2007), 26–31, 42–46.

3 Gregory P. A. Levine, *Daitokuji: The Visual Cultures of a Zen Monastery* (Seattle: University of Washington Press, 2005), 98–102.

4 Burton Watson, trans., *The Lotus Sutra* (New York: Columbia University Press), 170–181, 224–232; and *Myōhō rengenkyō,* TD, 9:32b–34b, 42a–44a.

5 Shōtarō Iida and Jane Goldstone, trans., *The Sutra That Expounds the Descent of Maitreya Buddha and His Enlightenment* (Moraga, CA: Bukkyō Dendō Kyōkai America, 2016), 5–25.

6 Raoul Birnbaum, *The Healing Buddha* (Boulder, CO: Shambhala Publications, 1979), 153–154. The sutra listing these twelve vows is the *Yakushi Rurikō nyorai hongan kudokukyō,* TD, 14:404–408.

7 Itō Shirō, *Yakushi Nyoraizō, Nihon no bijutsu* 242 (July 1986): 18–19.

8 A. Charles Muller and Kenneth K. Tanaka, trans., *The Brahma's Net Sutra* (Moraga, CA: Bukkyō Dendō Kyōkai America, 2017), 41; and *Bonmōkyō,* TD, 24:1003c–1004a.

9 Timothy Cleary, trans., *The Flower Ornament Scripture: A Translation of the Avatamsaka Sutra,* 3 vols. (Boston: Shambhala, 1985–1987), 1:256, 257; and *Daihōkō Butsu Kegonkyō,* TD, 10:54b26–27, 10:55a1–2.

10 Sawa Ryūken, *Butsuzō zuten, Zōhoban* (Tokyo: Yoshikawa Kōbunkan, 1990), 34–35; Nakamura Hajime, ed., *Zusetsu Bukkyōgo daijiten* (Tokyo: Tokyo Shoseki, 1988), 440, s.v. "Dainichi Nyorai"; and E. Dale Saunders,

Mudrā: A Study of Symbolic Gestures in Japanese Buddhist Sculpture (New York: Pantheon Books, 1960), 102–107.

11 Elizabeth ten Grotenhuis, *Japanese Mandalas: Representations of Sacred Geography* (Honolulu: University of Hawai'i Press, 1999), 60–66.

12 Ibid., 38–46.

13 Okazaki Jōji, ed., *Butsugu daijiten* (Tokyo: Kamakura Shinsho, 1982), 446–467.

14 Taikō Yamasaki links the two mandala to visualization practices in *Shingon: Japanese Esoteric Buddhism* (Boston: Shambhala, 1988), 123–149 and 198–210, whereas Robert H. Sharf, in "Visualization and Mandala in Shingon Buddhism," in *Living Images: Japanese Buddhist Icons in Context*, ed. Robert H. Sharf and Elizabeth Horton Sharf (Stanford, CA: Stanford University Press, 2001), 151–197, shows that visualization is not the function of the mandala in mainstream ritual. See also Cynthea J. Bogel, *With a Single Glance: Buddhist Icon and Early Mikkyō Vision* (Seattle: University of Washington Press, 2009), 218–224.

15 Hisao Inagaki, *The Three Pure Land Sutras: A Study and Translation* (Kyoto: Nagata Bunshodo, 1994), 3–57, 227–313; and Luis O. Gómez, trans., *The Land of Bliss: The Paradise of the Buddha of Measureless Light* (Honolulu: University of Hawai'i Press, 1996), 23–59, 153–222.

16 Elizabeth ten Grotenhuis, *The Revival of the Taima Mandala in Medieval Japan* (New York: Garland, 1985).

17 Jacqueline I. Stone, *Right Thoughts at the Last Moment: Buddhism and Deathbed Practices in Early Medieval Japan* (Honolulu: University of Hawai'i Press, 2016), 29–80.

CHAPTER 5: MIRACULOUS BODHISATTVAS

1 Sawa Ryūken, *Bukkyō bijutsu nyūmon* (Tokyo: Shakai Shisōsha, 1968), 62–66; Furuta Shōkin et al., eds., *Buddhica—Bukkyō daijiten* (Tokyo: Shōgakkan, 1988), 962–963, s.v. "Miroku Bosatsu"; Sekine Shun'ichi, ed., *Busson no jiten* (Tokyo: Gakken, 1997), 60–61; and Nara Kokuritsu Hakubutsukan, ed., *Butsuzō no katachi to gihō* (Nara: Nara Kokuritsu Hakubutsukan, 1988), 20.

2 M. W. de Wisser, *The Bodhisattva Ti-tsang (Jizō) in China and Japan* (Berlin: Oesterheld, 1914), 6–13; Hsüan Hua and Heng Ching, *Sūtra of the Past Vows of Earth Store Bodhisattva* (New York: Buddhist Text Translation Society and Institute for Advanced Studies of World Religions, 1974), 74, 88–89, 95, 126–127, 147, 188; *Jizō Bosatsu hongangyō*, TD, 13:777c–790a; and the *Daijō daishū Jizō jūringyō*, TD, 13:721a–777c.

3 Yoshiko Kurata Dykstra, "Jizō, the Most Merciful: Tales from *Jizō Bosatsu Reigenki*," *Monumenta Nipponica* 33, no. 2 (Summer 1978): 196–197.

4 Sarah J. Horton, *Living Buddhist Statues in Early Medieval and Modern Japan* (New York: Palgrave Macmillan, 2007), 112–155; William LaFleur, *Liquid Life: Abortion and Buddhism in Japan* (Princeton, NJ: Princeton University Press, 1992); and Bardwell Smith, *Narratives of Sorrow and Dignity: Japanese Women, Pregnancy Loss, and Modern Rituals of Grieving* (Oxford: Oxford University Press, 2013).

5 John R. McRae, trans., *The Vimalakīrti Sutra* (Berkeley: Bukkyō Dendō Kyōkai and Numata Center for Translation and Research, 2004), 55–179.

6 Pi-Cheng Lee, trans., *The Vows of Bodhisattva Samantabhadra Sutra* (Singapore: Golden Earth Design and Printing, 2004); Timothy Cleary, trans., *The Flower Ornament Scripture: A Translation of the Avatamsaka Sutra* (Boston: Shambhala, 1987), 3:387–394; and *Daihōkō Butsu kegonkyō*, TD, 10:442c–444c.

7 Cleary, *Flower Ornament Scripture*, 3:11–394; and *Daihōkō Butsu kegonkyō*, TD, 10:319–444.

8 Sawa, *Bukkyō bijutsu nyūmon*, 160–166; and Sekine, *Busson no jiten*, 76–77.

9 Burton Watson, trans., *The Lotus Sutra* (New York: Columbia University Press, 1993), 309–311, 319–324; and *Myōhō rengenkyō*, TD, 9:59a–b, 61a–62a. Also, see Nicole Fabricand-Person, "Demonic Female Guardians of the Faith: The Fugen Jūrasetsunyo Iconography in Japanese Buddhist Art," in *Engendering Faith: Women and Buddhism in Premodern Japan*, ed. Barbara Ruch (Ann Arbor: Center for Japanese Studies, University of Michigan, 2002), 343–382.

10 Watson, *Lotus Sutra*, 298–306; *Myōhō rengenkyō*, TD, 9:56c–58b; and Sawa Ryūken, *Butsuzō zuten, Zōhoban* (Tokyo: Yoshikawa Kōbunkan, 1990), 55–57.

11 Hisao Inagaki, *The Three Pure Land Sutras: A Study and Translation* (Kyoto: Nagata Bunshodo, 1994), 275, 334–337, 339–343; *Muryōjukyō*, TD, 12:273b; and *Kanmuryōjukyō*, TD, 12:343c–344b, 344c–345b.

12 For examples, *Sengen senpi Kanzeon Bosatsu darani jinjukyō*, TD, 20:83b–96b; *Jūichimen Kanzeon jinjukyō*, TD, 20:149a–152a; *Batō Kannon shin darani*, TD, 20:170ab; *Shichiguchi Butsumoshin Dai Juntei daranikyō*, TD, 20:185a–186b; *Kanzeon Bosatsu himitsuzō nyoirin darani jinjukyō*, TD, 20:197b–200a; and *Fukūkenjaku jukyō*, TD, 20:399a–402b.

13 Sekine, *Busson no jiten*, 64–65; Sawa, *Butsuzō zuten, Zōhoban*, 53–54; and Louis Frédéric, *Buddhism: Flammarion Iconographic Guides* (Paris: Flammarion, 1995), 155–156.

14 Tove E. Neville, *Eleven-Headed Avalokiteśvara—Chenresigs, Kuan-yin or Kannon Bodhisattva: Its Origin and Iconography* (New Delhi: Munshiram Manoharlal, 1998), 14–15.
15 Frédéric, *Buddhism,* 163–169.
16 Sherry D. Fowler, *Accounts and Images of Six Kannon in Japan* (Honolulu: University of Hawai'i Press, 2016), 17–28; Frédéric, *Buddhism,* 156–162; Sawa, *Butsuzō zuten, Zōhoban,* 72–74, 76; Sawa, *Bukkyō bijutsu nyūmon,* 148–151.
17 Nakamura Hajime, ed., *Zusetsu Bukkyōgo daijiten* (Tokyo: Tokyo Shoseki, 1988), 646–647, s.v. "Maria Kannon."
18 Horton, *Living Buddhist Statues,* 77–111.

CHAPTER 6: OTHER MYTHIC BUDDHIST FIGURES

1 Kumada Yumiko, ed., *Butsuzō no jiten* (Tokyo: Seibidō Shuppan, 2006), 52–57.
2 Robert E. Morrell, *Sand and Pebbles (Shasekishū): The Tales of Mujū Ichien. A Voice for Pluralism in Kamakura Buddhism* (Albany: State University of New York Press, 1985), 116. This is an English paraphrase of the original text rather than an exact translation.
3 Bernard Faure, *Gods of Medieval Japan,* vol. 1, *The Fluid Pantheon* (Honolulu: University of Hawai'i Press, 2016), 115–151.
4 Faure, *Fluid Pantheon,* 167–198.
5 Sawa Ryūken, *Bukkyō bijutsu nyūmon* (Tokyo: Shakai Shisōsha, 1968), 200–202.
6 Kumada, *Butsuzō no jiten,* 66–67.
7 Nishimura Kōchō, *Yoku wakaru Butsuzō no mikata: Yamatoji no Butsutachi* (Tokyo: Shōgakkan, 1999), 36–39.
8 Sawa Ryūken, *Butsuzō zuten, Zōhoban* (Tokyo: Yoshikawa Kōbunkan, 1990), 133–135.
9 Nishimura, *Yoku wakaru Butsuzō no mikata,* 40–43.
10 Raoul Birnbaum, *The Healing Buddha* (Boulder, CO: Shambhala Publications, 1979), 169, 208.
11 Nishimura, *Yoku wakaru Butsuzō no mikata,* 56–59.
12 Sawa, *Butsuzō zuten, Zōhoban,* 137–138.
13 Kyoko Motomochi Nakamura, trans., *Miraculous Tales from the Japanese Buddhist Tradition: The* Nihon ryōiki *of the Monk Kyōkai* (Cambridge, MA: Harvard University Press, 1973), 178.
14 Louis Frédéric, *Buddhism: Flammarion Iconographic Guides* (Paris: Flammarion, 1995), 221–223, 238–240.

15 Ibid., 252–254.

16 Sekine Shun'ichi, ed., *Busson no jiten* (Tokyo: Gakken, 1997), 212–213, 217–218.

17 Nakamura Hajime, ed., *Zusetsu Bukkyōgo daijiten* (Tokyo: Tokyo Shoseki, 1988), 420–421, s.v. "Sōgyō Hachiman shin."

18 Sekine, *Busson no jiten*, 226–227; and Sōhonzan Kinpusenji, ed., *Yamabushi Shugendō Zaō Gongen nyūmon* (Tokyo: Sōhonzan Kinpusenji and Kokusho Kankōkai, 2010), 10–17, 72–80.

CHAPTER 7: BUDDHIST ICONS AS LIVING ENTITIES

1 Horiike Shunpō, *Tōdaijishi e no izanai* (Kyoto: Shōwadō, 2004), 34–46; Nara Kokuritsu Hakubutsukan et al., eds., *Daibutsu kaigen 1250 nen: Tōdaiji no subete* (Tokyo: Asahi Shinbunsha, 2002), 10–12; Tsuji Zennosuke, *Nihon Bukkyōshi* (Tokyo: Iwanami Shoten, 1944–1955), 1:164–167, 174–178; Roger Goepper, "Icon and Ritual in Japanese Buddhism," in *Enlightenment Embodied: The Art of the Japanese Buddhist Sculptor (7th–14th Centuries)* (New York: Japan Society, 1997), 75; and Nara Kokuritsu Hakubutsukan, ed., *Shōsōin ten rokujukkai no ayumi* (Nara: Nara Kokuritsu Hakubutsukan, 2008), 40, 149.

2 Donald K. Swearer, *Becoming the Buddha: The Ritual of Image Consecration in Thailand* (Princeton, NJ: Princeton University Press, 2004), 77–121; Richard Gombrich, "The Consecration of a Buddhist Image," *Journal of Asian Studies* 26, no. 1 (November 1966): 23–36; Yael Bentor, *Consecration of Images and Stūpas in Indo-Tibetan Tantric Buddhism* (Leiden: E. J. Brill, 1996), 13–19; Fujii Masao, ed., *Shinsōban Bukkyō girei jiten* (Tokyo: Tōkyōdō, 2001), 39–40, 177–195; and Bernard Faure, *Visions of Power: Imagining Medieval Japanese Buddhism* (Princeton, NJ: Princeton University Press, 1996), 249–255.

3 Concerning these issues, see Robert H. Sharf, "Prolegomenon to the Study of Japanese Buddhist Icons," in *Living Images: Japanese Buddhist Icons in Context*, ed. Robert H. Sharf and Elizabeth Horton Sharf (Stanford, CA: Stanford University Press, 2001), 15-16; and "On the Allure of Buddhist Relics," *Representations* 66 (Spring 1999): 85-92.

4 Swearer, *Becoming the Buddha*, 212–218.

5 Gregory Henderson and Leon Hurvitz, "The Buddha of Seiryōji: New Finds and New Theory," *Artibus Asiae* 19, no. 1 (1956): 5–9, 22–35, 47–49; Helmut Brinker, *Secrets of the Sacred: Empowering Buddhist Images in Clear, in Code, and in Cache* (Lawrence: Spencer Museum of Art, University of

Kansas, 2011), 33–45; and Sarah J. Horton, *Living Buddhist Statues in Early Medieval and Modern Japan* (New York: Palgrave Macmillan, 2007), 26, 42–43. Also see Faure, *Visions of Power,* 248–249; Swearer, *Becoming the Buddha,* 197, 206–207, 226–228; and Gombrich, "Consecration of a Buddhist Image," 36.

6 Daisetz Teitaro Suzuki, *Essays in Zen Buddhism (First Series)* (London: Rider, 1949), 330–334. The locus classicus of this story is *Keitoku dentōroku,* TD, 51:310c13–16.

7 Horton, *Living Buddhist Statues,* 39–40.

8 Yamagishi Tsuneto, *Tō to Butsudō no tabi: Jiin kenchiku kara rekishi o yomu* (Tokyo: Asahi Shinbunsha, 2005), 9–12, 62–66; and Martin Collcutt, *Five Mountains: The Rinzai Zen Monastic Institution in Medieval Japan* (Cambridge, MA: Council on East Asian Studies, Harvard University, 1981), 171–220.

9 Yamagishi, *Tō to Butsudō no tabi,* 12–24, 42–60, 78–90; and Soejima Hiromichi, ed., *Butsuzō kanshō gaido: A Guide to Japanese Buddhist Sculpture* (Tokyo: Ikeda Shoten, 2008), 18.

10 Monica Bethe, "Butsuzen to sono shūhen" (Worship Sanctuary: Altars and Their Surroundings), in *Amamonzeki jiin no sekai,* ed. Chūsei Nihon Kenkyūjo et al. (Tokyo: Sankei Shinbunsha, 2009), 136–151; and Robert H. Sharf, "Visualization and Mandala in Shingon Buddhism," in Sharf and Sharf, *Living Images,* 158–159.

11 Burton Watson, trans., *The Lotus Sutra* (New York: Columbia University Press, 1993), 80.

12 Kosho Yamamoto, trans., *The Mahayana Mahaparinirvana Sutra,* Karin Buddhological Series 5 (1973; PDF reprint, ed. Tony Page, 2007), 139. http://lirs.ru/do/Mahaparinirvana_Sutra,Yamamoto,Page,2007.pdf.

13 Fujii, *Shinsōban Bukkyō girei jiten,* 231–265. For a video of the morning ceremony at Sōjiji Zen Monastery in Yokohama, see Sōtōshū Daihonzan Sōjiji Chōka, accessed October 14, 2018, https://www.youtube.com/watch?v=BBF2q0p9pdg.

14 Bukkyō Ryōri Kenkyūkai, ed., *Shōjin ryōri daijiten,* vols. 1–2 (Tokyo: Yūzankaku, 1983).

15 Horton, *Living Buddhist Statues,* 135–136.

16 Richard Karl Payne, *The Tantric Ritual of Japan, Feeding the Gods: The Shingon Fire Ritual* (Delhi: International Academy of Indian Culture and Aditya Prakashan, 1991), 88–191; and Sharf, "Visualization and Mandala," 157–192.

17 Uehara Shōichi et al., *Kurashi no naka no Butsuji Bukkyō hyakka* (Tokyo: Shūeisha, 1989), 182–191; and Sagawa Sōgen and Yoshioka Sachio, *Tōdaiji,* Koji junrei Nara 3 (Kyoto: Tankōsha, 2010), 138.

18 Mori Seihan and Tanabe Seiko, *Kiyomizudera,* Koji junrei Kyōto 26 (Kyoto: Tankōsha, 2008), 88–94.

19 Horton, *Living Buddhist Statues,* 156–192; and Mori and Tanabe, *Kiyomizudera,* 36.

20 Donald F. McCallum, *Zenkōji and Its Icon: A Study in Medieval Japanese Religious Art* (Princeton, NJ: Princeton University Press, 1994), 3–16.

21 Komatsu Shigemi, ed., *Shigisan engi,* Nihon emaki 4 (Tokyo: Chūō Kōronsha, 1987) 82–85, 109–112; and Takahata Isao, *Jūni seiki no animeeshon: Kokuhō emakimono ni miru eiga teki anime teki narumono* (Tokyo: Tokuma Shoten, 2008), 40.

CHAPTER 8: BEYOND THE BUDDHA IMAGE

1 Brian D. Ruppert, "Relics and Relics Cults," in *The Encyclopedia of Buddhism,* ed. Robert E. Buswell, Jr. (New York: Macmillan Reference, 2004), 2:715; H. L. Seneviratne, *Rituals of the Kandyan State* (London: Cambridge University Press, 1978), 1–37; and Robert H. Sharf, "The Buddha's Finger Bones at Famensi and the Art of Chinese Esoteric Buddhism," *Art Bulletin* 93, no. 1 (March 2011): 38–59.

2 Nakamura Hajime, *Gotama Buddha—A Biography Based on the Most Reliable Texts* (Tokyo: Kosei, 2005), 2:177–192; and John S. Strong, *Relics of the Buddha* (Princeton, NJ: Princeton University Press, 2004), 98–125.

3 Fu Xinian et al., *Chinese Architecture* (New Haven, CT: Yale University Press, 2002), 85–87; and Laurence G. Liu, *Chinese Architecture* (New York: Rizzoli, 1989), 56–73.

4 William E. Deal, "Buddhism and the State in Early Japan," in *Buddhism in Practice,* ed. Donald S. Lopez, Jr. (Princeton, NJ: Princeton University Press, 1995), 218–220; and W. G. Aston, trans., *Nihongi: Chronicles of Japan from the Earliest Times to A.D. 697* (Tokyo: Charles E. Tuttle, 1972), 2:65, 101–102.

5 Nara Kokuritsu Hakubutsukan, ed., *Shari to hōju: Shaka o shitau kokoro* (Nara: Nara Kokuritsu Hakubutsukan, 2001), 44, 199.

6 Edward Kamens, *The Three Jewels: A Study and Translation of Minamoto Tamenori's Sanbōe* (Ann Arbor: Center for Japanese Studies, University of Michigan, 1988), 302.

7 Imaizumi Yoshio, ed., *Nihon Bukkyōshi jiten* (Tokyo: Yoshikawa Kōbunkan, 1999), s.v. "Shari," "Shariden," "Sharitō," and "Busshari," 447–448, 893; and James L. Ford, *Jōkei and Buddhist Devotion in Early Medieval Japan* (New York: Oxford University Press, 2006), 121–122.

8 Strong, *Relics of the Buddha,* 10–12; and Nara Kokuritsu Hakubutsukan, *Shari to hōju,* 51, 53, 54, 56, 71–73, 76, 78, 83, 103, 104, 118, 121–123, 125–128.

9 Strong, *Relics of the Buddha,* 124–149; Brian D. Ruppert, *Jewel in the Ashes: Buddha Relics and Power in Early Medieval Japan* (Cambridge, MA: Harvard University Asia Center, 2000); and Nara Kokuritsu Hakubutsukan, *Shari to hōju,* 52, 77, 80, 84, 86, 90, 97–102, 108.

10 Strong, *Relics of the Buddha,* 8; and Gregory Henderson and Leon Hurvitz, "The Buddha of Seiryōji: New Finds and New Theory," *Artibus Asiae* 19, no. 1 (1956): 12, 27–31, 48.

11 Burton Watson, trans., *The Lotus Sutra* (New York: Columbia University Press, 1993). 161.

12 John Kieschnick, *The Impact of Buddhism on Chinese Material Culture* (Princeton, NJ: Princeton University Press, 2003), 164–176.

13 Bunsaku Kurata and Yoshirō Tamura, eds., *Art of the Lotus Sutra: Japanese Masterpieces* (Tokyo: Kōsei Publishing, 1987), illustrations 20, 59, 66, 67, 68.

14 Heather Elizabeth Blair, "Peak of Gold: Place, Trace, and Religion in Heian Japan" (PhD diss., Harvard University, 2008), 67–73, 77–97, 107–116, 151–188; and Kurata and Tamura, *Art of the Lotus Sutra,* illustrations 100, 101, 104, 105.

15 Jacqueline I. Stone, *Original Enlightenment and the Transformation of Medieval Japanese Buddhism* (Honolulu: University of Hawai'i Press, 1999), 280.

16 Ibid., 272–288.

17 James C. Dobbins, "Portraits of Shinran in Medieval Pure Land Buddhism," in *Living Images: Japanese Buddhist Icons in Context,* ed. Robert H. Sharf and Elizabeth Horton Sharf (Stanford, CA: Stanford University Press, 2001), 22–24, 25–27; and Chiba Jōryū, "Sōsetsu," in *Shinshū jūhō shūei,* vol. 1, "Myōgō honzon," ed. Chiba Jōryū (Kyoto: Dōbōsha, 1988), 185–197.

18 Gregory P. A. Levine, *Daitokuji: The Visual Cultures of a Zen Monastery* (Seattle: University of Washington Press, 2005), 145–159.

19 Bernard Faure, *The Rhetoric of Immediacy: A Cultural Critique of Chan/Zen Buddhism* (Princeton, NJ: Princeton University Press, 1991), 148–178.

20 Dobbins, "Portraits of Shinran," 33–48.

21 Uehara Shōichi et al., *Kurashi no naka no Butsuji Bukkyō hyakka* (Tokyo: Shūeisha, 1989), 51–53.

22 Ibid., 48–50; and Okazaki Jōji, ed., *Butsugu daijiten* (Tokyo: Kamakura Shinsho, 1982), 406–413.

AFTERWORD

1 Yamamoto Tsutomu, *Butsuzō no himitsu* (Tokyo: Asahi Shuppansha, 2006).

2 Fukuchi Makoto, ed., *Kimochi ii Bukkyō* (Tokyo: Yōsensha, 2004).

3 Kawahara Yoshio, ed., *Butsuzō no mikata miwakekata* (Tokyo: Shufu to Seikatsu Sha, 2002).

4 John M. Rosenfield, "Japanese Buddhist Art: Alive in the Modern Age," in Michael R. Cunningham, *Buddhist Treasures from Nara* (Cleveland: Cleveland Museum of Art, 1998), 232–244.

5 Alice Y. Tseng, *The Imperial Museums of Meiji Japan: Architecture and the Art of the Nation* (Seattle: University of Washington Press, 2008), 104–123.

6 Ibid., 141–148.

7 James Clifford, *Routes: Travel and Translation in the Late Twentieth Century* (Cambridge, MA: Harvard University Press, 1997), 188–219; and Mary Louise Pratt, *Imperial Eyes: Travel Writing and Transculturation* (London: Routledge, 1992), 1–11.

8 The exhibition occurred at the Cleveland Museum of Art from August 9 to September 27, 1998, and is documented in Cunningham, *Buddhist Treasures from Nara.*

SELECTED BIBLIOGRAPHY

BUDDHIST ICONOGRAPHY AND ART

Ariga Yoshitaka. *Butsuga no kanshō kiso chishiki.* Tokyo: Shibundō, 1996.

Bijutsu Shuppansha, ed. *Butsuzō gaido.* Tokyo: Bijutsu Shuppansha, 1966.

Bogel, Cynthea J. *With a Single Glance: Buddhist Icon and Early Mikkyō Vision.* Seattle: University of Washington Press, 2009.

Brinker, Helmut. *Secrets of the Sacred: Empowering Buddhist Images in Clear, in Code, and in Cache.* Lawrence: Spencer Museum of Art, University of Kansas, 2011.

Carter, Martha L. *The Mystery of the Udayana Buddha.* Supplement no. 64 agli Annali—vol. 50, fasc. 3. Napoli: Instituto Universitario Orientale, 1990.

Chicarelli, Charles F. *Buddhist Art: An Illustrated Introduction.* Chiang Mai, Thailand: Silkworm Books, 2004.

Coomaraswamy, Ananda K. *Elements of Buddhist Iconography.* Cambridge, MA: Harvard University Press, 1935.

———. *The Origin of the Buddha Image.* Delhi: Munshiram Manoharlal, 1972.

Cummings, Mary. *The Lives of the Buddha in the Art and Literature of Asia.* Ann Arbor: Center for South and Southeast Asian Studies, University of Michigan, 1982.

Cunningham, Michael R. *Buddhist Treasures from Nara.* Cleveland: Cleveland Museum of Art, 1998.

Daihōinkaku Henshūbu, ed. *Zukai Butsuga no yomikata.* Tokyo: Daihōinkaku, 1990.

Dehejia, Vidya. "Aniconism and the Multivalence of Emblems." *Ars Orientalis* 21 (1991): 45–66.

———. *Discourse in Early Buddhist Art: Visual Narratives of India.* New Delhi: Munshiram Manoharlal, 1997.

Epprecht, Katharina, ed. *Kannon: Divine Compassion. Early Buddhist Art From Japan.* Zurich: Museum Reitberg Zurich, 2007.

Fabricand-Person, Nicole. "Demonic Female Guardians of the Faith: The Fugen Jūrasetsunyo Iconography in Japanese Buddhist Art." In *Engen-*

dering Faith: Women and Buddhism in Premodern Japan, edited by Barbara Ruch, 343–382. Ann Arbor: Center for Japanese Studies, University of Michigan, 2002.

Fisher, Robert E. *Buddhist Art and Architecture.* London: Thames and Hudson, 1993.

Foucher, Alfred. *The Beginnings of Buddhist Art and Other Essays in Indian and Central Asian Archaeology.* London: Milford, 1918.

Fowler, Sherry D. *Accounts and Images of Six Kannon in Japan.* Honolulu: University of Hawai'i Press, 2016.

———. *Murōji: Rearranging Art and History at a Japanese Buddhist Temple.* Honolulu: University of Hawai'i Press, 2005.

Frédéric, Louis. *Buddhism: Flammarion Iconographic Guides.* Paris: Flammarion, 1995.

Fu Xinian et al. *Chinese Architecture.* New Haven, CT: Yale University Press, 2002.

Graham, Patricia Jane. *Faith and Power in Japanese Buddhist Art, 1600–2005.* Honolulu: University of Hawai'i Press, 2007.

Guth, Christine M.E. "The Pensive Prince of Chūgūji: Maitreya Cult and Image in Seventh-Century Japan." In *Maitreya, The Future Buddha,* edited by Alan Sponberg and Helen Hardacre, 191–213. Cambridge: Cambridge University Press, 1988.

Huntington, Susan L. "Aniconism and the Multivalence of Emblems: Another Look." *Ars Orientalis* 22 (1992): 111–156.

———. "Early Buddhist Art and the Theory of Aniconism." *Art Journal* 49, no. 4 (Winter 1990): 401–408.

Itō Shirō. *Yakushi Nyoraizō. Nihon no bijutsu* 242 (July 1986).

Kageyama, Haruki. *The Arts of Shinto.* Tokyo and New York: Weatherhill and Shibundo, 1973.

Karetzky, Patricia E. *Early Buddhist Narrative Art: Illustrations of the Life of the Buddha from Central Asia to China, Korea and Japan.* Lanham, MD: University Press of America, 2000.

Karlsson, Klemens. *Face to Face With the Absent Buddha: The Formation of Buddhist Aniconic Art.* Historia Religionium 15. Uppsala: Uppsala University Library, 1999.

Kawahara Yoshio, ed. *Butsuzō no mikata miwakekata.* Tokyo: Shufu to Seikatsu Sha, 2002.

Kumada Yumiko, ed. *Butsuzō no jiten.* Tokyo: Seibidō Shuppan, 2006.

Lee, Sherman E. "The Golden Image of the New-Born Buddha." *Artibus Asiae* 18, no. 3–4 (1955): 225–237.

Leidy, Denise Patry. *The Art of Buddhism: An Introduction to Its History and Meaning.* Boston: Shambhala, 2008.

Liu, Laurence G. *Chinese Architecture.* New York: Rizzoli, 1989.

McArthur, Meher. *Reading Buddhist Art: An Illustrated Guide to Buddhist Signs and Symbols.* London: Thames and Hudson, 2002.

McCallum, Donald F. *Zenkōji and Its Icon: A Study of Medieval Japanese Religious Art.* Princeton, NJ: Princeton University Press, 1994.

Morse, Samuel C., and Anne Nishimura Morse, eds. *Object as Insight: Buddhist Art and Ritual.* Katonah, NY: Katonah Museum of Art, 1995.

Nakamura Hajime, ed. *Zusetsu Bukkyōgo daijiten.* Tokyo: Tokyo Shoseki, 1988.

Nakano Teruo. *Enma Jūō zō. Nihon no bijutsu* 313 (June 1992).

Narain, A. K. "First Images of the Buddha and Bodhisattvas: Ideology and Chronology." In *Studies in Buddhist Art of South Asia,* edited by A. K. Narain, 1–21. New Delhi: Kanak Publications, 1985.

Nara Kokuritsu Hakubutsukan, ed. *Butsuzō no katachi to gihō.* Nara: Nara Kokuritsu Hakubutsukan, 1988.

———. *Shari to hōju: Shaka o shitau kokoro.* Nara: Nara Kokuritsu Hakubutsukan, 2001.

———. *Shōsōin ten rokujukkai no ayumi.* Nara: Nara Kokuritsu Hakubutsukan, 2008.

Neville, Tove E. *Eleven-Headed Avalokiteśvara—Chenresigs, Kuan-yin or Kannon Bodhisattva: Its Origin and Iconography.* New Delhi: Munshiram Manoharlal, 1998.

Nishimura Kōchō. *Yoku wakaru Butsuzō no mikata: Yamatoji no Butsutachi.* Tokyo: Shōgakkan, 1999.

Okazaki, Jōji. *Pure Land Buddhist Painting.* Tokyo: Kodansha International and Shibundo, 1977.

Rowland, Benjamin, Jr. "A Note on the Invention of the Buddha Image." *Harvard Journal of Asiatic Studies* 11, no. 1–2 (June 1948): 181–186.

Saunders, E. Dale. *Mudrā: A Study of Symbolic Gestures in Japanese Buddhist Sculpture.* New York: Pantheon Books, 1960.

Sawa Ryūken. *Bukkyō bijutsu nyūmon.* Tokyo: Shakai Shisōsha, 1968.

———. *Butsuzō zuten, Zōhoban.* Tokyo: Yoshikawa Kōbunkan, 1990.

Sekine Shun'ichi, ed. *Busson no jiten.* Tokyo: Gakken, 1997.

Sharf, Robert H., and Elizabeth Horton Sharf, eds. *Living Images: Japanese Buddhist Icons in Context.* Stanford, CA: Stanford University Press, 2001.

Soejima Hiromichi, ed. *Butsuzō kanshō gaido: A Guide to Japanese Buddhist Sculpture.* Tokyo: Ikeda Shoten, 2008.

ten Grotenhuis, Elizabeth. *Japanese Mandalas: Representations of Sacred Geography.* Honolulu: University of Hawai'i Press, 1999.

———. *The Revival of the Taima Mandala in Medieval Japan.* New York: Garland, 1985.

Washizuka Hiromitsu and Roger Goepper. *Enlightenment Embodied: The Art of the Japanese Buddhist Sculptor (7th–14th Centuries).* New York: Japan Society, 1997.

Yamagishi Tsuneto. *Tō to Butsudō no tabi: Jiin kenchiku kara rekishi o yomu.* Tokyo: Asahi Shinbunsha, 2005.

Yamamoto Tsutomu. *Butsuzō no himitsu.* Tokyo: Asahi Shuppansha, 2006.

Yiengpruksawan, Mimi Hall. *Hiraizumi: Buddhist Art and Regional Politics in Twelfth-Century Japan.* Cambridge, MA: Harvard University Asia Center, 1998.

Zimmer, Heinrich. *The Art of Indian Asia: Its Mythology and Transformations,* 2 vols. Princeton, NJ: Princeton University Press, 1983.

BUDDHIST TEMPLES AND RITUALS

Bethe, Monica. "Worship Sanctuary: Altars and Their Surroundings." In *Amamonzeki jiin no sekai,* edited by Chūsei Nihon Kenkyūjo et al., 148–151. Tokyo: Sankei Shinbunsha, 2009.

Chūsonji, ed. *Sekai isan Chūsonji.* Hiraizumi: Chūsonji, 2010.

Fujii Masao, ed. *Shinsōban Bukkyō girei jiten.* Tokyo: Tōkyōdō, 2001.

Henderson, Gregory, and Leon Hurvitz. "The Buddha of Seiryōji: New Finds and New Theory." *Artibus Asiae* 19, no. 1 (1956): 5–55.

Horiike Shunpō. *Tōdaijishi e no izanai.* Kyoto: Shōwadō, 2004.

Horton, Sarah J. *Living Buddhist Statues in Early Medieval and Modern Japan.* New York: Palgrave Macmillan, 2007.

Kidder, J. Edward, Jr. *The Lucky Seventh: Early Hōryū-ji and Its Time.* Tokyo: International Christian University, Hachiro Yuasa Memorial Museum, 1999.

Kurata, Bunsaku. *Hōryū-ji: Temple of the Exalted Law. Early Buddhist Art from Japan.* New York: Japan Society, 1981.

Levine, Gregory P. A. *Daitokuji: The Visual Cultures of a Zen Monastery.* Seattle: University of Washington Press, 2005.

MacWilliams, Mark. "Living Icons: 'Reizō' Myths of the Saikoku Kannon Pilgrimage." *Monumenta Nipponica* 59, no. 1 (Spring 2004): 35–82.

Matsuno Junkō, ed. *Bukkyō gyōji to sono shisō*. Tokyo: Daizō Shuppan, 1984.

McCallum, Donald. "The Replication of Miraculous Icons: The Zenkōji Amida and the Seiryōji Shaka." In *Images, Miracles, and Authority in Asian Religious Traditions,* edited by Richard Davis, 207–226. Boulder: Westview Press, 1998.

Mino, Yutaka, ed. *The Great Eastern Temple: Treasures of Japanese Buddhist Art from Tōdaiji.* Chicago: Art Institute of Chicago, 1986.

Mori Seihan and Tanabe Seiko. *Kiyomizudera.* Koji junrei Kyōto 26. Kyoto: Tankōsha, 2008.

Nara Kokuritsu Hakubutsukan, Tōdaiji, and Asahi Shinbunsha, eds. *Daibutsu Kaigan 1250 nen Tōdaiji no subete.* Tokyo: Asahi Shinbunsha, 2002.

Okazaki Jōji, ed. *Butsugu daijiten*. Tokyo: Kamakura Shinsho, 1982.

Sagawa Sōgen and Yoshioka Sachio. *Tōdaiji.* Koji junrei Nara 3. Kyoto: Tankōsha, 2010.

Sasaki, Kōzō. *Seiryōji.* Tokyo: Chūō Kōron Bijutsu Shuppan, 2001.

Sharf, Robert H. "The Buddha's Finger Bones at Famensi and the Art of Chinese Esoteric Buddhism." *Art Bulletin* 93, no. 1 (March 2011): 38–59.

Sōhonzan Kinpusenji, ed. *Yamabushi Shugendō Zaō Gongen nyūmon.* Tokyo: Sōhonzan Kinpusenji and Kokusho Kankōkai, 2010.

Tōkyō Kokuritsu Hakubutsukan, ed. *Hōryūji hōmotsukan.* Tokyo: Tōkyō Kokuritsu Hakubutsukan, 1999.

Walley, Akiko. *Constructing the Dharma King: The Hōryūji Shaka Triad and the Birth of the Prince Shōtoku Cult.* Leiden: Brill, 2015.

Weinstein, Lucie Ruth. "The Hōryūji Canopies and Their Continental Antecedents." PhD diss., Yale University, 1978.

Wong, Dorothy C., ed., *Hōryūji Reconsidered.* Newcastle: Cambridge Scholars Publishing, 2008.

INDIAN AND SOUTHEAST ASIAN BUDDHISM

Bentor, Yael. *Consecration of Images and Stūpas in Indo-Tibetan Tantric Buddhism.* Leiden: Brill, 1996.

Davis, Richard H. *Lives of Indian Images.* Princeton, NJ: Princeton University Press, 1997.

Eck, Diana L. *Darśan: Seeing the Divine Image in India.* 3rd ed. New York: Columbia University Press, 1993.

Eckel, Malcolm David. *To See the Buddha: A Philosopher's Quest for the Meaning of Emptiness.* San Francisco: Harper Collins, 1992.

Gombrich, Richard. "The Consecration of a Buddhist Image." *Journal of Asian Studies* 26, no. 1 (November, 1966): 23–36.

Hirakawa, Akira. *A History of Indian Buddhism From Śākyamuni to Early Mahāyāna.* Honolulu: University of Hawai'i Press, 1990.

Kawamura, Leslie S., ed. *The Bodhisattva Doctrine in Buddhism.* Waterloo, Canada: Wilfrid Laurier University Press, 1981.

Kinnard, Jacob N. *Imaging Wisdom: Seeing and Knowing in the Art of Indian Buddhism.* Surrey, U.K.: Curzon Press, 1999.

Kloetzli, W. Randolph. *Buddhist Cosmology—From Single World System to Pure Land: Science and Theology in the Images of Motion and Light.* Delhi: Motilal Banarsidass, 1983.

Nakamura, Hajime. *Gotama Buddha—A Biography Based on the Most Reliable Texts,* 2 vols. Tokyo: Kosei, 2000 and 2005.

Schopen, Gregory. "Burial *Ad Sanctos* and the Physical Presence of the Buddha in Early Indian Buddhism: A Study in the Archaeology of Religions." In *Bones, Stones, and Buddhist Monks: Collected Papers on the Archaeology, Epigraphy, and Texts of Monastic Buddhism in India,* 114–147. Honolulu: University of Hawai'i Press, 1997.

———. "The Phrase *sa pṛthivīpradeśaś caityabhūto bhavet* in the *Vajracchedikā:* Notes on the Cult of the Book in Mahāyāna." In *Figments and Fragments of Mahāyāna Buddhism in India,* 25–62. Honolulu: University of Hawai'i Press, 1997.

Seneviratne, H. L. *Rituals of the Kandyan State.* London: Cambridge University Press, 1978.

Strong, John S. *Relics of the Buddha.* Princeton, NJ: Princeton University Press, 2004.

Swearer, Donald K. *Becoming the Buddha: The Ritual of Image Consecration in Thailand.* Princeton, NJ: Princeton University Press, 2004.

Thomas, Edward J. *The Life of Buddha as Legend and History.* London: Routledge and Kegan Paul, 1949.

JAPANESE AND CHINESE BUDDHISM

Anesaki, Masaharu. *Buddhist Art in Its Relation to Buddhist Ideals—With Special Reference to Buddhism in Japan.* 1923. Reprint, New York: Hacker Art Books, 1978.

———. *History of Japanese Religion: With Special Reference to the Social and Moral Life of the Nation.* London: K. Paul, Trench, Trubner, and Co., 1930.

Blair, Heather. *Real and Imagined: The Peak of Gold in Heian Japan.* Cambridge, MA: Harvard University Press, 2015.

Casal, U. A. "The Saintly Kōbō Daishi in Popular Lore (A.D. 774–835)." *Asian Folklore Studies* 18 (1959): 95–144.

Chiba Jōryū. "Sōsetsu." In *Myōgō honzon,* vol. 1 of *Shinshū jūhō shūei,* edited by Chiba Jōryū, 185–197. Kyoto: Dōbōsha, 1988.

Collcutt, Martin. *Five Mountains: The Rinzai Zen Monastic Institution in Medieval Japan.* Cambridge, MA: Council on East Asian Studies, Harvard University, 1981.

de Wisser, M. W. *The Bodhisattva Ti-tsang (Jizō) in China and Japan.* Berlin: Oesterheld, 1914.

Dobbins, James C. *Jōdo Shinshū: Shin Buddhism in Medieval Japan.* Honolulu: University of Hawai'i Press, 2002.

———. "Portraits of Shinran in Medieval Pure Land Buddhism." In Sharf and Sharf, *Living Images: Japanese Buddhist Icons in Context,* 19–48.

Faure, Bernard. *Gods of Medieval Japan. Vol. 1, The Fluid Pantheon.* Vol. 2, *Protectors and Predators.* Honolulu: University of Hawai'i Press, 2016.

———. *The Rhetoric of Immediacy: A Cultural Critique of Chan/Zen Buddhism.* Princeton, NJ: Princeton University Press, 1991.

———. *Visions of Power: Imagining Medieval Japanese Buddhism.* Princeton, NJ: Princeton University Press, 1996.

Ford, James L. *Jōkei and Buddhist Devotion in Early Medieval Japan.* New York: Oxford University Press, 2006.

Foulk, T. Griffith, and Robert H. Sharf. "On the Ritual Use of Chan Portraiture in Medieval China." In *Chan Buddhism in Ritual Context,* edited by Bernard Faure, 74–150. London: Routledge and Curzon, 2003.

Fukuchi Makoto, ed. *Kimochi ii Bukkyō.* Tokyo: Yōsensha, 2004.

Glassman, Hank. *The Face of Jizō: Image and Cult in Medieval Japanese Buddhism.* Honolulu: University of Hawai'i Press, 2012.

Hayashi Eiichi. *Jizōbon: Juyō to tenkai no yōshiki.* Sakai: Hatsushiba Bunko, 1997.

Imaizumi Yoshio, ed. *Nihon Bukkyōshi jiten.* Tokyo: Yoshikawa Kōbunkan, 1999.

Inagaki, Hisao. *Jōdo Mandala.* Kyoto: Nagata Bunshōdō, 1998.

Kawamura, Leslie S., ed. *The Bodhisattva Doctrine in Buddhism.* Waterloo, Canada: Wilfrid Laurier University Press, 1981.

Kieschnick, John. *The Impact of Buddhism on Chinese Material Culture.* Princeton, NJ: Princeton University Press, 2003.

Kitagawa, Joseph M. *Religion in Japanese History.* New York: Columbia University Press, 1966.

Kurata, Bunsaku, and Yoshirō Tamura, eds. *Art of the Lotus Sutra: Japanese Masterpieces.* Tokyo: Kōsei Publishing, 1987.

LaFleur, William. *Liquid Life: Abortion and Buddhism in Japan.* Princeton, NJ: Princeton University Press, 1992.

Lopez, Donald S., Jr., ed. *Religions of China in Practice.* Princeton, NJ: Princeton University Press, 1996.

Lowe, Bryan D. *Ritualized Writing: Buddhist Practice and Scriptural Cultures in Ancient Japan.* Honolulu: University of Hawai'i Press, 2017.

Miyazaki Enjun. *Shinran to sono montei.* Kyoto: Nagata Bunshōdō, 1956.

Moerman, D. Max. *Localizing Paradise: Kumano Pilgrimage and the Religious Landscape of Premodern Japan.* Cambridge, MA: Harvard University Asia Center, 2005.

Payne, Richard Karl. *The Tantric Ritual of Japan, Feeding the Gods: The Shingon Fire Ritual.* Delhi: International Academy of Indian Culture and Aditya Prakashan, 1991.

Rambelli, Fabio. *Buddhist Materiality: A Cultural History of Objects in Japanese Buddhism.* Stanford: Stanford University Press, 2007.

Ruppert, Brian D. *Jewel in the Ashes: Buddha Relics and Power in Early Medieval Japan.* Cambridge, MA: Harvard University Asia Center, 2000.

Sharf, Robert H. "Prolegomenon to the Study of Japanese Buddhist Icons." In Sharf and Sharf, *Living Images: Japanese Buddhist Icons in Context,* 1–18.

———. "The Scripture in Forty-Two Sections." In Lopez, *Religions of China in Practice,* 360–371.

———. "The Scripture on the Production of Buddhist Images." In Lopez, *Religions of China in Practice,* 261–267.

———. "Visualization and Mandala in Shingon Buddhism." In Sharf and Sharf, *Living Images: Japanese Buddhist Icons in Context,* 151–197.

Smith, Bardwell. *Narratives of Sorrow and Dignity: Japanese Women, Pregnancy Loss, and Modern Rituals of Grieving.* Oxford: Oxford University Press, 2013.

Sponberg, Alan, and Helen Hardacre, eds. *Maitreya, The Future Buddha.* Cambridge: Cambridge University Press, 1988.

Stone, Jacqueline I. *Original Enlightenment and the Transformation of Medieval Japanese Buddhism.* Honolulu: University of Hawai'i Press, 1999.

———. *Right Thoughts at the Last Moment: Buddhism and Deathbed Practices in Early Medieval Japan.* Honolulu: University of Hawai'i Press, 2016.

Suzuki, Daisetz Teitaro. *Essays in Zen Buddhism (First Series).* London: Rider, 1949.

Tamura Yoshirō. *Nichiren: Junkyō no nyoraishi.* Tokyo: Nihon Hōsō Shuppan Kyōkai, 1975.

Teiser, Stephen F. *The Scripture of the Ten Kings and the Making of Purgatory in Medieval Chinese Buddhism.* Honolulu: University of Hawai'i Press, 1994.

Tsuji Zennosuke. *Nihon Bukkyōshi,* 10 vols. Tokyo: Iwanami Shoten, 1944–1955.

Warner, Langdon. *The Long Old Road in China.* Garden City, NJ, and New York: Doubleday, Page, 1926.

Uehara Shōichi et al. *Kurashi no naka no Butsuji Bukkyō hyakka.* Tokyo: Shūeisha, 1989.

———, eds. *Zusetsu Nihon Bukkyō no sekai,* 8 vols. Tokyo: Shūeisha, 1988–1989.

Yamasaki, Taikō. *Shingon: Japanese Esoteric Buddhism.* Boston: Shambhala, 1988.

MUSEUMS AND POSTCOLONIAL STUDIES

Abe, Stanley K. "Inside the Wonder House: Buddhist Art and the West." In *Curators of the Buddha,* edited by Donald S. Lopez, Jr., 63–106. Chicago: University of Chicago Press, 1995.

Clifford, James. *Routes: Travel and Translation in the Late Twentieth Century.* Cambridge, MA: Harvard University Press, 1997.

Faure, Bernard. "The Buddhist Icon and the Modern Gaze." *Critical Inquiry* 24 (Spring 1998): 768–813.

Graham, Patricia J. "Langdon Warner's Vision of the Japanese Collection at the Nelson-Atkins Museum of Art, 1930–35." *Journal of the History of Collections* 28, no. 3 (2016): 367–382.

Hopkirk, Peter. *Foreign Devils on the Silk Road.* Amherst: University of Massachusetts Press, 1980.

Karp, Ivan, and Steven D. Lavine, eds. *Exhibiting Cultures: The Poetics and Politics of Museum Display.* Washington: Smithsonian Institution Press, 1991.

Lopez, Donald S., Jr. *From Stone to Flesh: A Short History of the Buddha.* Chicago: University of Chicago Press, 2013.

Payne, Crispin. *Religious Objects in Museums: Private Lives and Public Duties.* London: Bloomsbury, 2013.

Pratt, Mary Louise. *Imperial Eyes: Travel Writing and Transculturation.* London: Routledge, 1992.

Rosenfield, John M. "Japanese Buddhist Art: Alive in the Modern Age." In Cunningham, *Buddhist Treasures from Nara,* 232–244.

Sharf, Robert H. "On the Allure of Buddhist Relics." *Representations* 66 (Spring 1999): 75–99.

Sullivan, Bruce M. *Sacred Objects in Secular Spaces: Exhibiting Asian Religions in Museums.* London: Bloomsbury, 2015.

Tseng, Alice Y. *The Imperial Museums of Meiji Japan: Architecture and the Art of the Nation.* Seattle: University of Washington Press, 2008.

RELIGIOUS TEXTS

Aston, W. G., trans. *Nihongi: Chronicles of Japan from the Earliest Times to A.D. 697.* Tokyo: Charles E. Tuttle, 1972.

Birnbaum, Raoul. *The Healing Buddha.* Boulder: Shambhala Publications, 1979.

Cleary, Timothy, trans. *The Flower Ornament Scripture: A Translation of the Avatamsaka Sutra,* 3 vols. Boston: Shambhala, 1985–1987.

Deal, William E. "Buddhism and the State in Early Japan." In *Buddhism in Practice,* edited by Donald S. Lopez, Jr., 216–227. Princeton, NJ: Princeton University Press, 1995.

Dobbins, James C. "Genshin's Deathbed Nembutsu Ritual in Pure Land Buddhism." In *Religions of Japan in Practice,* edited by George J. Tanabe, Jr., 166–175. Princeton, NJ: Princeton University Press, 1999.

Dykstra, Yoshiko Kurata. "Jizō, the Most Merciful: Tales from *Jizō Bosatsu Reigenki.*" *Monumenta Nipponica* 33, no. 2 (Summer 1978): 179–200.

———. "Tales of the Compassionate Kannon: The *Hasedera Kannon Genki.*" *Monumenta Nipponica* 31, no. 2 (1976): 113–143.

Gómez, Luis O., trans. *The Land of Bliss: The Paradise of the Buddha of Measureless Light.* Honolulu: University of Hawai'i Press, 1996.

Hua, Hsüan, and Heng Ching. *Sūtra of the Past Vows of Earth Store Bodhisattva.* New York: Buddhist Text Translation Society and the Institute for Advanced Studies of World Religions, 1974.

Iida, Shōtarō, and Jane Goldstone, trans. *The Sutra That Expounds the Descent of Maitreya Buddha and His Enlightenment.* Moraga, CA: Bukkyō Dendō Kyōkai America, 2016.

Inagaki, Hisao. *The Three Pure Land Sutras.* Kyoto: Nagata Bunshodo, 1994.

Kako genzai ingakyō. In *Kokuyaku issaikyō,* edited by Iwano Shin'yu, 32:1–120. Tokyo: Daitō Shuppansha, 1929.

Kamens, Edward. *The Three Jewels: A Study and Translation of Minamoto Tamenori's Sanbōe.* Ann Arbor: Center for Japanese Studies, University of Michigan, 1988.

Komatsu Shigemi, ed. *Shigisan engi.* Nihon emaki 4. Tokyo: Chūō Kōronsha, 1987.

Lee, Pi-Cheng, trans. *The Vows of Bodhisattva Samantabhadra Sutra.* Singapore: Golden Earth Design and Printing, 2004.

McRae, John R., trans. *The Vimalakīrti Sutra.* Berkeley: Bukkyō Dendō Kyōkai and Numata Center for Translation and Research, 2004.

Morrell, Robert E. *Sand and Pebbles (Shasekishū): The Tales of Mujū Ichien. A Voice for Pluralism in Kamakura Buddhism.* Albany: State University of New York Press, 1985.

Muller, A. Charles, and Kenneth K. Tanaka, trans. *The Brahma's Net Sutra* (Moraga, CA: Bukkyō Dendō Kyōkai America, 2017.

Nakamura, Kyoko Motomochi, trans. *Miraculous Tales from the Japanese Buddhist Tradition: The* Nihon ryōiki *of the Monk Kyōkai.* Cambridge, MA: Harvard University Press, 1973.

Okudaira Hideo, ed. *Shigisan engi.* Nihon emakimono zenshū 3. Tokyo: Kadokawa Shoten, 1976.

Takahata Isao. *Jūni seiki no animeeshon: Kokuhō emakimono ni miru eiga teki anime teki narumono.* Tokyo: Tokuma Shoten, 2008.

Ury, Marian. *Tales of Times Now Past: Sixty-Two Stories from a Medieval Japanese Collection.* Berkeley: University of California Press, 1979.

Watson, Burton, trans. *The Lotus Sutra.* New York: Columbia University Press, 1993.

Yamamoto, Kosho, trans. *The Mahayana Mahaparinirvana Sutra.* Karin Buddhological Series 5. 1973. PDF reprint, edited and revised by Tony Page, 2007. http://lirs.ru/do/Mahaparinirvana_Sutra,Yamamoto,Page,2007.pdf.

ILLUSTRATION CREDITS

Cover. Seated Amida Nyorai, 12th cent. By permission of Kyoto National Museum.

Part title pages: Amida Nyorai, ca. 1250. Metropolitan Museum of Art, New York. Rogers Fund, 1919.

Figure 1. Gallery of Hōryūji Treasures, Tokyo National Museum. Photo by author.

Figure 2. Grand altar, Seiryōji Temple. By permission of Seiryōji Temple, Kyoto.

Figure 3. Eight Men Ferrying a Statue of the Buddha (from Mogao Cave 323, Dunhuang, Gansu province), 7th cent. Harvard Art Museums/Arthur M. Sackler Museum, First Fogg Expedition to China (1923–1924), 1924.41. Photo: Imaging Department © President and Fellows of Harvard College.

Figure 4. Buddhist Temple, Museum of Fine Arts, Boston. Photo © 2020 Museum of Fine Arts, Boston.

Figure 5. Buddha of Infinite Life and Light (Amida Nyorai), 1269. Kōshun, Kōshin, and Jōshun. Kamakura period (1185–1333). Cypress wood with lacquer, color, gold, cut gold, rock crystal inlaid eyes, and quartz; h. 94.6 cm. The Cleveland Museum of Art. John L. Severance Fund, 1960.197. Photo © The Cleveland Museum of Art.

Figure 6. Great Buddha Hall, Tōdaiji Temple. National Treasure. By permission of Tōdaiji Temple, Nara. Photo by author.

Figure 7. Great Buddha, Tōdaiji Temple. National Treasure. By permission of Tōdaiji Temple, Nara. Photo by Cheryl Cottine.

Figure 8. Great Buddha Hall, Hōkōji Temple, Kyoto. Detail of *Rakuchū Rakugai Zu Byōbu,* 18th cent. By permission of Otani University Museum, Kyoto.

Figure 9. "Giant Standing Buddhas of Bamiyan Still Cast Shadows." Courtesy of Defense Visual Information Distribution Service. Photo by Sgt. Ken Scar, 7th Mobile Public Affairs Detachment, June 17, 2012. Bamiyan province, Afghanistan. The appearance of U.S. Department of Defense (DoD) visual information does not imply or constitute DoD endorsement.

Figure 10. Seated Buddha Amida, Zōjōji Temple. By permission of Zōjōji Temple, Tokyo.

Figure 11. Śākyamuni Buddha at birth, Tōdaiji Temple. National Treasure. By permission of Tōdaiji Temple, Nara.

Figure 12. Śākyamuni entertained by palace maidens. Section from *Eingakyō* Illustrated Scroll, 8th cent. Important Cultural Property. By permission of Nara National Museum.

Figure 13. Śākyamuni encountering the monk. Section from *Eingakyō* Illustrated Scroll, 8th cent. Important Cultural Property. By permission of Nara National Museum.

Figure 14. Śākyamuni seeking consent to become a religious mendicant. Section from *Eingakyō* Illustrated Scroll, 8th cent. Important Cultural Property. By permission of Nara National Museum.

Figure 15. Śākyamuni coming out of the mountains, 14th cent. By permission of Nara National Museum.

Figure 16. Śākyamuni Buddha's enlightenment, 13th cent. Scene from the Illustrated Sutra of Past and Present Karma (*Kako genzai e-inga-kyō*; Matsunaga Version). Metropolitan Museum of Art, New York. Mary Griggs Burke Collection, Gift of the Mary and Jackson Burke Foundation, 2015.

Figure 17. Śākyamuni Buddha preaching, 8th cent. A section from the Illustrated Sutra of Past and Present Karma (*Kako genzai inga kyō emaki*). Metropolitan Museum of Art, New York. Purchase, Louis V. Bell, Harris Brisbane Dick, Fletcher, and Rogers Funds and Joseph Pulitzer Bequest; The Vincent Astor Foundation and Mary and James G. Wallach Foundation Gifts, 2016.

Figure 18. Death of the Buddha, 1730s. Nishimura Shigenobu. Allen Memorial Art Museum, Oberlin College, Ohio. Mary A. Ainsworth Bequest, 1950.

Figure 19. Amarāvatī, two-sided drum-slab (back), 1st cent. BCE. Amarāvatī Stupa, India. Carved limestone. © Trustees of the British Museum, London.

Figure 20. Buddha Shakyamuni, 2nd–early 3rd cent. Gandhara region, Pakistan, Gray schist, 47½ × 16 × 19½ in. (120.65 × 40.64 × 49.53 cm). Los Angeles County Museum of Art. Gift of Mr. and Mrs. Eric Lidow in honor of the museum's twenty-fifth anniversary (M.91.90). Photo © Museum Associates/LACMA.

Figure 21. Śākyamuni Buddha, Seiryōji Temple. National Treasure. By permission of Seiryōji Temple, Kyoto.

Figure 22. Seated Amida Nyorai, 12th cent. By permission of Kyoto National Museum.

Figure 23. Kannon Bosatsu, 12th cent. Japan. Carved wood (a-c): 85 × 32½ × 36 in. (215.9 × 82.55 × 91.44 cm). Los Angeles County Museum of Art. Mr. and Mrs. Allan C. Balch Fund (M.62.6a-c). Photo © Museum Associates/LACMA.

Figure 24. Standing Amida Nyorai, 13th cent. By permission of Nara National Museum.

Figure 25. Embroidery of Shaka Nyorai preaching (detail), 8th cent. National Treasure. By permission of Nara National Museum.

Figure 26. Shakyamuni, late 1800s. Japan, Meiji period (1868–1912). Wood with traces of lacquer and gilding; h. 33.5 cm. The Cleveland Museum of Art. Gift from the Collection of George Gund III, 2015.501. Photo © The Cleveland Museum of Art.

Figure 27. Amida Nyorai (detail), 12th cent. By permission of Nara National Museum.

Figure 28. Nyoirin Kannon, 9th–10th cent. Important Cultural Property. By permission of Nara National Museum.

Figure 29. Seated Yakushi Nyorai, 9th cent. National Treasure. By permission of Nara National Museum.

Figure 30. Buddhist home altar. Wada House, Shirakawa-gō village, Gifu prefecture. Photo by author.

Figure 31. Interior of Kondō Hall, Hōryūji Temple. National Treasure. By permission of Hōryūji Temple, Ikaruga. Photos by Askaen Co., Nara. This view of the temple's interior has been created digitally from three photos, so the spacing between images is compressed and inexact.

Figure 32. Replica of the Seiryōji Śākyamuni Buddha, 13th cent. Important Cultural Property. By permission of Nara National Museum.

Figure 33. *Lotus Sutra* Mandala, 14th cent. By permission of Nara National Museum.

Figure 34. Seated Miroku (Maitreya) Buddha, 11th cent. Important Cultural Property. By permission of Nara National Museum.

Figure 35. Healing Buddha with Lotus, ca. 1150. Wood, Japanese cypress (Hinoki); Buddha: 39½ × 12 × 11 in. Lotus: 4 × 14 × 14 in. Dallas Museum of Art. Gift of The Eugene McDermott Foundation, 1985.116.A-C.

Figure 36. Great Buddha, Tōdaiji Temple. National Treasure. By permission of Tōdaiji Temple, Nara. Photo by Wai Wah Sung.

Figure 37. Etching on lotus petal of the Great Buddha, Tōdaiji Temple. National Treasure. By permission of Tōdaiji Temple, Nara.

Figure 38. Dainichi, the Buddha of Infinite Illumination, 1149. Camphor wood with gold; joined woodblock construction. Height of figure: 141.6 cm (55¾ in.). Museum of Fine Arts, Boston. Denman Waldo Ross Collection, 09.531a-c. Photo © 2020 Museum of Fine Arts, Boston.

Figure 39. Taizokai Mandala, 13th cent. Freer Gallery of Art and Arthur M. Sackler Gallery, Smithsonian Institution, Washington, DC. Purchase—Charles Lang Freer Endowment, F1998.1.

Figure 40. Mandala of the Diamond World. Tanio Nakamura (Japanese), Muromachi period (1392–1573). Ink and colors on silk. Asian Art Museum of San Francisco. The Avery Brundage Collection, B60D24+. Photo © Asian Art Museum of San Francisco.

Figure 41. Seated Amida Buddha, Byōdōin Temple. National Treasure. By permission of and © Byōdōin Temple, Kyoto. Photo by Askaen Co., Nara.

Figure 42. Taima Mandala, 1750. Metropolitan Museum of Art, New York. Charles Steward Smith Collection, Gift of Mrs. Charles Steward Smith, Charles Steward Smith, Jr., and Howard Caswell Smith, in memory of Charles Steward Smith, 1914.

Figure 43. The Welcoming Descent of Amida Buddha and Twenty-five Bodhisattvas, 1668. Metropolitan Museum of Art, New York. Bequest of Lettice Sands Phelps Stokes, 1988.

Figure 44. Miroku, 7th cent. Freer Gallery of Art and Arthur M. Sackler Gallery, Smithsonian Institution, Washington, DC. Gift of Charles Lang Freer, F1909.338.

Figure 45. Miroku (Maitreya), 1300s. Japan, Nanbokuchō period (1336–1392). Hanging scroll, ink and color with gold and cut gold on silk. Mounted: 115.57 × 41.35 cm. The Cleveland Museum of Art. Gift of Rosemarie and Leighton Longhi in memory of Robert P. Bergman, 1999.195. Photo © The Cleveland Museum of Art.

Figure 46. Jizō Bosatsu, late 12th–mid-13th cent. Metropolitan Museum of Art, New York. Rogers Fund, 1918.

Figure 47. Child-saving Jizō Bodhisattvas, Zōjōji Temple, Tokyo. Photo by author.

Figure 48. Monju Bodhisattva riding a lion, with attendant figures, Jionji Temple. Important Cultural Property. By permission of Jionji Temple, Yamagata.

Figure 49. Fugen Bodhisattva riding an elephant, with attendant figures, Jionji Temple. Important Cultural Property. By permission of Jionji Temple, Yamagata.

Figure 50. Eleven-headed Kannon Bodhisattva, 8th–9th cent. Important Cultural Property. By permission of Nara National Museum.

Figure 51. Eleven-headed thousand-armed Kannon Bodhisattva, Sanjūsangendō Temple. National Treasure. By permission of Sanjūsangendō Honbō Myōhōin Monzeki Temple, Kyoto.

Figure 52. White-Robed Kannon, from a set of White-Robed Kannon with Landscape and Tiger. Kano Tan'yū, 1602–1674. Ink on paper, $47\frac{15}{16} \times 19\frac{13}{16}$ in. (121.76 × 50.32 cm). Minneapolis Institute of Art. The John Cowles Family Fund, 2002.142.2. Photo: Minneapolis Institute of Art.

Figure 53. Eleven-headed thousand-armed Kannon Bodhisattvas, Sanjūsangendō Temple. Important Cultural Properties. By permission of Sanjūsangendō Honbō Myōhōin Monzeki Temple, Kyoto.

Figure 54. Fudō Myōō, 13th cent. Metropolitan Museum of Art, New York. Mary Griggs Burke Collection, Gift of the Mary and Jackson Burke Foundation, 2015.

Figure 55. Aizen Myōō, 13th cent. Important Cultural Property. By permission of Nara National Museum.

Figure 56. Kujaku Myōō, 14th cent. Freer Gallery of Art and Arthur M. Sackler Gallery, Smithsonian Institution, Washington, DC. Gift of Charles Lang Freer, F1907.544.

Figure 57. Tamonten (11th–12th cent.) and Zōchōten (13th cent.), two of the Four Heavenly Kings. Important Cultural Properties. By permission of Nara National Museum.

Figure 58. Bishamonten, 15th cent. Japanese, Muromachi period. Woodblock print; ink on paper, with hand applied color. 96.8 × 35 cm (38 1/8 × 13 3/4 in.). Museum of Fine Arts, Boston. Gift of Robert T. Paine, Jr., 60.1381. Photo © 2020 Museum of Fine Arts, Boston.

Figure 59. Twin Benevolent Kings, Tōdaiji Temple. National Treasures. By permission of Tōdaiji Temple, Nara.

Figure 60. Yakushi, the Healing Buddha, and the Twelve Divine Generals, 16th cent. Japanese, Muromachi period. Panel; ink, color, and gold on silk. 108 × 66.7 cm (42 1/2 × 26 1/4 in.). Museum of Fine Arts, Boston. Fenollosa-Weld Collection. Photo © 2020 Museum of Fine Arts, Boston.

Figure 61. Benzaiten, a Hanging Scroll Painting, 14th cent. © Trustees of the British Museum, London.

Figure 62. Emma-O, late 16th–early 17th cent. Wood, lacquer, gold gilt, and glass. 45 × 40 × 30 in. Dallas Museum of Art. Wendover Fund in memory of Alfred and Juanita Bromberg and the Cecil and Ida Green Acquisition Fund, 2008.25.A-H.

Figure 63. Zaō Gongen, 14th cent. Metropolitan Museum of Art, New York. Gift of Marielle Bancou-Segal, in memory of the vision of William Segal, 2002.

Figure 64. Great Buddha Hall. Illustration from *Tōdaiji Engi,* 16th cent. By permission of Nara National Museum.

Figure 65. Great Buddha, Tōdaiji Temple. National Treasure. By permission of Tōdaiji Temple, Nara. Photo by Wai Wah Sung.

Figure 66. Seiryōji Śākyamuni Buddha, Seiryōji Temple. National Treasure. By permission of Seiryōji Temple, Kyoto.

Figure 67. The Monk from Danxia Burning a Wooden Image of the Buddha. Unkoku Tōgan (1547–1618). Japan, late 16th–early 17th cent. Hanging scroll; ink on paper. Image: 44 × 19 in. (111.76 × 48.26 cm); Mount: 74 7/8 × 19 3/4 in. (190.18 × 50.17 cm). Los Angeles County Museum of Art. Gift of Anna Bing Arnold, Museum Acquisition Fund, and the Far Eastern Art Council. (M.90.21). Photo © Museum Associates/LACMA.

Figure 68. Myōshinji Zen monastery, Kyoto. Illustration from *Miyako meisho zue*, 1786. By permission of the International Research Center for Japanese Studies, Kyoto.

Figure 69. Konjikidō Hall, Chūsonji Temple. National Treasure. By permission of Chūsonji Temple, Hiraizumi.

Figure 70. Eleven-headed thousand-armed Kannon Bodhisattva, Sanjūsangendō Temple. National Treasure. By permission of Sanjūsangendō Honbō Myōhōin Monzeki Temple, Kyoto.

Figure 71. Jizō Bodhisattva, Denkōji Temple. Important Cultural Property. By permission of Denkōji Temple, Nara.

Figure 72. Shingon *goma* ceremony, Tōji Temple, Kyoto. Photo by Shii Wikimedia Commons CC BY-SA 3.0, slightly cropped.

Figure 73. Founder Memorial Service (Gyoki Daie), Zōjōji Temple. By permission of Zōjōji Temple, Tokyo.

Figure 74. Zenkōji Amida Triad, 13th–14th cent. Kamakura period. Bronze. Buddha: H with base 17¾ in., H of figure 14¼ in., diam. of base 5¾ in. Two Bosatsu: H with base 12 in., H of figure 9 in., diam. of base 4¼ in. John C. Weber Collection. Photo by John Bigelow Taylor.

Figure 75. Illustration from *Shigisan Engi*. National Treasure. By permission of Shigisan Chōgosonshiji Temple, Ikoma.

Figure 76. Central altar of the Daihondō, Kuonji Temple. By permission of Minobusan Kuonji Temple, Minobu.

Figure 77. Temple of the Tooth (Daḷadā Māligāwa), Kandy. Photo by author.

Figure 78. Five-tiered pagoda, Kōfukuji Temple, Nara. National Treasure. Photo by 663highland Wikimedia Commons CC BY-SA 3.0, edited to adjust vertical orientation and remove a trace of the moon overhead.

Figure 79. Buddhist reliquary in the form of a five-element stupa, 15th cent. By permission of Nara National Museum.

Figure 80. Buddhist Reliquary in the Shape of a Wish-Granting Jewel, 16th–17th cent. Gilt bronze, rock crystal, 7¼ × 3½ × 3¾ in. (18.42 × 8.89 × 9.53 cm). Minneapolis Institute of Art. Louis W. Hill, Jr., Fund and Gifts of Funds in Memory of John Austin O'Keeffe, 2006.42. Photo: Minneapolis Institute of Art.

Figure 81. Chapter 21 of the *Lotus Sutra,* 12th cent. Important Cultural Property. By permission of Kyoto National Museum.

Figure 82. Sutra canister, 12th cent. By permission of Nara National Museum.

Figure 83. Great Mandala and Principal Object of Reverence at the Time of Passing (*Rinmetsu Doji Daimandara Gohonzon*). By permission of Hikigayatsu Myōhonji Temple, Kamakura.

Figure 84. Six-character inscription of Amida's name, Hongwanji Temple. By permission of Hongwanji Temple, Kyoto.

Figure 85. Portrait of Hottō Enmyō Kokushi, ca. 1286–1333. Japan, Kamakura period (1185–1333). Hinoki cypress wood with lacquer; h. 91.4 cm. The Cleveland Museum of Art. Leonard C. Hanna, Jr., Fund, 1970.67. Photo © The Cleveland Museum of Art.

Figure 86. Portrait of Kūkai (Kōbō Daishi), from Kongōbuji on Mount Kōya, 18th–19th cent. Edo period–Meiji era. Woodblock print; ink on paper with hand-applied color. 24 × 17.2 cm (9 7/16 × 6¾ in.). Museum of Fine Arts, Boston. Gift of Robert T. Paine, Jr., RES.60.17.38. Photo © 2020 Museum of Fine Arts, Boston.

Figure 87. Roadside Buddhist shrine, Iwakura, Kyoto. Photo by author.

Figure 88. Graves of Takeda Katsuyori, his wife Hōjō Masako, and his son Takeda Nobukatsu, 1775, Keitokuin Temple, Kōshū. Photo by Sakaori Wikimedia Commons CC BY-SA 3.0.

Figure 89. Kyoto National Museum. Important Cultural Property. Photo by author.

Figure 90. Portrait of the Priest Shinran, 13th–14th cent. Important Cultural Property. By permission of Nara National Museum.

INDEX

Page numbers in **bold** refer to figures.

ABOUT THE AUTHOR

James C. Dobbins is the Fairchild Professor Emeritus of Religion and East Asian Studies at Oberlin College in Ohio. His major publications include *Jōdo Shinshū: Shin Buddhism in Medieval Japan; Letters of the Nun Eshinni: Images of Pure Land Buddhism in Medieval Japan;* and *Selected Works of D. T. Suzuki, Vol. 2, Pure Land.* Dobbins has served as the coeditor of *The Journal of Japanese Studies* and as the chair of the Associated Kyoto Program.